Solicitors' Accounts—
A Practical Guide

Solicitors' Accounts— A Practical Guide

Dale Kay
Solicitor (Hons)

and

Janet Baker
LLB (Hons), Solicitor

OXFORD
UNIVERSITY PRESS

Great Clarendon Street, Oxford OX2 6DP

Oxford University Press is a department of the University of Oxford.
It furthers the University's objective of excellence in research, scholarship,
and education by publishing worldwide in

Oxford New York

Auckland Cape Town Dar es Salaam Hong Kong Karachi
Kuala Lumpur Madrid Melbourne Mexico City Nairobi
New Delhi Shanghai Taipei Toronto

With offices in

Argentina Austria Brazil Chile Czech Republic France Greece
Guatemala Hungary Italy Japan Poland Portugal Singapore
South Korea Switzerland Thailand Turkey Ukraine Vietnam

Oxford is a registered trade mark of Oxford University Press
in the UK and in certain other countries

Published in the United States
by Oxford University Press Inc., New York

© Dale Kay and Janet Baker 2006

The moral rights of the authors have been asserted
Database right Oxford University Press (maker)

Crown copyright material is reproduced under Class Licence
Number C01P0000148 with the permission of OPSI
and the Queen's Printer for Scotland

First edition 1997
Second edition 1998
Third edition 1999
Fourth edition 2000
Fifth edition 2001
Sixth edition 2002
Seventh edition 2003
Eighth edition 2004
Ninth edition 2005
Tenth edition 2006

All rights reserved. No part of this publication may be reproduced,
stored in a retrieval system, or transmitted, in any form or by any means,
without the prior permission in writing of Oxford University Press,
or as expressly permitted by law, or under terms agreed with the appropriate
reprographics rights organization. Enquiries concerning reproduction
outside the scope of the above should be sent to the Rights Department,
Oxford University Press, at the address above

You must not circulate this book in any other binding or cover
and you must impose the same condition on any acquirer

British Library Cataloguing in Publication Data
Data available

Library of Congress Cataloging in Publication Data
Data available

Typeset by Newgen Imaging Systems (P) Ltd., Chennai, India
Printed in Great Britain
on acid-free paper by
Antony Rowe Limited, Chippenham

ISBN 0-19-928959-X   978-0-19-928959-2

10 9 8 7 6 5 4 3 2 1

OUTLINE CONTENTS

Detailed contents vii
Preface xi
Online resources to accompany this book xii

1	Introduction to solicitors' accounts and basic bookkeeping	1
2	The Trial Balance	19
3	Final accounts	27
4	Adjustments to final accounts	39
5	Further adjustments to final accounts	53
6	Partnership accounts	71
7	Basic accounting concepts and trading accounts	95
8	Company accounts	103
9	Group companies and consolidated accounts	127
10	Interpretation of accounts and accounting ratios	141
11	Basic solicitors' accounts	161
12	Transfers and mixed money	181
13	Value added tax	193
14	Financial statements and property transactions	205
15	Deposit interest and interest payable to clients	239
16	Probate transactions	251
17	Further transactions	257
18	Short-answer questions and revision questions on solicitors' accounts	267

Index 277

DETAILED CONTENTS

Preface x
Online resources to accompany this book xii

1 Introduction to solicitors' accounts and basic bookkeeping 1

1.1 Introduction 1
1.2 Overview of accounts 1
1.3 The purpose of keeping accounts 2
1.4 An introduction to double-entry bookkeeping 3
1.5 Classification of accounts 5
1.6 Worked example on double entry 12
1.7 Check list 14
1.8 Exercises on double-entry bookkeeping 14
1.9 Suggested answers to exercises on double-entry bookkeeping 15

2 The Trial Balance 19

2.1 The Trial Balance 19
2.2 Check list 21
2.3 Exercises on double-entry bookkeeping and Trial Balance 21
2.4 Suggested answers to exercises on the Trial Balance 22
2.5 Full exercise on the Trial Balance 23
2.6 Suggested answers to exercise on double-entry bookkeeping and Trial Balance 24

3 Final accounts 27

3.1 Introduction 27
3.2 Closing the accounts 28
3.3 Presentation of final accounts 29
3.4 The Balance Sheet 29
3.5 Check list 33
3.6 Exercises on basic final accounts 33
3.7 Suggested answers to exercises on basic final accounts 35

4 Adjustments to final accounts 39

4.1 The need for adjustments 39
4.2 Outstanding expenses adjustment 39
4.3 Payment in advance 41
4.4 Closing stocks 43
4.5 Work in progress 44
4.6 Summary of adjustments 47
4.7 Check list 48
4.8 Exercises on adjustments and final accounts 48
4.9 Suggested answers to exercises on adjustments and final accounts 49

5 Further adjustments to final accounts 53

5.1 Introduction 53
5.2 Bad debts and doubtful debts adjustments 53
5.3 Depreciation 57
5.4 Sale of assets 60
5.5 Summary 61
5.6 Check list 62
5.7 Exercises on adjustments and final accounts 62
5.8 Suggested answers to exercises on adjustments and final accounts 65

6 Partnership accounts 71

6.1 The accounts kept by a partnership—introduction 71
6.2 Final accounts 71
6.3 Drawings 72
6.4 Partnership changes 76
6.5 Check list 77
6.6 Exercises on partnership final accounts 78
6.7 Suggested answers to exercises on partnership final accounts 82
6.8 Test on partnership final accounts 90
6.9 Suggested answer to test on partnership final accounts 91

7 Basic accounting concepts and trading accounts 95

7.1 Introduction 95
7.2 Financial accounting concepts 95
7.3 Accounting bases and policies 96
7.4 Trading accounts 97
7.5 Check list 99
7.6 Practice exercises 99
7.7 Suggested answers to practice exercises 100

8 Company accounts 103

8.1 Introduction 103
8.2 Accounts of limited companies 103
8.3 Limited companies' Profit and Loss accounts 107

8.4	The form of the Balance Sheet	117		13.5	Agency method—summary	199
8.5	Check list	120		13.6	Principle method—summary	199
8.6	Practice exercises	120		13.7	VAT relief for bad debts	200
8.7	Suggested answers to practice exercises	123		13.8	Check list	201
				13.9	Exercises on ledger accounts including VAT	201
				13.10	Suggested answers to exercises on ledger accounts including VAT	202

9 Group companies and consolidated accounts — 127

9.1	Introduction	127
9.2	The consolidated Balance Sheet	128
9.3	The consolidated Profit and Loss account	132
9.4	Where a company holds a majority interest in the subsidiary	134
9.5	Check list	136
9.6	Practice exercises	136
9.7	Suggested answers to practice exercises	138

10 Interpretation of accounts and accounting ratios — 141

10.1	Introduction	141
10.2	Use of accounts	141
10.3	Check factors outside the accounts	142
10.4	General areas to look at	142
10.5	Trends	143
10.6	Ratios	143
10.7	Example	152
10.8	Check list	155
10.9	Exercise	156
10.10	Suggested answer to exercise	158

11 Basic solicitors' accounts — 161

11.1	Introduction	161
11.2	The Solicitors' Accounts Rules 1998 (SAR)	161
11.3	Basic entries	168
11.4	Payments out of petty cash—office account	171
11.5	Profit costs and VAT	173
11.6	Record keeping and compliance	174
11.7	Check list	175
11.8	Practice exercises	176
11.9	Answers to practice exercises	176

12 Transfers and mixed money — 181

12.1	Introduction	181
12.2	Transfers	181
12.3	Check list	186
12.4	Exercises on basic ledger entries	186
12.5	Suggested answers to exercises on basic ledger entries	188

13 Value added tax — 193

13.1	Introduction	193
13.2	VAT—a brief overview	193
13.3	Registering for VAT	193
13.4	Accounting to HM Revenue and Customs for VAT	194

14 Financial statements and property transactions — 205

14.1	Introduction	205
14.2	Financial statements to clients	205
14.3	Property transactions—a summary	206
14.4	Receipt of deposit on exchange of contracts	207
14.5	Mortgage advances	209
14.6	Mortgage repayment	213
14.7	Completion	214
14.8	Check list	226
14.9	Exercises on property transactions	226
14.10	Suggested answers to exercises on property transactions	230

15 Deposit interest and interest payable to clients — 239

15.1	Introduction	239
15.2	Paying interest to the client, rules 24 and 25	239
15.3	Earning interest on clients' money on a general deposit account	246
15.4	Solicitor/Trustees	247
15.5	Check list	247
15.6	Exercises on deposit interest and interest payable	248
15.7	Suggested answers to exercises on deposit interest and interest payable	248

16 Probate transactions — 251

16.1	Introduction	251
16.2	Exercises on probate transactions	251
16.3	Suggested answers to exercises on probate transactions	254

17 Further transactions — 257

17.1	Introduction	257
17.2	Abatements	257
17.3	Dishonoured cheques	258
17.4	Small transactions	261
17.5	Bad debts—a reminder	261
17.6	Check list	261
17.7	Exercises on further transactions	262
17.8	Suggested answers to exercises on further transactions	263

18 Short-answer questions and revision questions on solicitors' accounts — 267

18.1	Introduction	267
18.2	Revision questions—Set A	267

18.3	Suggested answers to revision questions—Set A	268	18.8 Test on ledger accounts including VAT	275
18.4	Self-assessment questions—Set B	268	18.9 Suggested answer to test on ledger accounts including VAT	276
18.5	Suggested answers to self-assessment questions—Set B	269		
18.6	Test on further transactions	273		
18.7	Suggested answer to test on further transactions	274	*Index*	277

PREFACE

I would like to thank Janet Baker, whose original book still forms a basis for this Guide. My thanks also go to my husband, Roger, to all my former students, my colleagues and ex-colleagues, to all the helpful and supportive team at Oxford University Press, including Lucy Graham and Anna Read.

Dale Kay
April 2006
Manchester

ONLINE RESOURCES TO ACCOMPANY THIS BOOK...

Online Resource Centres are developed to provide students and lecturers with ready-to-use teaching and learning resources. They are free-of-charge, designed to complement the textbook and offer additional materials that are suited to electronic delivery. The Online Resource Centre to accompany this book can be found at:

www.oxfordtextbooks.co.uk/orc/lpcsolicitorsaccounts06_07/

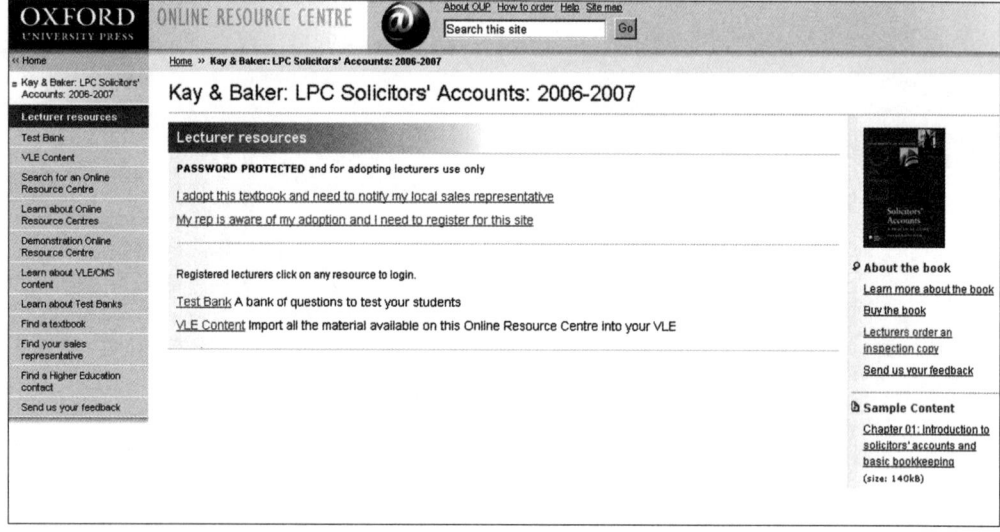

Lecturer resources

Password-protected to ensure only lecturers adopting this book can access these resources, each registration is personally checked to ensure the security of the site. Use these resources to complement your own teaching notes and the resources you provide for your LPC students.

Registering is easy: click on 'Lecturer Resources' on the Online Resource Centre, complete a simple registration form which allows you to choose your own username and password, and access will be granted within 48 hours (subject to verification).

Test bank of multiple choice questions

Using your lecturer password, you can gain access to a fully customisable bank of multiple choice questions offering a versatile way to test your students' knowledge and understanding of the accounting methods and principles covered in this book. The questions are downloadable into Questionmark Perception, Blackboard, WebCT and most other virtual learning environments capable of importing QTI XML. The questions are also available in print format.

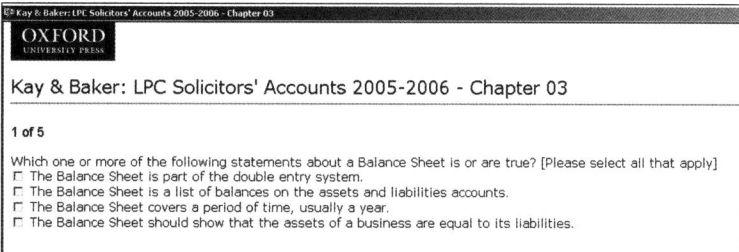

Student resources

Students can access several interactive exercises without the need for a password. These exercises offer an excellent interactive way to test your knowledge and understanding of the accounting principles.

1

Introduction to solicitors' accounts and basic bookkeeping

1.1 Introduction

This chapter includes:

1. An introduction to accounts.
2. The purpose of keeping accounts.
3. An explanation of the double-entry bookkeeping system with worked examples.
4. Practical self-test exercises in drawing up accounts using the double-entry system.

1.2 Overview of accounts

Accounts on the Legal Practice Course is regarded as a pervasive subject, although it is separately assessed. A word of encouragement at the start. Although initially Accounts can seem daunting, most students do well, and even manage to enjoy the time they spend on Accounts. Do not worry if you did not enjoy GCSE maths; the only maths involved here is very basic arithmetic.

Do practice using the exercises in the book and those given to you on your course. This is the best way to come to grips with the subject. The questions at the end of each chapter are graded, starting with easier exercises and working up to more challenging questions.

The following web sites may be useful to you, and will also be mentioned in the relevant chapters:

www.lawsociety.org.uk in respect of solicitors accounts;
www.companieshouse.gov.uk in respect of company accounts;
www.dti.gov.uk in respect of company accounts;
www.hmrc.gov.uk Customs and Excise in respect of VAT, Inland Revenue.

1.2.1 Why study Accounts?

You may think that Accounts is the last subject a prospective solicitor needs to know. However, there are very good reasons why it is included. Solicitors can be struck off as solicitors if they breach the Solicitors' Accounts Rules—have a look in the *Law Society Gazette* and see how often this is a reason. They look after large sums of money on behalf of their clients, and must be trusted to do so. They are ultimately responsible and cannot totally rely on the skill or honesty of others.

Solicitors are also running a business; they must be able to understand how the accounts are kept, and, as partners, be able to read their Profit and Loss accounts and Balance Sheets each year.

Solicitors will often need some understanding of accounts when giving advice, whether to corporate clients, or, for example, to matrimonial clients when advising on asset distribution.

1.2.2 How to study Accounts

Accounts is a practical subject, it involves understanding the principles and applying them. The best way to do this is by reading the explanation and then working through the exercises. Only when you are satisfied that you understand what you are doing should you move on to the next section. Repetition of exercises will consolidate your understanding. Once you understand the basic principles the later sections should fall into place.

1.2.3 The main areas of study

Accounts on this course falls into two main sections:

1. Business Accounts
2. Solicitors' Accounts.

Business Accounts

This includes basic double-entry bookkeeping, the Trial Balance, and preparation of Final Accounts, being the Profit and Loss and Balance Sheet. The Final Accounts can be prepared for a sole owner, a partnership or a company.

Solicitors' Accounts

This covers the Solicitors' Accounts Rules, the difference between office and client account, controlled trust money, and the bookkeeping entries required. It also covers how to prepare a simple Financial Statement for a client, and the particular bookkeeping entries required for certain types of work, for example property or probate work.

1.3 The purpose of keeping accounts

All businesses need to keep a day-to-day record of all their financial transactions, so that they can see what is happening. From these records they will be able to draw up final accounts.

These fall into two main sections:

The Profit and Loss account

This will record all income less expenses, to give the profit or loss for the period.

The Balance Sheet

This will show what the business OWNS—its assets and what the business OWES—its liabilities.

Different people will use the accounts for different purposes, for example:

- The owners—will need to know what is happening financially, this will help them with planning for the business
- The Inland Revenue or Customs and Excise—for tax purposes
- Any person or company that has lent money to the business, for example the bank
- A buyer of the business
- A new partner coming into a partnership.

1.4 An introduction to double-entry bookkeeping

Basic accounts are merely records or histories of financial transactions. The normal method of keeping day-to-day accounts is that of double entry, which will be used in this book. This means that TWO entries are made for every SINGLE FINANCIAL TRANSACTION.

1.4.1 The principle of double-entry bookkeeping

The system of double-entry bookkeeping operates on the basis that when the business is involved in a transaction there are two sides to the transaction:

1. the business receives value from the transaction;
2. the business gives consideration for the value received.

The double-entry system records both sides of the transaction so that somewhere in the accounts both parts of the transactions will be shown—the double entry.

For example, if a firm buys a computer for £1,000 cash, it has gained an asset, but has lost cash. If the business provides legal services and is paid £500, then it has gained cash of £500, but given consideration of the work done, which is the source of the income.

The benefit received is shown on the left hand side of the account and called the **DEBIT** entry, the consideration given is shown on the right hand side of the account, and called the **CREDIT** entry.

DEBIT   CREDIT
BENEFIT RECEIVED   CONSIDERATION GIVEN

This may seem strange or wrong at this stage, as you may associate credit with receipts, and debit with payments out, usually based on your bank statement sent out from the bank, where payments out of your account are shown as debit entries and receipts are shown as credit entries.

EXAMPLE

Jane pays £1,000 into her bank account with the Northern Bank PLC. The Northern Bank will draw up its accounts as follows:

Northern Bank PLC cash account

	Benefit received DEBIT	Consideration given CREDIT	Balance
Jane	1,000		1,000 DR

Jane account

	Benefit received DEBIT	Consideration given CREDIT	Balance
Cash		1,000	1,000 CR

The bank has followed the rules given above, but all Jane sees is her account, which is one part of the double entry. From Jane's point of view the credit entry records a receipt. From the Bank's point of view the receipt was DEBITED on the Bank's cash account and Jane's account was CREDITED to show that Jane has given the cash. Jane is a creditor of the Bank—see later.

Remember that the two entries made DO record the same SINGLE transaction. The principle of double-entry bookkeeping is therefore: *for every debit entry in one account there must be a corresponding credit entry in another account.*

1.4.2 The layout of an account

There are several methods of drawing an account. The method adopted in this book is as follows.

Name of account

Date	Details	DR	CR	Balance

Note the following:

(a) This layout has five columns.

(b) There is one column each for date and details. Note that the details column must indicate clearly the name of the account which forms the other part of the double entry.

(c) The column headed 'DR' (abbreviation of debit) is always on the LEFT. Debit entries are made in this column.

(d) The column headed 'CR' (abbreviation of credit) is always on the RIGHT. Credit entries are made in this column.

(e) There is a balance column which gives a running balance on the account after each transaction is completed. The balance is the difference between the debit and credit entries. If the debit side is heavier than the credit side then there is a debit balance, and vice versa.

Note that for solicitors, Rule 32(5) of the Solicitors' Accounts Rules 1998 imposes an obligation to show the current balance on each client's ledger, or the balance must be readily ascertainable from the records kept.

1.4.3 An example of double-entry bookkeeping

On 1 March the business buys a car for £3,000 and pays by cheque drawn on the firm's bank account. The two sides to this transaction are:

1. the receipt of value in the form of an asset acquired by the business, i.e, the car;

2. the giving of consideration, i.e., reducing the firm's bank balance by £3,000.

To record this transaction the firm will use two accounts:

1. the motor cars account;
2. the cash account.

Motor cars account

Date	Details	Dr	Cr	Balance
1 March	Cash—purchase of car	3,000		

Cash account

Date	Details	Dr	Cr	Balance
		Received	Paid	
1 March	Motor cars		3,000	

1.5 Classification of accounts

All financial transactions will therefore need to be recorded by double entry in the ledger (day-to-day) accounts of a business. These ledger accounts can be divided into three groups:

1. Personal accounts—accounts for each individual, business or company dealing with the business;
2. Asset (real) accounts—accounts showing each asset or set of assets (e.g, cars) of the business;
3. Nominal accounts
   (a) Income accounts name the source of the income;
   (b) Expense accounts name the source of the loss.

Using the double-entry system there are set rules for these accounts, set out below. These rules can be memorised, and followed for every entry you will ever need to make on ledger accounts. Once you have used these rules for some time, you will find that the accounts do always follow the two-fold aspect of benefit and consideration mentioned previously.

A summary of the rules for these groups of accounts is set out briefly below, then a more detailed explanation is given.

1. ASSET(real) accounts

   DEBIT when business receives an asset or assets are increased.

   CREDIT when the business disposes of an asset or if the assets are reduced.

2. Nominal INCOME or EXPENSE accounts

   CREDIT Income accounts—they name the source of the income.

   DEBIT—Expense accounts—they name the source of the loss.

3. PERSONAL accounts

   DEBIT—the personal account which receives goods, cash or services from the business.

   CREDIT—the personal account which has given goods, cash or services to the business.

1.5.1 Personal accounts

A separate account must be kept for each person, firm or company with which the business has dealings, for example, each debtor and creditor.

The rule for making entries in a personal account is:

DEBIT   When goods, cash or services are received by that person or company from the business, i.e. they are being charged for the goods, etc.
(They are then a DEBTOR)

CREDIT   When that person or company gives goods, cash or services to the business, i.e. the business owes them money for the goods, etc.
(They are then a CREDITOR)

1.5.2 The personal accounts of the business owner

As the accounts look at a transaction from the point of view of the business, the business and its owner are treated as separate entities. This principle holds good for a solicitor's practice. The accounts which record transactions between the business and its owner are personal accounts. These accounts are:

1.5.2.1 The owner's Captial

When a person sets up in business he or she will introduce assets, e.g., money, premises, car and equipment. When this happens:

(a) DEBIT the relevant asset account.

(b) CREDIT the Capital account, which will show the amount due to the owner.

EXAMPLE

On 1 January Harry starts up in practice as a sole practitioner. He introduces £8,000 cash, a car valued at £5,000 and office equipment worth £2,000. These opening entries will be recorded as follows:

Cash account—Asset account/personal account with bank

Date	Details	DR	CR	Balance
		(Received)	(Paid)	
1 Jan	Capital introduced by Harry	8,000		8,000 DR

Car account—Asset account

Date	Details	DR	CR	Balance
1 Jan	Capital introduced by Harry	5,000		5,000 DR

Office equipment account—Asset account

Date	Details	DR	CR	Balance
1 Jan	Capital introduced by Harry	2,000		2,000 DR

Capital account—personal account of the owner

Date	Details	DR	CR	Balance
1 Jan	Cash		8,000	8,000 CR
	Car		5,000	13,000 CR
	Office equipment		2,000	15,000 CR

1.5.2.2 Drawings account

From time to time the owner will take money out of the business either in cash or by paying private expenses, for example, a home gas bill. These are called drawings and are usually recorded in a personal account, the drawings account.

The drawings account will always be DEBITED.

EXAMPLE

On 31 January Harry draws £1,000 out of the firm's bank account for his own use and pays his personal tax of £500. The entries to record these transactions are as follows:

Drawings account—Personal account

Date	Details	DR	CR	Balance
31 Jan	Cash—drawings	1,000		
31 Jan	Cash—personal tax	500		1,500 DR

Cash account—Asset/personal account with bank

Date	Details	DR	CR	Balance
	Balance			8,000 DR
31 Jan	Drawings—cash		1,000	7,000 DR
	Drawings—personal tax		500	6,500 DR

The credit balance on the capital account shows the amount which the business owes to its owner, i.e., the amount he has invested. The debit balance on the drawings account shows the amount the owner owes the business.

1.5.3 Asset/real accounts

These will show the assets at the price paid for them (cost price).

It is not always easy to decide whether a purchase should be recorded as an asset, or as an expense. For example if the business buys office furniture, this is likely to last for some time and so will be recorded as an asset. However, if the business buys stationery, this will be used up in a fairly short time, and so it will be recorded as an expense.

The cash account

This is not only a real account, it is also a personal account with the bank.

The business will usually place most of its cash in the bank, it will pay all cheques received into the bank, and make most payments out by cheque or transfer. Any cash in the bank will be an asset. However if the business went overdrawn at the bank, then the overdraft would be a liability.

The petty cash account

This deals with cash payments made by the firm. A cash sum will be taken out of the bank each week as a cash float. This can be used to make payments out, and topped up when required.

The rule for making entries in an asset account is:

DEBIT   receipt of an asset.
CREDIT reduction of an asset.

EXAMPLE   ASSET ACCOUNTS

Assume that a firm has £10,000 cash in the bank.
The firm purchases office furniture for £2,000.
DEBIT the increase on the office furniture account.
CREDIT the decrease on the Cash Account.

Office furniture account

Date	Details	DR	CR	Balance
	Cash	2,000		2,000 DR

Cash account

Date	Details	DR	CR	Balance
	Balance			10,000 DR
	Office Furniture		2,000	8,000 DR

The balances on the accounts show the shift in assets from cash to office furniture; at first the firm had £10,000 cash, now it has £8,000 cash and office furniture worth £2,000.

1.5.4 Income and expense accounts

(a) INCOME ACCOUNTS These record the receipt of income by the firm. The following are examples of income accounts kept by a solicitor:
  (i) Profit costs account—this account shows the profit costs charged to clients. It is based on the bills sent to clients.
  (ii) Interest received account—this account shows interest received by the firm on money held in a deposit account.
  (iii) Rent received account—this account shows rent received by the firm if it leases out any of its surplus office accommodation.

Income accounts are CREDITED with income received and will therefore always have CREDIT balances.

EXAMPLE

A firm lets its surplus office premises for which it receives rent of £800 per month. On 1 January the firm receives the first month's rent.

CREDIT   Rent received account.
DEBIT   Cash Book.

Rent received account

Date	Details	DR	CR	Balance
1 Jan	Cash		800	800 CR

Cash account

Date	Details	DR	CR	Balance
1 Jan	Rent received	800		800 DR

EXAMPLE

The firm does work for Basil, for which the charge is £500. When the bill is sent to Basil, the income (work done) account will be credited; it shows what the business has given in return for the gain. Note that in solicitors' firms the income account based on the bills sent out is usually called the Profit Costs account. Basil's personal account will be debited, showing that Basil has received £500 worth of services. The debit balance will show that Basil is a debtor of the firm; he owes £500.

CREDIT   Profit costs account.
DEBIT   Basil account.

Profit Costs account (work done account)
Income

Date	Details	DR	CR	Balance
	Basil—bill		500	500 CR

Basil account (personal account)

Date	Details	DR	CR	Balance
	Profit costs—bill	500		500 DR

When Basil pays the bill, the entries will be:

DEBIT   The Cash account (real account).
CREDIT   Basil's account.

Cash account

Date	Details	DR	CR	Balance
	Balance say			8,000 DR
	Basil	500		8,500 DR

Basil account

Date	Details	DR	CR	Balance
	Balance			500 DR
	Cash you		500	—

The debt of £500 due from Basil has been paid and converted into cash.

Note: the balance on Basil's account was £500 debit, the balance is now nil as the amount owed has been paid.

(b) EXPENSE ACCOUNTS. These record the payment of business expenses.

   (i) A separate expense account is opened for each type of expense which the firm has; for example, most firms will have rent, council tax, electricity, telephone and salaries accounts.

   (ii) An expense account is DEBITED each time the firm pays a business expense.

EXAMPLE

On 30 November the firm pays an office electricity bill of £500.

DEBIT   Electricity account.
CREDIT   Cash account.

Electricity account

Date	Details	DR	CR	Balance
30 Nov	Cash	500		500 DR

Cash account

Date	Details	DR (Received)	CR (Paid out)	Balance
	Balance say			5,000 DR
30 Nov	Electricity		500	4,500 DR

Payments made under any leasing or rental agreement are business expenses and are recorded in an expense account.

EXAMPLE

A firm leases word processors from Computer Supplies Ltd. The quarterly rental is £100. On 1 April the first instalment is paid. Assume the firm has a cash balance of £5,000 at the bank.

DEBIT   Rental account.
CREDIT Cash account.

Word processors rentals account

Date	Details	DR	CR	Balance
1 Apr	Cash	100		100 DR

Cash account

Date	Details	DR	CR	Balance
1 Apr	Balance Word processors rentals		100	5,000 DR 4,900 DR

Expense accounts will always have DEBIT balances.

1.5.5 Trading accounts

Manufacturing and trading accounts are dealt with in more detail in **Chapter 7**, where the same principles apply. Where goods are purchased as part of the trading cycle, e.g. goods are purchased for £6,500 cash, the entries would be:

CREDIT the cash account £6,500.
DEBIT the Purchases (expense account) £6,500.

On the assumption that the firm starts with £16,500 cash then the accounts would be as follows:

Cash account

Date	Details	DR	CR	Balance
	Balance Purchases		6,500	16,500 DR 10,000 DR

Purchases account

Date	Details	DR	CR	Balance
	Cash	6,500		6,500 DR

When the goods are sold a separate sales account will be opened. This will be CREDITED.

EXAMPLE

Assume the business has £10,000 Cash.
Goods are sold for £9,000 cash.

DEBIT   The cash account £9,000.
CREDIT The sales account (an income account) £9,000.

Cash account

Date	Details	DR	CR	Balance
	Balance			10,000 DR
	Sales	9,000		19,000 DR

Sales account (nominal income account)

Date	Details	DR	CR	Balance
	Cash		9,000	9,000 CR

1.5.6 Solicitors and accounts

Note that as solicitors will usually be holding large sums of money on behalf of clients they will have at least two bank accounts, one dealing with the firm's own money, called OFFICE ACCOUNT and the other dealing with clients' money called CLIENT ACCOUNT. For further details see Chapter 11 onwards.

1.6 Worked example on double entry

Fiona, a sole practitioner, sets up her practice on 1 February with £10,000 cash, office equipment worth £1,000 and premises valued at £140,000.

During the month of February the practice engages in the following transactions:

1. It pays her secretary's salary of £1,300.
2. It receives one month's rent from the tenant occupying part of the office premises—£800.
3. It buys a desk for £500.
4. It buys a car on credit from Karsales Ltd for £9,000.
5. Fiona draws £1,000 out of the bank for her own use.
6. The firm sends a bill to Jim for £500, re profit costs for work done.
7. Jim pays the bill of £500.

Cash account

Date	Details	DR	CR	Balance
Feb	Capital introduced	10,000		10,000 DR
	Salaries		1,300	8,700 DR
	Rent received	800		9,500 DR
	Office furniture		500	9,000 DR
	Drawings (cash)		1,000	8,000 DR
	Jim	500		8,500 DR

A real account/personal account with the bank.

Office equipment account

Date	Details	DR	CR	Balance
Feb 1	Capital introduced	1,000		1,000 DR

A real/asset account.

Premises account

Date	Details	DR	CR	Balance
Feb 1	Capital introduced	140,000		140,000 DR

A real/asset account.

Capital account

Date	Details	DR	CR	Balance
Feb	Cash		10,000	10,000 CR
	Office equipment		1,000	11,000 CR
	Premises		140,000	151,000 CR

A personal account.

Salaries account

Date	Details	DR	CR	Balance
Feb	Cash (secretary)	1,300		1,300 DR

A nominal expense account.

Rent received account

Date	Details	DR	CR	Balance
Feb	Cash		800	800 CR

A nominal income account.

Office furniture account

Date	Details	DR	CR	Balance
Feb	Cash (desk)	500		500 DR

A real/asset account.

Motor vehicles account

Date	Details	DR	CR	Balance
Feb	Karsales Ltd (car)	9,000		9,000 DR

A real/asset account.

Karsales Ltd account

Date	Details	DR	CR	Balance
Feb	Motor vehicles (car)		9,000	9,000 CR

A personal account.

Drawings account

Date	Details	DR	CR	Balance
Feb	Cash (drawings)	1,000		1,000 DR

A personal account.

Profit costs income account

Date	Details	DR	CR	Balance
	Jim—bill		500	500 CR

A nominal income account.

Jim

Date	Details	DR	CR	Balance
	Profit costs—bill	500		500 DR
	Cash—you		500	—

A personal account.

1.7 Check list

By the end of this chapter you should be able to:

1. appreciate that for ONE financial transaction there will be TWO entries—A DEBIT ENTRY on one account; and A CREDIT ENTRY on another account;
2. identify the main types of account being: INCOME accounts and EXPENSE accounts; ASSET (REAL) accounts; PERSONAL accounts;
3. understand which of these accounts will be debited or credited;
4. complete all the self-test exercises at the end of the chapter. Once you have done these, move on to the Trial Balance (Chapter 2).

1.8 Exercises on double-entry bookkeeping

1. Allow 5 to 10 minutes for this.

    State the double entry that would be made in the following transactions:

    (a) Kirk starts a business and introduces cash of £5,000.

    (b) Little and Co. receive cash of £600 in payment of work done.

    (c) North pays out £300 in respect of an electricity bill.

    (d) Fishwick pays an employee's salary of £500.

    (e) Grayling draws £1,000 from her business for her own use.

    (f) Morris purchases a car for his business for £15,000 on credit from Stockton Garage Ltd.

2 Allow 5 to 10 minutes for this.

   Blears starts in business on 1 January as a solicitor, and introduces cash of £6,000 and office furniture worth £4,000. Show the accounts to record this.

3 Allow 10 minutes for this.

   Latter starts a business with £5,000 cash on 10 November. He then buys a computer for £800 on 11 November. He sends a bill for £1,000 to a customer, Howard, for work done on 20 November.

   Show the accounts to record this.

4 Allow 20 to 30 minutes for this.

   Paula starts in practice as a solicitor on 1 July with cash of £10,000, a car worth £16,000 and premises worth £128,000. During the month of July the following transactions occur:

1 July	Pays council tax £900.
3 July	Buys office furniture £1,800. Pays by cheque.
8 July	Pays secretary's salary £1,500.
10 July	Receives £12,500 as a loan from her brother-in-law Ted, to be repaid in three years without interest.
14 July	Draws £2,500 for her own use.

   Prepare accounts to record the above transactions.

1.9 Suggested answers to exercises on double-entry bookkeeping

1
   (a) DEBIT the Cash Account £5,000.
       CREDIT the Capital Account (for Kirk) £5,000.
   (b) DEBIT the Cash Account £600.
       CREDIT the Profit costs (work done) account (income account) £600.
   (c) CREDIT Cash Account £300.
       DEBIT Electricity account (expense account) £300.
   (d) CREDIT Cash Account £500.
       DEBIT Salaries account (expense account) £500.
   (e) CREDIT Cash Account £1,000.
       DEBIT Drawings account (personal account) £1,000.
   (f) DEBIT Car account (asset account) £15,000.
       CREDIT Stockton Garage Ltd account (personal account) £15,000.

2 **Cash account**

Date	Details	DR	CR	Balance
1 Jan	Capital	6,000		6,000 DR

Office furniture account

Date	Details	DR	CR	Balance
1 Jan	Capital	4,000		4,000 DR

Capital account

Date	Details	DR	CR	Balance
1 Jan	Cash Office furniture		6,000 4,000	6,000 CR 10,000 CR

3 Cash account

Date	Details	DR	CR	Balance
10 Nov	Capital	5,000		5,000 DR
11 Nov	Computer		800	4,200 DR

Capital account

Date	Details	DR	CR	Balance
10 Nov	Cash		5,000	5,000 CR

Computer account

Date	Details	DR	CR	Balance
11 Nov	Cash	800		800 DR

Howard account

Date	Details	DR	CR	Balance
20 Nov	Profit costs –bill	1,000		1,000 DR

Profit costs

Date	Details	DR	CR	Balance
20 Nov	Howard–bill		1,000	1,000 CR

4 Cash account

Date	Details	DR	CR	Balance
1 July	Capital	10,000		10,000 DR
	Council tax		900	9,100 DR
3 July	Office furniture		1,800	7,300 DR
8 July	Salary		1,500	5,800 DR
10 July	Loan: Ted	12,500		18,300 DR
14 July	Drawings		2,500	15,800 DR

Car account

Date	Details	DR	CR	Balance
1 July	Capital	16,000		16,000 DR

Premises account

Date	Details	DR	CR	Balance
1 July	Capital	128,000		128,000 DR

Capital account

Date	Details	DR	CR	Balance
1 July	Cash		10,000	10,000 CR
	Car		16,000	26,000 CR
	Premises		128,000	154,000 CR

Council tax account

Date	Details	DR	CR	Balance
1 July	Cash	900		900 DR

Office furniture account

Date	Details	DR	CR	Balance
3 July	Cash	1,800		1,800 DR

Salaries account

Date	Details	DR	CR	Balance
8 July	Cash (secretary)	1,500		1,500 DR

Loan account: Ted

Date	Details	DR	CR	Balance
10 July	Cash		12,500	12,500 CR

Drawings account

Date	Details	DR	CR	Balance
14 July	Cash	2,500		2,500 DR

The Trial Balance

2.1 The Trial Balance

Note that this is only a LIST of all the balances at the end of each account—it is not an account.

2.1.1 Purpose of the Trial Balance

The Trial Balance is used:

1. to check the accuracy of the double entry bookkeeping;
2. as a first stage in drawing up the Final accounts.

2.1.2 Preparation of the Trial Balance

As two entries are always made for each single transaction, one debit and one credit, then all the debit entries must equal all the credit entries. Provided all the entries are correct, then all the debit balances at the end of the accounts should equal all the credit balances at the end of the accounts.

To check the accuracy of the double entries that have been made a Trial Balance is drawn up. This will be done regularly, and also before the final accounts are prepared. All the balances at the end of each account are listed. There will be one column for all the debit balances and one column for all the credit balances. Each column will be added up.

On the Trial Balance
The DEBIT column will show EITHER assets OR expense accounts.
The CREDIT column will show EITHER liabilities OR income accounts.

2.1.3 Suspense accounts

If the debit and credit columns do not agree, even after checking all the entries, it may be necessary to adjust for the difference by opening a Suspense account until the difference can be found. Thus, if the credit balances exceed the debit balances by £100 a Suspense account can be opened with a debit balance of £100.

> **EXAMPLE TRIAL BALANCE**
>
> On 31 October the bookkeeper extracts the following balances from the accounts of A. Solicitor:
>
> | | |
> |---|---:|
> | Profit costs | 16,000 |
> | Capital account | 15,000 |
> | Motor cars account | 20,000 |
> | Office furniture account | 5,000 |
> | Rent paid account | 1,300 |
> | General expenses account | 200 |

Council tax account	1,250
Postage account	100
Stationery account	80
Salaries account	1,600
Drawings account	800
Cash account	4,500 DR
Petty cash account	170
Loan account	4,000

The following trial balance is then prepared.

A. Solicitor: Trial Balance as at 31 October

Name of account	DR	CR
Profit costs		16,000
Capital amount due to owner		15,000
Motor cars—asset/real account	20,000	
Office furniture—asset/real	5,000	
Rent—expense	1,300	
General expenses—expense	200	
Council tax—expense	1,250	
Postage—expense	100	
Stationery—expense	80	
Salaries—expense	1,600	
Drawings—amount taken out by owner—personal	800	
Cash—asset/real	4,500	
Petty cash—asset/real	170	
Loan—liabiity		4,000
Totals	35,000	35,000

You can see from the above that the DEBIT balances show either ASSET accounts or EXPENSE accounts. The CREDIT balances show either LIABILITIES (e.g. due to the owner of the business or creditors) or INCOME accounts.

2.1.4 Errors not revealed by the Trial Balance

The fact that the total debit and total credit balances agree does not mean that the bookkeeper has not made any mistakes. There are some errors which will not be revealed by the trial balance, for example:

(a) Errors of entry—the same incorrect entry is made in both accounts used to record the transaction.

EXAMPLE

The firm buys a typewriter for £500. The bookkeeper inadvertently makes a debit entry in the office equipment account of £50 and a credit entry of £50 in the cash account.

(b) Compensating errors—the bookkeeper makes two separate errors which cancel each other out.

> **EXAMPLE**
>
> The bookkeeper incorrectly totals one account by £100 too much on the credit side and another by £100 too much on the debit side.

(c) Errors of omission—the bookkeeper leaves out both parts of the double entry from the accounts.

(d) Errors of commission—the bookkeeper makes the right entry but in the wrong account.

> **EXAMPLE**
>
> The firm buys office equipment costing £1,000. Instead of debiting the office equipment account with £1,000 the bookkeeper debits the office furniture account.

(e) Errors of principle—the bookkeeper makes an entry in the wrong type of account.

> **EXAMPLE**
>
> The purchase of office equipment is shown in the general expenses account, i.e., a nominal instead of a real account. If this error remains undetected at the time the firm's final accounts are prepared the business expenses will be overstated in the profit and loss account and the value of the assets will be understated in the balance sheet.

2.2 Check list

By the end of this chapter you should:

1. understand the nature of the Trial Balance and its limitations;
2. be able to categorise the types of accounts listed on the Trial Balance;
3. identify which accounts would have a debit balance and which a credit balance (note for those accounts which could have either a credit or a debit balance you will be told whether it is a debit or a credit balance);
4. have completed all the self-test exercises at the end of the chapter.

2.3 Exercises on double-entry bookkeeping and Trial Balance

Once you have completed these exercises, move on to Final Accounts (Chapter 3).

1 Allow 10 to 15 minutes for this exercise.

The bookkeeper has extracted the following balances from the accounts of Hooper, a sole practitioner, on 30 September. From the balances you are asked to prepare a Trial Balance. State what each account is, for example an asset account, a personal account, or an income or expense account.

Salaries	1,000
Leasehold property	15,000
Capital	35,000
Drawings	2,000
Administration expenses	4,000
Motor cars	12,500
Cash account	500 DR

2 Allow 15 to 20 minutes for this exercise.

From the following information, extracted as at 30 June, prepare a trial balance for Timothy, a sole practitioner.

General expenses	200
Salaries	1,200
Drawings	4,000
Rent	1,250
Council tax	150
Electricity	800
Creditors	2,500
Office furniture	7,000
Bank overdraft	2,300
Loan account	9,000
Car	7,700
Capital	8,500

3 Allow 20 to 25 minutes for this exercise.

The bookkeeper has extracted the following balances from the accounts of Sally Jones, a sole practitioner, on 31 January. From the balances you are asked to prepare a Trial Balance.

Salaries	3,000
Office equipment	15,000
Freehold property	235,000
Capital	220,000
Drawings	13,200
Midshire Bank—loan account	20,000
Cash—office account	1,000 DR
Cash—client account	125,000 DR
Council tax	900
General expenses	1,400
Debtors	2,000
Creditors	1,500
Rent received	2,000
Profit costs	30,000
Due to clients	125,000
Bank interest paid	2,000

2.4 Suggested answers to exercises on the Trial Balance

1 Hooper: Trial Balance as at 30 September

Name of account	DR	CR
Salaries—expense	1,000	
Leasehold property—asset	15,000	
Capital—personal		35,000
Drawings—personal	2,000	
Administration expenses—expense	4,000	
Motor cars—asset	12,500	
Cash account—asset/personal	500	
Totals	35,000	35,000

2 **Timothy: Trial Balance as at 31 June**

Name of account	DR	CR
General expenses	200	
Salaries	1,200	
Drawings	4,000	
Rent	1,250	
Council tax	150	
Electricity	800	
Creditors		2,500
Office furniture	7,000	
Cash		2,300
Loan account		9,000
Car	7,700	
Capital		8,500
Totals	22,300	22,300

3 **Sally Jones: Trial Balance as at 31 January**

Name of account	DR	CR
Salaries	3,000	
Office equipment	15,000	
Freehold property	235,000	
Capital		220,000
Drawings	13,200	
Loan account		20,000
Cash (office)	1,000	
Cash (client)	125,000	
Council tax	900	
General expenses	1,400	
Debtors	2,000	
Creditors		1,500
Rent received		2,000
Profit costs		30,000
Due to clients		125,000
Bank interest paid	2,000	
Totals	398,500	398,500

2.5 Full exercise on the Trial Balance

Allow about 40 minutes to complete this exercise.

Jane starts in practice as a solicitor on 1 January. She introduces £15,000 into the firm's bank account and a car worth £8,200. During the month of January the following transactions take place:

4 January   Pays rent of £1,000.
5 January   Pays salary £1,200 to secretary.

6 January Buys a computer costing £650 on credit from Wylie Ltd.
22 January Buys stationery for £80.
24 January Pays instalment of £65 to Wylie Ltd.
25 January Draws £1,600 for her own use.

Prepare accounts to record the above transactions, and prepare a trial balance as at 31 January.

2.6 Suggested answers to exercise on double-entry bookkeeping and Trial Balance

Cash account

Date	Details	DR Receipts	CR Payments Out	Balance
1 Jan	Capital	15,000		15,000 DR
4 Jan	Rent		1,000	14,000 DR
5 Jan	Salaries		1,200	12,800 DR
22 Jan	Stationery		80	12,720 DR
24 Jan	Wylie Ltd		65	12,655 DR
25 Jan	Drawings		1,600	11,055 DR

Capital account

Date	Details	DR	CR	Balance
1 Jan	Cash		15,000	15,000 CR
	Car		8,200	23,200 CR

Car account

Date	Details	DR	CR	Balance
1 Jan	Capital	8,200		8,200 DR

Rent account

Date	Details	DR	CR	Balance
4 Jan	Cash	1,000		1,000 DR

Salaries account

Date	Details	DR	CR	Balance
5 Jan	Cash (secretary)	1,200		1,200 DR

Office equipment account—computer account

Date	Details	DR	CR	Balance
6 Jan	Wylie Ltd (computer)	650		650 DR

Wylie Ltd

Date	Details	DR	CR	Balance
6 Jan	Office equipment		650	650 CR
24 Jan	Cash	65		585 CR

Stationery account

Date	Details	DR	CR	Balance
22 Jan	Cash	80		80 DR

Drawings account

Date	Details	DR	CR	Balance
25 Jan	Cash	1,600		1,600 DR

Jane: Trial Balance as at 31 January

Name of account	DR	CR
Cash	11,055	
Capital		23,200
Car	8,200	
Rent	1,000	
Salaries	1,200	
Office equipment	650	
Wylie Ltd		585
Stationery	80	
Drawings	1,600	
Totals	23,785	23,785

3

Final accounts

3.1 Introduction

Basic final accounts consist of:

(1) the Profit and Loss account;

(2) the Balance Sheet.

Final accounts are usually prepared annually at the end of the firm's financial year.

Immediately before the final accounts are prepared a trial balance is drawn up listing the balances on the accounts. Each balance shown on the trial balance will EITHER be:

(a) transferred to the Profit and Loss account;

OR

(b) shown on the Balance Sheet.

3.1.1 Profit and Loss account

Note that this is a double-entry account, i.e., it is part of the double-entry system.

Its function is to calculate the net profit or loss made by the practice during the financial year. It shows income less expenses.

3.1.2 Balance Sheet

The Balance Sheet is a statement of the firm's assets and liabilities on a given date, usually the last day of the financial year. It shows what the firm owns and what it owes.

The Balance Sheet is NOT an account and is therefore not part of the double-entry system. It is a list of the balances on the asset and liability accounts.

At any time the assets of a business should equal its liabilities. This is because each time the business acquires something of value it gives consideration.

EXAMPLE

X, a solicitor, commences in practice with £2,000 in cash which is placed in the firm's bank account. Immediately X has a balance sheet; it is:

Liability		Asset	
Capital	2,000	Cash at bank	2,000

X's practice is thus shown to own £2,000 cash (an asset) all of which is owed to X, the owner of the practice (a liability).

3.2 Closing the accounts

(a) Before preparing the final accounts the Income and Expense accounts are closed by transferring the balance on each account to the Profit and Loss account.

(b) Expense accounts have DEBIT balances and so to transfer from an expense account to the Profit and Loss account, the bookkeeping entries are:
   (i) CREDIT the nominal expense account.
   (ii) DEBIT the profit and loss account.

All you have done is move the debit balance to the Profit and Loss account.

EXAMPLE

At the end of the year the firm's salaries account has a debit balance of £15,000. The balance is transferred to the Profit and Loss account on 31 December.

Salaries account

Date	Details	DR	CR	Balance
	Balance			15,000 DR
31 Dec	Profit and Loss account: transfer		15,000	—

(c) Income accounts have CREDIT balances and so to transfer from an income account to the Profit and Loss account, the bookkeeping entries are:
   (i) DEBIT the income account.
   (ii) CREDIT the Profit and Loss account.

EXAMPLE

At the end of the year the firm's Profit Costs account has a credit balance of £300,000. On 31 December the balance is transferred to the Profit and Loss account.

Costs account

Date	Details	DR	CR	Balance
	Balance			300,000 CR
31 Dec	Profit and Loss account: transfer	300,000		—

(d) These transfer entries close the Income and Expense accounts.

(e) The Balance Sheet, unlike the Profit and Loss account, is not an account of double entry and so the balances on the asset and liability accounts are not transferred to the Balance Sheet. They are merely listed on the Balance Sheet. The asset and liability accounts are ongoing and will be kept open for as long as the asset is owned by the firm or for as long as the liability remains unsettled.

3.3 Presentation of final accounts

3.3.1 Vertical format: Profit and Loss account

There are two methods of presenting final accounts: the horizontal format and the vertical format. In this book, the vertical format will be used. A basic vertical format Profit and Loss account is shown in the following example:

Sally Jones: Profit and Loss account for the year ended 30 September 200—

INCOME		
Profit costs	300,000	
ADD ADDITIONAL INCOME		
Rent received	20,000	
TOTAL INCOME		320,000
LESS EXPENSES		
Salaries	60,000	
Rates	9,000	
General expenses	14,000	
Bank interest charged	2,000	85,000
NET PROFIT		235,000

This is only a very basic example of a Profit and Loss account. You will see in the next chapter that adjustments will be made to give a more accurate picture of the profit or loss.

3.3.2 Notes on the Profit and Loss account

(a) At the end of the financial year the Income and Expense accounts are closed. The credit balances from the Income accounts are transferred to the Income part of the Profit and Loss account. The debit balances from the Expense accounts are transferred to the Expenses part of the Profit and Loss account.

(b) The balance left after deducting total Expenses from total Income is net profit (or loss). If a profit is made this is credited to the Capital account in the case of a sole owner. If a loss is made this is debited to the Capital account. For the position in the case of a partnership see **Chapter 6**.

(c) Note that Drawings made by the owner are appropriations of profit, NOT business expenses. Thus the balance on the Drawings account is NOT transferred to the Profit and Loss account, but will be shown on the Balance Sheet.

3.4 The Balance Sheet

3.4.1 Definitions

3.4.1.1 Assets

A business may own all kinds of assets, for example:

   Premises—freehold or leasehold

   Office furniture

Office equipment

Machinery

Stocks of goods

Cars

Work in Progress (the value of work done but not yet billed)

Debtors (they will pay and convert the debts into cash)

Cash at the Bank

Cash in hand (petty cash)

Note that assets are split into two groups:

FIXED ASSETS

CURRENT ASSETS.

Fixed Assets

These are assets which are held long term, they are not part of the day to day working cycle. Examples would be:

Premises

Factory Machinery

Office equipment

Office furniture

Library

Cars.

Current assets

Also known as circulating assets. These arise from the day-to-day trading or working cycle of the business, they represent cash, or are intended for conversion into cash, or they have a short life, e.g., stationery. They include: cash at the bank, petty cash, debtors, work in progress and payments in advance (see later). If the firm is a trading one, then goods (stock) intended for resale will be a current asset.

Those assets which are cash, or assets which can be easily converted into cash, e.g. debtors, are known as liquid assets.

3.4.1.2 Liabilities

Money owed by the business in respect of loans to the business, e.g. capital, bank loans, mortgages, or money owed for goods or services supplied to the firm, i.e. creditors.

Like assets liabilities can be broken down into groups:

(a) Capital;

(b) Long-term liabilities;

(c) Current liabilities.

3.4.1.3 Capital

This is the amount due to the owner of the business. It will include the value of any assets the owner introduced to the business. Any profit made will also belong to the owner, less any drawings that the owner has taken out over the year.

This will be shown as follows:
For a sole owner

> CAPITAL
> PLUS PROFIT
> LESS DRAWINGS
> equals TOTAL DUE TO OWNER.

Note that the Drawings account is a personal account, showing that the proprietor is a debtor of the business. It is not an expense account and should never be shown on the Profit and Loss account. Think of it as a personal account which will reduce the amount due to the owner.

Long-term liabilities

Usually some formal loan from an individual, bank or other financial institution, repayable over, or after, a stated number of years. These would include long-term bank loans (not usually overdrafts), private loans, mortgages.

Current liabilities

If a liability has to be settled in the short term, then it is a current liability. Current liabilities include: creditors, bank overdrafts, outstanding expenses.

3.4.2 The form of the Balance Sheet

The form more commonly used now is the vertical form. The Balance Sheet is in two halves.

The first half will show NET ASSETS.
The second half will show THE TOTAL DUE TO THE OWNER.
The two totals should be equal.

3.4.3 Listing assets and liabilities on the Balance Sheet

There is a common set order in listing the assets and liabilities on the balance sheet.

Assets

Fixed assets are shown first and then Current assets. The general rule is that you start at the top with the most permanent asset and work down to the least permanent. The top asset on the list will be the most difficult to turn into cash, the bottom will be the most liquid asset, e.g. cash itself. (The order of liquidity is reversed.)

For example, fixed assets may start with premises, which are usually the most permanent fixed asset belonging to the firm, and end with motor cars which are usually the least permanent fixed asset. Current assets start with work in progress which is the least liquid current asset, as it needs two stages to be converted into cash; first it would have to be billed, then the debtors will have to pay.

Current liabilities are deducted from the Current Assets, to give a figure known as Net Current Assets, or Working Capital, being that part of the capital invested in the business which is left to run the business after providing the Fixed Assets. This important figure is then added to the Fixed Assets.

Long-term liabilities will then be deducted from this total, which gives the total Net Assets.

The total achieved should equal the Capital due to the owner of the business.

A summary of the vertical form Balance Sheet is as follows:

NAME OF BUSINESS
BALANCE SHEET as at 31 December 200—

```
FIXED ASSETS
ADD
NET CURRENT ASSETS
(BEING CURRENT ASSETS
LESS CURRENT LIABILITIES)
                                        TOTAL

LESS LONG-TERM LIABILITIES
                                        FINAL TOTAL, i.e., NET ASSETS

CAPITAL EMPLOYED
CAPITAL
ADD NET PROFIT
         SUB TOTAL
LESS DRAWINGS
                                        FINAL TOTAL—AMOUNT DUE TO OWNER(S)
```

3.4.4 The solicitor and client money

When a solicitor handles money on behalf of his/her clients, it is the client's money and not the solicitor's. The Solicitors' Accounts Rules 1998 say that a solicitor must keep the records showing dealings with this money totally separate from the solicitor's own money. To do this the solicitor must have a separate bank account (or accounts) for clients' money called the Client Account. The money held in the client bank account(s) must always equal the amount that is shown due to clients.

This can be shown at the end of the balance sheet.

3.4.5 An example of vertical format: Balance Sheet

Sally Jones: Balance Sheet as at 30 September 200—

FIXED ASSETS		
Freehold property	235,000	
Office equipment	15,000	
		250,000
CURRENT ASSETS		
Debtors	20,000	
Cash (office bank account)	10,000	
	30,000	
LESS CURRENT LIABILITIES		
Creditors	15,000	

NET CURRENT ASSETS		15,000
		265,000
LESS LONG-TERM LIABILITIES		
Midshire Bank loan		40,000
TOTAL NET ASSETS		225,000
CAPITAL EMPLOYED		
Capital	200,000	
Add net profit	64,000	
		264,000
Less drawings		39,000
TOTAL DUE TO OWNER		225,000
CLIENT ACCOUNT		
Cash at bank client current account	300,000	
deposit account	200,000	500,000
Due to clients		500,000

3.5 Check list

By the end of this chapter you should be able to:

1. understand the functions of a Profit and Loss account and a Balance Sheet;
2. identify which accounts on a Trial Balance will go to Profit and Loss account and which accounts will be shown on the Balance Sheet;
3. appreciate that the Profit and Loss account shows the total income for the period less the total expenses;
4. understand that the vertical form Balance Sheet shows the total net assets of a business, which should equal the amount due to the owner or owners of the business;
5. draw up a simple Profit and Loss account showing the total income and total expenditure and the resulting net profit;
6. draw up a Balance Sheet in vertical form;
7. complete all the self-test exercises at the end of the chapter.

3.6 Exercises on basic final accounts

When you have completed these exercises you should know the structure of a basic Profit and Loss account and a Balance Sheet and can move on to adjustments to these in Chapter 4.

1 Allow 20 to 30 minutes for this.
   From the following Trial Balance dated 31 December 200— draw up a Profit and Loss account and Balance Sheet for the owner, Smith.

	DR	CR
Profit costs		82,500
General expenses	24,000	
Wages	22,000	
Drawings	34,000	

Cash at Bank	5,250	
Freehold premises	150,000	
Capital		154,000
Creditors		2,950
Debtors	4,130	
Petty cash	70	
	239,450	239,450

2 Allow 30 to 35 minutes for this.

From the Trial Balance of North drawn up on 31 December 200— and set out below, draw up a Profit and Loss account and a Balance Sheet.

	DR	CR
Freehold premises	140,000	
Profit costs		62,920
Office furniture	5,000	
Car	15,000	
Interest received		1,450
Creditors		1,200
Cash at bank	2,500	
Petty cash	150	
Salaries	20,000	
Drawings	25,000	
Capital		110,000
General expenses	10,578	
Administrative expenses	4,642	
Debtors	1,700	
Long-term loan		49,000
	224,570	224,570

3 Allow about 45 minutes for this.

From the following balances extracted from the accounts of Alexandra on 30 September 200— prepare:

(a) a Trial Balance;

(b) a Profit and Loss account;

(c) a Balance Sheet.

Profit costs	130,000
Light and heat	3,600
Drawings	55,000
Creditors	4,969
Cash at bank (office)	19,230 DR
Cash at bank (client)	750,000 DR
Premises	220,000
Insurance commission received	3,000
Council tax	1,700
Salaries	48,000
Stationery	2,000
Capital	100,400
Bank loan	120,000
Debtors	7,960
Petty cash	879
Due to clients	750,000

3.7 Suggested answers to exercises on basic final accounts

1 Smith Profit and Loss account for the year ending 31 December 200—

INCOME		
Profit costs		82,500
ADD ADDITIONAL INCOME		—
LESS EXPENSES		82,500
General expenses	24,000	
Wages	22,000	
Total expenses		46,000
NET PROFIT		36,500

Smith Balance Sheet as at 31 December 200—

FIXED ASSETS			
Freehold premises			150,000
CURRENT ASSETS			
Debtors	4,130		
Cash at bank	5,250		
Petty cash	70		
		9,450	
LESS			
CURRENT LIABILITIES			
Creditors		2,950	
NET CURRENT ASSETS			6,500
			156,500
LESS LONG-TERM LIABILITIES			—
TOTAL NET ASSETS			156,500
CAPITAL EMPLOYED			
Capital	154,000		
ADD NET PROFIT	36,500		
	190,500		
LESS drawings	34,000		
TOTAL DUE TO OWNER			156,500

2 North Profit and Loss account for the year ending 31 December 200—

INCOME		
Profit costs		62,920
ADD ADDITIONAL INCOME		
Interest received		1,450
		64,370
LESS EXPENSES		
General expenses	10,578	
Administrative expenses	4,642	
Salaries	20,000	
		35,220
NET PROFIT		29,150

North Balance Sheet as at 31 December 200—

FIXED ASSETS		
Freehold premises	140,000	
Office furniture	5,000	
Car	15,000	
		160,000
CURRENT ASSETS		
Debtors	1,700	
Cash at bank	2,500	
Petty cash	150	
	4,350	
LESS CURRENT LIABILITIES		
Creditors	1,200	
NET CURRENT ASSETS		3,150
		163,150
LESS LONG-TERM LIABILITIES		
Long-term loan		49,000
TOTAL NET ASSETS		114,150
CAPITAL EMPLOYED		
Capital	110,000	
ADD NET PROFIT	29,150	
	139,150	
LESS drawings	25,000	
TOTAL DUE TO OWNER		114,150

3 Alexandra: Trial Balance as at 30 September 200—

Name of account	DR	CR
Profit costs		130,000
Light and heat	3,600	
Drawings	55,000	
Creditors		4,969
Cash at bank (office)	19,230	
Cash at bank (client)	750,000	
Premises	220,000	
Insurance commission received		3,000
Council tax	1,700	
Salaries	48,000	
Stationery	2,000	
Capital		100,400
Bank loan		120,000
Debtors	7,960	
Petty cash	879	
Due to clients		750,000
Totals	1,108,369	1,108,369

Profit and Loss account for the year ended 30 September 200—

INCOME		
Profit costs	130,000	
ADD ADDITIONAL INCOME		
Insurance commission received	3,000	133,000
LESS EXPENSES		
Light and heat	3,600	
Council tax	1,700	
Salaries	48,000	
Stationery	2,000	55,300
NET PROFIT		77,700

Alexandra: Balance Sheet as at 30 September 200—

FIXED ASSETS			
Premises			220,000
CURRENT ASSETS			
Debtors	7,960		
Cash (office bank account)	19,230		
Petty cash	879		
		28,069	
LESS CURRENT LIABILITIES			
Creditors		4,969	
NET CURRENT ASSETS			23,100
			243,100
LESS LONG-TERM LIABILITIES			
Bank loan			120,000
TOTAL NET ASSETS			123,100
CAPITAL EMPLOYED			
Capital	100,400		
ADD Net profit	77,700		
		178,100	
LESS drawings		55,000	
TOTAL DUE TO OWNER			123,100
CLIENT ACCOUNT			
Client bank balance	750,000		
LESS due to clients	750,000		

4

Adjustments to final accounts

4.1 The need for adjustments

The balances on the income and expenses accounts do not show all the income earned, or all the expenses actually incurred during the year. Adjustments are made to make sure:

1. that income includes the value of work done during the current year, even though it has not yet been billed;
2. that expenses include those which have been incurred in the current year, even though they have not yet been billed or paid;
3. that expenses do not include those which have been paid in the current year but which relate to the next year.

In this chapter we will look at the following adjustments:

(a) Outstanding expenses;

(b) Payment in advance;

(c) Closing stocks;

(d) Work in Progress.

Note that for all adjustments two entries are made on the same account; the first entry will affect the Profit and Loss account and the second will affect the Balance Sheet.

4.2 Outstanding expenses adjustment

There are expenses incurred during the current financial year but where payment will not be made until the next financial year, for example, gas, electricity and telephone charges.

At the end of the financial year, a provision is made for this. If a bill has not already been received the provision will be an estimate. The relevant expense will be INCREASED by the provision to give the true expense for the year.

Thus the adjustment is made on the relevant expense account by:

1. DEBITING the expense for the current year (increases the expense).
2. CREDITING the expense for the next year (reduces next year's expense).

These entries will therefore shift the expense from one year to the next.

The effect on the Profit and Loss account and the Balance Sheet for the current year will be:

1. Profit and Loss account—INCREASE expenses;
2. Balance Sheet—show the outstanding expense as a CURRENT LIABILITY.

EXAMPLE

A solicitor prepares final accounts on 31 October. At that date the telephone account has a debit balance of £600. This represents cash paid for telephone charges over the year. It is decided to make a provision of £200 for telephone charges due but unpaid. The provision carried down (1) will be debited to the telephone account.

Telephone account

Date	Details	DR	CR	Balance
31 Oct	Balance Provision carried down (c/d) (1)	200		600 DR 800 DR

The balance on the expense account, including the provision made at the end of the financial year, is transferred to the Profit and Loss account and the nominal expense account is closed. Continuing the example:

Telephone account

Date	Details	DR	CR	Balance
31 Oct	Balance Provision c/d (1) Profit and Loss account: transfer	200	800	600 DR 800 DR —

The provision is brought down as a credit entry (2) in the expense account at the start of the next financial year. The provision will be set off against payment of the bill in the next financial year. Continuing the example, on 10 November the bill of £200 is paid.

Telephone account

Date	Details	DR	CR	Balance
31 Oct	Balance Provision c/d (1) Profit and Loss account: transfer	200	800	600 DR 800 DR —
1 Nov 10 Nov	Provision brought down (b/d) (2) Cash	200	200	200 CR —

Profit and Loss account for the year ended 31 October

EXPENSES
Telephones   600
Add outstanding expenses   200
                                                        ———
                                                        800

The provision brought down for outstanding expenses is shown on the Balance Sheet as a current liability because on the date on which the Balance Sheet is prepared, it is expenditure incurred but not yet paid. Continuing the example:

Balance Sheet as at 31 October

FIXED ASSETS		XX
CURRENT ASSETS	XX	
LESS CURRENT LIABILITIES		
Outstanding expenses—telephone	200	
		XX
		XX
CAPITAL EMPLOYED		
		XX

4.3 Payment in advance

If a payment is made in the current financial year for a service which will not be used until the next financial year, for example, council tax, then, at the end of the financial year, the appropriate expense account is credited with the amount paid in advance. This has the effect of REDUCING the expenses and increasing the profit. The corresponding debit entry is made in the same account at the start of the next financial year. This time the double entry shifts the expense out of the current year into the next year.

The adjustment is made on the relevant expense account by:

1. CREDITING the expense for the current year (reducing expenses);
2. DEBITING the expense for the next year (increasing next year's expenses).

The effect on the Profit and Loss account and the Balance Sheet for the current year will be:
THE PROFIT AND LOSS ACCOUNT;

REDUCE expenses.

THE BALANCE SHEET;

Show as a CURRENT ASSET.

EXAMPLE

A solicitor pays council tax of £4,000 per annum by two equal instalments, in advance, on 31 March and 30 September each year. Final accounts are prepared on 31 December each year. Thus a payment in advance of £1,000 for council tax is being made because the £2,000 paid on 30 September is for council tax from 1 October to 31 March.

Council tax account

Date	Details	DR	CR	Balance
31 Mar	Cash	2,000		2,000 DR
30 Sept	Cash	2,000		4,000 DR
31 Dec	Payment in advance c/d (1)		1,000	3,000 DR

The balance on the expense account is transferred to the Profit and Loss account at the end of the year. Continuing the example:

Council tax account

Date	Details	DR	CR	Balance
31 Mar	Cash	2,000		2,000 DR
30 Sept	Cash	2,000		4,000 DR
31 Dec	Payment in advance c/d (1)		1,000	3,000 DR
	Profit and Loss account: transfer		3,000	—

Note that the firm is charging to the Profit and Loss account as a business expense only the amount spent on council tax from 1 January to 31 December, i.e. in the current financial year.

The payment in advance is brought down as a debit entry on the expense account at the start of the next financial year, which is when the service that has been paid for in the current financial year will be used. Continuing the example:

Council tax account

Date	Details	DR	CR	Balance
31 Mar	Cash	2,000		2,000 DR
30 Sept	Cash	2,000		4,000 DR
31 Dec	Payment in advance c/d (1)		1,000	3,000 DR
	Profit and Loss account: transfer		3,000	—
1 Jan	Payment in advance b/d (2)	1,000		1,000 DR

Profit and Loss account for the year ending 31 December

EXPENSES
Council tax   4,000
Less payment in advance   1,000

                                                        3,000

The payment in advance is shown on the Balance Sheet as a current asset. In theory the person to whom the payment has been made is a debtor of the firm for the service which is to be supplied. Continuing the example:

Balance Sheet as at 31 December

FIXED ASSETS   XX
CURRENT ASSETS
Payments in advance
Council tax   1,000
                                                        XX
LESS CURRENT LIABILITIES
                                                        XX
                                                        --
                                                        XX
CAPITAL EMPLOYED
                                                        XX

4.4 Closing stocks

Where a business has paid for items used over the year, for example stationery or pens, then only the cost of the items actually used during the year should be shown as an expense. Thus the value of any items left will be DEDUCTED from the relevant expense account, to give the true expense.

The adjustment is made on the relevant expense account by:

CREDITING expense for the current year (thus reducing expenses).

DEBITING the expense for the next year (increasing next year's expenses).

Again this shifts the expense from the current year to the next year.
The effect on the Profit and Loss account and the Balance Sheet will be:

THE PROFIT AND LOSS ACCOUNT;

REDUCE expenses.

THE BALANCE SHEET;

Show as a CURRENT ASSET.

EXAMPLE

During the year the firm pays the following amounts for stationery:

31 March	£40
16 October	£25
8 December	£35

Final accounts are prepared on 31 December. On 31 December the firm has a stock of stationery paid for but unused, valued at £30.

Stationery account

Date	Details	DR	CR	Balance
31 Mar	Cash	40		40 DR
16 Oct	Cash	25		65 DR
8 Dec	Cash	35		100 DR
31 Dec	Closing stock c/d (1)		30	70 DR

At the end of the year the nominal expense account is closed and the balance on it is transferred to the Profit and Loss account. Continuing the example:

Stationery account

Date	Details	DR	CR	Balance
31 Mar	Cash	40		40 DR
16 Oct	Cash	25		65 DR
8 Dec	Cash	35		100 DR
31 Dec	Closing stock c/d (1)		30	70 DR
	Profit and Loss account: transfer balance		70	—

Note that only the cost of stationery used during the current financial year is transferred to the Profit and Loss account as a business expense.

The value of the closing stock is brought down as a Debit entry in the expense account at the start of the next financial year. Continuing the example:

Stationery account

Date	Details	DR	CR	Balance
31 Mar	Cash	40		40 DR
16 Oct	Cash	25		65 DR
8 Dec	Cash	35		100 DR
31 Dec	Closing stock c/d (1)		30	70 DR
	Profit and Loss account: transfer		70	—
1 Jan	Opening stock b/d (2)	30		30 DR

Note from the above account that at the start of the next financial year the closing stock from the previous year will be the opening stock.

Profit and Loss account for the year ending 31 December

EXPENSES
Stationery   100
Less closing stock   30
                                                                                          70

On the Balance Sheet the value of the closing stock is shown as a current asset. Continuing the example:

Balance Sheet as at 31 December

FIXED ASSETS   XX
CURRENT ASSETS
(Closing) Stock of stationery   30
                                                                                XX
LESS CURRENT LIABILITIES
                                                                                XX
                                                                                XX
CAPITAL EMPLOYED
                                                                                XX

4.5 Work in Progress

For solicitors, the main source of income is from bills delivered in respect of work done for clients. The Profit costs account will record all of the billed work. However, at the end of the year the firm will have done work for clients which has not yet been billed. As this work has been carried out in the current year it can be valued and shown as income earned during the year. This will be added to the current year's income and deducted from the next year's income.

The adjustment will be made to the Profit Costs account by:

CREDITING the account for the current year (increasing income);

DEBITING the account for the next year (reducing next year's income).

The effect on the Profit and Loss account and the Balance Sheet will be as follows:

THE PROFIT AND LOSS ACCOUNT;

INCREASE the Profit Costs by the Work in Progress for the end of the year.

THE BALANCE SHEET;

Show the Work in Progress at the end of the year as a CURRENT ASSET.

Year 2

As shown above, the Work in Progress brought forward reduces the Profit Costs income. Thus the Profit and Loss account for year 2 would show:

Profit Costs

LESS Work in Progress at the START of the year;

ADD Work in Progress at the END of the year.

This gives the VALUE OF WORK DONE during the year.

The Balance Sheet would show:

the Work in Progress at the END of the year as a CURRENT ASSET.

EXAMPLE YEAR 1

The firm prepares its final accounts on 31 December each year. On 31 December the Profit Costs account has a credit balance of £30,000. Work in progress is valued at £5,000.

Profit costs account

Date	Details	DR	CR	Balance
31 Dec	Balance			30,000 CR
	Closing Work in Progress c/d (1)		5,000	35,000 CR

At the end of the financial year the Profit Costs account is closed and the balance on the account is transferred to the Profit and Loss account. At the start of the new financial year the closing work in progress is brought down on the DR side as opening work in progress. Continuing the example:

Profit costs account

Date	Details	DR	CR	Balance
31 Dec	Balance			30,000 CR
	Closing Work in Progress c/d (1)		5,000	35,000 CR
	Profit and loss account: transfer	35,000		—
1 Jan	Opening Work in Progress b/d (2)	5,000		5,000 DR

The value of the closing Work in Progress is shown on the balance sheet as a current asset. Continuing the example:

Balance Sheet as at 31 December

FIXED ASSETS		XX
CURRENT ASSETS		
Work in Progress at the end of year	5,000	
		XX
LESS CURRENT LIABILITIES		XX
		XX
CAPITAL EMPLOYED		
		XX

Year 2

In the following year the Profit costs account begins with the debit entry for opening work in progress. This reduces the income from profit costs in that year (as the profit costs figure includes bills delivered which include costs for work carried out in the previous year). The movement on the Profit costs account will be shown in the Profit and Loss account, which will give the value of work done during the year.

EXAMPLE

Work in Progress at start of Year 2	£15,000
Profit costs for the year	£125,000
Work in Progress at end of Year 2	£20,000

Profit and Loss account for the year

INCOME

Profit costs (based on bills delivered)	125,000	
ADD closing Work in Progress at 31 Dec	20,000	145,000
LESS opening Work in Progress at 1 Jan		15,000
VALUE OF WORK DONE		
		130,000

Note: only the Work in Progress figure at the *end* of the year is shown in the Balance Sheet.

Note: you should show each subtotal after adding the closing Work in Progress and then deducting the opening Work in Progress. Any additional income, e.g., rent received, interest received, insurance commission received, should be shown after the Work in Progress adjustments have been made.

4.5.1 Worked example on closing Work in Progress adjustment

A firm of solicitors prepares its final accounts on 30 June each year. The firm's Profit Costs account shows an opening debit balance on 1 July 2004 of £35,000. During the year ending 30 June 2005, bills have been delivered to clients totalling £175,000. The firm estimates that the value of work done during the year ending 30 June 2005, in respect of which bills have not yet been delivered, is £45,000. The accounts to record the above will appear as follows:

Profit Costs account

Date	Details	DR	CR	Balance
2004 1 July	Opening Work in Progress b/d	35,000		35,000 DR
2005 30 June	Sundry profit costs		175,000	140,000 CR
	Closing Work in Progress c/d (1)		45,000	185,000 CR
	Profit and Loss account: transfer	185,000		—
1 July	Opening Work in Progress b/d (2)	45,000		45,000 DR

Profit and Loss account for the year ended 30 June 2005

INCOME
Profit costs   175,000
ADD Closing Work in Progress   45,000
                                                          ———
                                                          220,000
LESS Opening Work in Progress   35,000
                                                          ———
VALUE OF WORK DONE   185,000

Note: by convention the detailed movement on the Profit Costs account is shown on the Profit and Loss account.

Balance Sheet as at 30 June 2005

FIXED ASSETS   XX
CURRENT ASSETS
Work in Progress (at end of year)   45,000
                                                                              XX

4.6 Summary of adjustments

Outstanding expenses:

> Profit and Loss account;
> INCREASE expenses.
> Balance Sheet;
> CURRENT LIABILITY.

Payments in advance:

> Profit and Loss account;
> REDUCE expenses.
> Balance Sheet;
> CURRENT ASSET.

Closing stock:

> Profit and Loss account;
> REDUCE expenses.

Balance Sheet;
CURRENT ASSET.

Work in Progress:

Profit and Loss account;

DEDUCT Work in Progress at the START of the year from Profit costs;

ADD Work in Progress at the END of the year to Profit costs.

Balance Sheet;

Show Work in Progress at the END of the year as a CURRENT ASSET.

4.7 Check list

By the end of this chapter you should be able to:

1. understand the reasons for adjustments;
2. appreciate that adjustments made will affect both the Profit and Loss account and the Balance Sheet and that they will also be carried forward to the next accounting period;
3. know the effect of each adjustment in this chapter on the Profit and Loss account and the Balance Sheet;
4. use entries on a Trial Balance together with information supplied in respect of adjustments to draw up a Profit and Loss account and a Balance Sheet;
5. complete all the self-test exercises at the end of the chapter.

4.8 Exercises on adjustments and final accounts

Once you have completed these exercises in the time allowed, move on to further adjustments to final accounts (Chapter 5).

1 Allow 5 to 10 minutes.
On 31 October 200— the firm's light and heat account has a debit balance of £5,000. The firm estimates that a further £250 worth of gas has been used.

Show the state of the light and heat account on 1 November 200— and the entries which you would make in the final accounts which are prepared on 31 October 200—.

2 Allow 10 to 15 minutes.
The firm pays council tax of £1,000 on 1 April and 1 October 2004 for the following six months. The firm's final accounts are prepared on 31 December each year.

Show the rates account at 1 January 2005 and the entries you would make in the final accounts for the year ended 31 December 2004.

3 Allow about 10 minutes.
Final accounts are prepared on 30 June each year. On 30 June 2005 the stationery account shows a debit balance of £800. On checking the stationery it is discovered that there is £200 worth left.

Show the stationery account at 1 July 2005 and the entries in the final accounts for the year ended 30 June 2005.

4 Allow about 20 minutes.
At the end of its financial year, 31 December 2003, Grace & Co. had profit costs of £180,000 and its work in progress was valued at £18,000. At the end of its second year, 31 December 2004, the firm had delivered bills totalling £220,000 and its work in progress was valued at £25,000.

Show the Profit costs account and also the final accounts for the year ended 31 December 2004.

5 Allow about 45 minutes.

The Trial Balance of Torr, a solicitor, is set out below.

	31 December 200—	
	DR	CR
Capital		65,000
Office equipment	6,330	
Car	14,900	
Leasehold property	95,000	
General expenses	38,290	
Rent paid	4,800	
Salaries	27,000	
Mortgage		45,000
Drawings	30,570	
Cash at bank office account	2,210	
Cash at bank client account	67,900	
Amount due to clients		67,900
Creditors		3,650
Amount due from clients (debtors)	2,000	
Profit costs		110,000
Work in Progress at 1 Jan 200—	5,000	
Commission received		2,450
	294,000	294,000

Work in Progress as at 31 December 200— is £6,000. Payments in advance are £1,200, and outstanding expenses are £540. Draw up the Profit and Loss account for the year ending 31 December 200— and the Balance Sheet as at that date.

4.9 Suggested answers to exercises on adjustments and final accounts

1 Light and heat account

Date	Details	DR	CR	Balance
200—				
31 Oct	Balance			5,000 DR
	Provision: Gas c/d	250		5,250 DR
	Profit and Loss: transfer		5,250	—
1 Nov	Provision: Gas b/d		250	250 CR

Profit and Loss account for the year ended 31 October 200—

INCOME			XX
LESS EXPENSES			
Light and heat	5,000		
Add provision	250	5,250	

Balance Sheet as at 31 October 200—

FIXED ASSETS		XX
CURRENT ASSETS	XX	

LESS CURRENT LIABILITIES	
Provision for light and heat	250
	XX
	XX
CAPITAL EMPLOYED	
	XX

2 Council tax account

Date	Details	DR	CR	Balance
2004				
1 Apr	Cash	1,000		1,000 DR
1 Oct	Cash	1,000		2,000 DR
31 Dec	Payment in advance c/d		500	1,500 DR
	Profit and Loss: transfer		1,500	—
2005				
1 Jan	Payment in advance b/d	500		500 DR

Profit and Loss account for the year ended 31 December 2004

INCOME			XX
LESS EXPENSES			
Council tax	2,000		
Less paid in advance	500	1,500	

Balance Sheet as at 31 December 2004

FIXED ASSETS		XX
CURRENT ASSETS		
Council tax paid in advance	500	
	XX	
LESS CURRENT LIABILITIES		
	XX	
	XX	
CAPITAL EMPLOYED		
	XX	

3 Stationery account

Date	Details	DR	CR	Balance
2005				
30 June	Balance			800 DR
	Closing stock c/d		200	600 DR
	Profit and Loss: transfer		600	—
1 July	Opening stock b/d	200		200 DR

Profit and Loss account for the year ended 30 June 2005

INCOME	XX
LESS EXPENSES	

Stationery		800	
Less closing stock		200	600

Balance Sheet as at 30 June 2005

FIXED ASSETS		XX
CURRENT ASSETS		
Closing stock of stationery	200	
		XX

4 Profit costs account

Date	Details	DR	CR	Balance
2003				
31 Dec	Balance (bills delivered)			180,000 CR
	Closing work in progress c/d		18,000	198,000 CR
	Profit and Loss: transfer	198,000		—
2004				
1 Jan	Opening work in progress b/d	18,000		18,000 DR
31 Dec	Profit costs		220,000	202,000 CR
	Closing work in progress c/d		25,000	227,000 CR
	Profit and Loss: transfer	227,000		—
2005				
1 Jan	Opening Work in Progress b/d	25,000		25,000 DR

Grace & Co: Profit and Loss account for the year ended 31 December 2004

INCOME			
Profit Costs		220,000	
ADD closing Work in Progress		25,000	
		245,000	
LESS opening Work in Progress		18,000	227,000
LESS EXPENSES			XX

Grace & Co: Balance Sheet as at 31 December 2004

FIXED ASSETS		XX
CURRENT ASSETS		
Work in Progress	25,000	
		XX

5 Torr Profit and Loss account for the year ending 31 December 200—

INCOME	
Profit costs	110,000
ADD Work in Progress at end of year	6,000
	116,000
LESS	
Work in Progress at start of year	5,000
VALUE OF WORK DONE	111,000

ADD ADDITIONAL INCOME		
Commission received		2,450
TOTAL INCOME		113,450
LESS EXPENSES		
General expenses	38,290	
Salaries	27,000	
Rent paid	4,800	
Outstanding expenses	540	
	70,630	
LESS payments in advance	1,200	
Total expenses		69,430
NET PROFIT		44,020

Torr Balance Sheet as at 31 December 200—

FIXED ASSETS			
Leasehold premises	95,000		
Office equipment	6,330		
Car	14,900		
			116,230
CURRENT ASSETS			
Work in Progress	6,000		
Debtors (due from clients)	2,000		
Cash at bank	2,210		
Payment in advance	1,200		
		11,410	
LESS CURRENT LIABILITIES			
Creditors	3,650		
Outstanding expenses	540		
		4,190	
NET CURRENT ASSETS			7,220
			123,450
LESS LONG-TERM LIABILITIES			
Mortgage			45,000
TOTAL NET ASSETS			78,450
CAPITAL EMPLOYED			
Capital	65,000		
ADD net profit	44,020		
		109,020	
LESS drawings		30,570	
TOTAL DUE TO OWNER			78,450
CLIENT ACCOUNT			
Cash at bank client account		67,900	
Amount due to clients		67,900	

5

Further adjustments to final accounts

5.1 Introduction

In this chapter we will look at:

(a) Bad and doubtful debts.

(b) Depreciation and sale of assets.

5.2 Bad debts and doubtful debts adjustments

5.2.1 Writing off bad debts

Debts owed to a business are assets. When the debtors pay, the debts will be converted into cash. However, some debtors will never pay and so the debts will be worthless. If a business knows that a particular debtor is never going to pay, for example, the debtor has disappeared or is bankrupt, then the business will write off the bad debt, showing that it is worthless. The firm has lost that debt and it will be recorded as an expense.

To write off a bad debt:

CREDIT the debtor's account (this wipes out the debt).

DEBIT the Bad Debts account (this shows the expense).

The effect on the Profit and Loss account and the Balance Sheet will be as follows:

On the Profit and Loss account;

Show the Bad Debts as an EXPENSE.

On The Balance Sheet

If the Trial Balance shows a figure for Bad Debts, then the debtor's figure will already have been reduced by the bad debts written off, so just use the debtor's figure shown.

Note

If, however, you are asked to write off a bad debt AFTER the Trial Balance has been drawn up, then you would have to reduce the debtor's figure for the Balance Sheet, as well as showing the Bad Debt as an expense on the Profit and Loss account above.

EXAMPLE

A bill delivered to Jack for £235 (including £35 VAT) has not been paid. At the end of the financial year 31 October the debt was written off.

Jack's account

Date	Details	DR	CR	Balance
31 Oct	Balance: amount due Bad debt: written off		235	235 DR —

Bad debts account

Date	Details	DR	CR	Balance
31 Oct	Jack: debt written off	235		235 DR

Note that VAT relief for bad debts is dealt with in Chapter 13 (**13.7**).

5.2.2 Recovery of a debt that has been written off

When a debt that has previously been written off as a bad debt is recovered, the following entries will be made in the account:

(a) DEBIT cash account.

(b) CREDIT Bad Debts account.

Continuing the example, assume that in the year after the debt has been written off, Jack pays his bill.

Cash account

Date	Details	DR	CR	Balance
15 Jan	Bad debts (recovered from Jack)	235		235 DR

Bad Debts account

Date	Details	DR	CR	Balance
15 Jan	Cash (debt recovered from Jack)		235	235 CR

No entry is made in Jack's account, although a note that he has paid could be useful.

5.2.3 Making a provision for doubtful debts

As well as writing off bad debts a business will also make provision for the debts that are unlikely to be paid. This provision is an estimated loss.

The provision is usually calculated as a percentage of the debtor's figure, after bad debts have been written off.

Effect on PROFIT AND LOSS ACCOUNT;

INCREASE expenses by this year's provision for doubtful debts.

EFFECT ON BALANCE SHEET;

REDUCE the debtors figure by this year's provision for doubtful debts.

The entries will be:

(1) DEBIT the Bad Debts account with the provision at the end of the current financial year.

(2) CREDIT the Bad Debts account with the provision at the start of the next financial year.

Note that the provision brought forward to the next year will reduce the expense of bad debts for the next year.

EXAMPLE

A. Solicitor prepares final accounts on 31 October. On that date the bad debts account has a debit balance of £1,500 in respect of bad debts written off during the year. Total debts owed to the practice amount to £20,000 and A. Solicitor decides to make a provision for doubtful debts of 5% of the total.

Bad Debts account

Date	Details	DR	CR	Balance
	Balance—bad debts previously written off			1,500 DR
31 Oct	Provision: doubtful debt c/d (1)	1,000		2,500 DR

5.2.4 Effect of bad debts on final accounts

At the end of the financial year the Bad Debts account will be closed and the balance will be transferred to the Profit and Loss account. If, at the end of the financial year, the Bad Debts account has a debit balance this will be transferred to the Profit and Loss account as an expense by making the following entries in the accounts:

(a) CREDIT the Bad Debts account.

(b) DEBIT the Profit and Loss account.

Continuing the example of A. Solicitor:

Bad Debts account

Date	Details	DR	CR	Balance
	Balance			1,500 DR
31 Oct	Provision: doubtful debts c/d (1)	1,000		2,500 DR
	Profit and Loss account: transfer		2,500	—

Profit and Loss account for the year ended 31 October 200—

INCOME —

Less EXPENSES
Bad debts 1,500
Provision for doubtful debts 1,000

2,500

At the start of the next financial year the provision will be carried down as a credit entry on the Bad Debts account. Continuing the example of A. Solicitor:

Bad Debts account

Date	Details	DR	CR	Balance
200— 31 Oct	Balance			1,500 DR
	Provision: doubtful debts c/d (1)	1,000		2,500 DR
	Profit and Loss account: transfer		2,500	—
1 Nov	Provision for doubtful debts b/d (2)		1,000	1,000 CR

The provision for doubtful debts made at the end of the financial year is shown as a deduction from the debtors figure on the current assets part of the Balance Sheet. Continuing the example of A. Solicitor:

Balance Sheet as at 31 October 200—

FIXED ASSETS XX
CURRENT ASSETS
Debtors 20,000
Less: Provision for doubtful debts 1,000

19,000
XX

Note: If the Bad Debts account has a credit balance at the end of the year because the firm has overestimated its provision for doubtful debts in previous years, then the credit balance is transferred to the Profit and Loss account as income by making the following entries:

(a) DEBIT Bad Debts account.
(b) CREDIT Profit and Loss account.

EXAMPLE

At the start of the financial year, 1 January 200—, a provision of £3,000 is brought down from the previous year. During the year bad debts of £5,000 are written off. At the end of the financial year, 31 December 200—, total debtors amount to £40,000. It is decided to make a provision for doubtful debts of 10%.

Bad Debts account

Date	Details	DR	CR	Balance
200—				
1 Jan	Last year's Provision b/d		3,000	3,000 CR
	Bad debts written off	5,000		2,000 DR
31 Dec	This year's Provision c/d	4,000		6,000 DR
	Profit and loss account: transfer		6,000	—

Profit and Loss account for the year ended 31 December 200—

EXPENSES
Bad debts   5,000
ADD this year's provision   4,000
                                                   9,000
LESS last year's provision   3,000   6,000

Balance sheet as at 31 December 200—

FIXED ASSETS   XX
CURRENT ASSETS
Debtors   40,000
Less this year's provision   4,000   36,000

Only one method of providing for bad debts and doubtful debts has been shown in this book. There are other, equally acceptable methods in use.

5.3 Depreciation

5.3.1 Introduction

The asset accounts show the cost price of the assets. Over time the cost price of an asset is unlikely to be its true value, as many assets go down in value, through wear and tear or obsolescence. Instead of waiting until the asset is sold to find out the loss, the business will spread the fall in value over time, showing an expense of depreciation each year.

Calculating depreciation

There are different ways of doing this: the simplest is known as the straight-line method. Depreciation can be calculated as a percentage of the cost price each year. For example, if a car cost £20,000, the business could calculate depreciation at 20% each year, being £4,000 a year.

Alternatively the formula for calculating depreciation by the straight-line method is:

$$\frac{\text{Cost of asset} - \text{value of asset at end of its life}}{\text{life expectancy of asset}}$$

EXAMPLE

A firm buys a car for £5,500. The car has an estimated life of five years, at the end of which its sale value will be £500. The annual provision for depreciation using the straight-line method of calculating depreciation will be:

$$\frac{£5,500 - £500}{5} = £1,000 \text{ loss/depreciation per year}$$

A separate depreciation account should be opened for each class of fixed assets to be depreciated. Using the straight-line method, depreciation may be calculated as a percentage of the cost price of the asset.

EXAMPLE

A firm buys a car for £16,000. Depreciation is calculated at 15% per annum on the cost price. Thus each year the depreciation will be £2,400.

Note: a further alternative method is to depreciate on the reducing balance of the asset rather than the cost price.

EXAMPLE

A firm buys a car for £16,000. Depreciation is calculated at 15% per annum on the reducing balance of the car. Thus in year 1 depreciation will be £2,400. In year 2 the reduced balance of the car will be:

Cost price	£16,000
Less depreciation	£2,400
	£13,600

Thus depreciation in year 2 will be £2,040.
   In year 3 the reduced balance of the car will be £11,560. Depreciation in year 3 will be £1,734.

Normally you should depreciate on the cost price of the asset rather than on the reducing balance.

5.3.2 Recording depreciation in the accounts

To record depreciation in the accounts at the end of the financial year, the following entries are made:

(a) CREDIT the appropriate accumulated depreciation account with depreciation charged on the fixed asset.
(b) DEBIT the Profit and Loss account with the current year's depreciation, as an expense.

Note that if an asset is bought part-way through the year, it is usual to depreciate it for a full year. Do this unless you are told otherwise.

EXAMPLE

The firm buys a car for £6,000 in March 200—. Depreciation on the car is 20% a year. The firm's financial year ends on 31 December 200—.

Accumulated depreciation (Cars) account

Date	Details	DR	CR	Balance
200— 31 Dec	Profit and Loss		1,200	1,200 CR

Accumulated depreciation is shown on the Balance Sheet as a deduction from the cost price of the asset. Continuing the example:

Profit and Loss account for year ended 31 December 200—

INCOME —

LESS EXPENDITURE
Depreciation: motor cars   1,200

Balance Sheet as at 31 December 200—

FIXED ASSETS
Motor cars at cost   6,000
LESS accumulated depreciation   1,200
                                                                         4,800

In year 2 the accounts would be shown as follows:

Accumulated depreciation (Cars) account

Date	Details	DR	CR	Balance
Year 1 31 Dec	Profit and Loss		1,200	1,200 CR
Year 2 31 Dec	Profit and Loss		1,200	2,400 CR

Profit and loss account for year 2

INCOME —

LESS EXPENDITURE
Depreciation: motor cars   1,200

Balance Sheet as at end year 2

FIXED ASSETS   XX
Motor cars at cost   6,000
LESS accumulated depreciation   2,400
                                                                         3,600

5.4 Sale of assets

When an asset is sold an asset disposal account will be opened. The cost price of the asset and its accumulated depreciation to date will be transferred to this account, and the sale price will be recorded. From this account you will be able to see whether the business has made a 'profit' or a 'loss' on the sale.

For example if a car had been purchased for £20,000 and the accumulated depreciation to date was £8,000, then the estimated current value of the car would be £12,000. If the car was sold for £13,000 a 'profit' of £1,000 has been made. This would be shown on the accounts as follows:

Car Asset disposal account

Date	Details	DR	CR	Balance
200—	Cost price of car	20,000		20,000 DR
	Accumulated depreciation on car		8,000	12,000 DR
	Cash on sale		13,000	1,000 CR

The credit balance is a 'profit', which will be shown as INCOME on the Profit and Loss account.

If the account came out with a debit balance this would be a loss/EXPENSE for the Profit and Loss account.

5.4.1 Disposing of part of a group of assets

The same principle as above will apply. As before the cost price of the asset being sold and the accumulated depreciation on the asset being sold will be transferred to the asset disposal account, leaving the cost price of the remaining assets, and the accumulated depreciation of the remaining assets behind.

EXAMPLE

Chandra, a solicitor, prepared final accounts on 31 December. The cost price of cars are shown on the Trial Balance as £80,000. Accumulated depreciation on all the cars is shown as £28,000. Depreciation on cars is calculated at 20% per annum. A car is sold during the current year for £13,000. The car cost £20,000, and accumulated depreciation on the car is £8,000, being two years depreciation at 20%. Chandra's accounts to record the above will be as follows:

Cars account

Date	Details	DR	CR	Balance
31 Dec	Balance			80,000 DR
	Asset disposal—cost price of car sold		20,000	60,000 DR

Accumulated depreciation account (motor cars)

Date	Details	DR	CR	Balance
1 Jan	Balance			28,000 CR
	Asset disposal	8,000		20,000 CR
31 Dec	Depreciation this year		12,000	32,000 CR

Asset disposal account (Car)

Date	Details	DR	CR	Balance
31 Dec	Car cost price	20,000		20,000 DR
	Depreciation		8,000	12,000 DR
	Cash		13,000	1,000 CR
	Profit and Loss account:			
	Transfer profit on sale	1,000		—

Profit and Loss account for the year ended 31 December

INCOME		XX
Profit on sale of car	1000	
LESS EXPENDITURE		
Depreciation: on remaining cars	12,000	

Balance Sheet as at 31 December

FIXED ASSETS		
Cars at cost	60,000	
LESS accumulated depreciation	32,000	
		28,000
CURRENT ASSETS		XX

Note: the current year's depreciation is calculated by taking the cost price of the car which has been sold (£20,000) from the balance on the motor cars account (£80,000), and finding 20% of the remainder (£60,000) = £12,000.

5.5 Summary

Bad debts

PROFIT AND LOSS ACCOUNT;

Show as an EXPENSE.

BALANCE SHEET;

Only reduce the debtor's figure by any bad debts which are written off after the Trial Balance. If bad debts are shown on the Trial Balance then the debtor's figure has already been reduced; it should not be changed.

Provision for doubtful debts

This year's provision:

PROFIT AND LOSS ACCOUNT;

Show as an EXPENSE.

BALANCE SHEET;

REDUCE debtor's figure by this year's provision.

Last year's provision:
> PROFIT AND LOSS ACCOUNT;
> REDUCE expense of bad debts by last year's provision.
> BALANCE SHEET;
> NO effect.

Depreciation

PROFIT AND LOSS ACCOUNT;
Show the depreciation for the current year only as an EXPENSE.
BALANCE SHEET;
Show the Cost price of the asset
LESS any accumulated depreciation from previous years
AND less the depreciation for the current year.

5.6 Check list

By the end of this chapter you should be able to:

1. understand that bad debts are an expense;
2. understand that a provision for doubtful debts is an adjustment, its effect on the Profit and Loss account and the Balance Sheet, and on the next year's accounts;
3. understand that depreciation records the fall in value of assets as an expense, its effect on the Profit and Loss account and the Balance Sheet, and on the next year's accounts;
4. note how a firm would deal with the sale of an asset or assets;
5. use information supplied in respect of bad debts and provision and depreciation in drawing up a Profit and Loss account and Balance Sheet;
6. complete all the self-test exercises at the end of the chapter.

5.7 Exercises on adjustments and final accounts

When you have completed these exercises in the time allocated, move on to Partnership accounts (Chapter 6).

1 Allow 10 to 15 minutes.

An extract from the Trial Balance of Lightfoot drawn up on 31 December 200— shows the following:

Name of account	DR	CR
Debtors	4,340	
Bad debts	625	

It is decided to make a provision for doubtful debts of £450 for the year. Show the figures for expenses on the Profit and Loss account for the year and the figures that would be shown on the Balance sheet as at 31 December 200—.

2 Allow about 10 minutes.

An extract from the Trial Balance of Davis drawn up on 31 March 200— shows the following:

Name of account	DR	CR
Cost price of cars	30,000	
Accumulated depreciation on cars		9,000

Depreciation for the year ending 31 March 200— is to be 15% of the cost price. Show the figure for expenses on Profit and Loss account and the details in respect of cars on the Balance Sheet.

3 Allow 30 to 40 minutes.

The Trial Balance for Karsh on 30 September 200— is set out below:

Name of account	DR	CR
Capital		170,000
Profit costs		90,000
Drawings	32,000	
Office furniture	8,500	
Accumulated depreciation on office furniture		2,550
Premises cost price	160,000	
General and administrative expenses	46,000	
Cash at bank office account	13,915	
Petty cash	165	
Creditors		1,980
Debtors	3,544	
Bad debts	406	
Cash at bank client account	249,000	
Due to clients		249,000
	513,530	513,530

Depreciation for the year on office furniture is 10% of the cost price. The provision for doubtful debts for the year is £360 and Work in Progress at the end of the year is £6,200. Draw up the Profit and Loss account for the year ending 30 September and Balance Sheet as at that date

4 Allow 40 to 50 minutes.

The trial balance of J. Milton, prepared on 31 December 200—, is as follows:

Trial balance as at 31 December 200—

Name of account	DR	CR
Drawings	19,000	
Fixtures and fittings	5,200	
Cars	20,600	
Accumulated depreciation (cars)		4,120
Accumulated depreciation (fixtures and fittings)		1,300
Premises	132,000	
Capital		140,000
Telephone/postage	1,300	
Council tax	2,950	
Light and heat	1,550	
Salaries	25,270	
Cash at bank:		
Office account	14,190	
Client account	315,000	
Petty cash	123	
Debtors	4,422	
Due to creditors		4,763
Due to clients		315,000
Profit costs		76,422
	541,605	541,605

In addition:

(a) Depreciation at 10% and 5% is to be charged against the cost price of cars and fixtures and fittings, respectively.

(b) At 31 December 200— electricity and telephone bills outstanding amount to £551 and £505, respectively.

(c) Included in the amount for debtors is £122 which is to be written off. A provision for doubtful debts of 5% of remaining debtors is to be made.

(d) Work in Progress at 31 December 200— is valued at £8,569.

Prepare final accounts for the year ended 31 December 200—.

5 Allow 50 minutes to 1 hour.

The following balances were taken from the accounts of C. Arnold, solicitor, on 31 December 200—.

Capital	223,059
Work in progress at 1 January 200—	16,582
Petty cash	55
Bank overdraft on office account	4,552
Bank client account	450,000
Debtors	12,009
Creditors	9,235
Car: cost price	20,000
Accumulated depreciation: car	8,000
Drawings	20,459
Fixtures and fittings at cost	8,000
Accumulated depreciation: fixtures and fittings	1,200
Profit costs	78,021
Rent and rates	2,626
Salaries	30,226
General expenses	12,500
Interest on overdraft	735
Insurance commission received	369
Freehold premises	200,500
Bad debts	2,400
Provision for doubtful debts b/d (last year's)	1,656
Due to clients	450,000

C. Arnold provides the following additional information about the practice:

(a) Work in Progress was valued at £14,270 on 31 December 200—.

(b) Salaries outstanding on 31 December 200— were £426.

(c) Council tax paid in advance on 31 December 200— amounted to £500.

(d) This year's provision for doubtful debts is to be increased to £2,600.

(e) Depreciation is to be charged at 20% per annum on cost of cars and 5% per annum on cost of fixtures and fittings.

Prepare a Profit and Loss account and balance sheet for the year ended 31 December 200—.

5.8 Suggested answers to exercises on adjustments and final accounts

1 Lightfoot Profit and Loss account for the year ending 31 December 200—

EXPENSES	
Bad debts	625
ADD this year's provision for doubtful debts	450
	1,075

Lightfoot Balance Sheet as at 31 December 200—

CURRENT ASSETS	
Debtors	4,340
LESS provision for doubtful debts	450
	3,890

2 Davis Profit and Loss account for the year ending 31 March 200—

EXPENSES	
Depreciation on cars	4,500
(15% of £30,000)	

Davis Balance Sheet as at 31 March 200—

FIXED ASSETS	
Cost price of cars	30,000
LESS total accumulated depreciation	
(being 9,000 plus 4,500)	13,500
	16,500

3 Karsh Profit and Loss account for the year ending 30 September 200—

INCOME		
Profit costs	90,000	
ADD		
Work in Progress at end of year	6,200	
VALUE OF WORK DONE	96,200	
ADDITIONAL INCOME	Nil	
TOTAL INCOME		96,200
LESS EXPENSES		
General and administrative expenses	46,000	
Depreciation on office furniture	850	
Bad debts	406	
Provision for doubtful debts	360	
Total expenses		47,616
NET PROFIT		48,584

Karsh Balance Sheet as at 30 September 200—

FIXED ASSETS			
Premises cost price		160,000	
Office furniture cost price	8,500		
Less total depreciation			
(2,550 + 850)	3,400		
		5,100	
			165,100
CURRENT ASSETS			
Work in Progress		6,200	
Debtors (due from clients)	3,544		
LESS provision for doubtful			
Debts	360		
		3,184	
Cash at bank office a/c		13,915	
Petty cash		165	
		23,464	
LESS CURRENT LIABILITIES			
Creditors		1,980	
NET CURRENT ASSETS			21,484
			186,584
LESS LONG-TERM LIABILITIES			
TOTAL NET ASSETS			186,584
Capital employed			
Capital	170,000		
ADD net profit	48,584		
		218,584	
LESS drawings		32,000	
TOTAL DUE TO OWNER			186,584
CLIENT ACCOUNT			
Cash at bank client account			249,000
Amount due to clients			249,000

4 J Milton: Profit and Loss account for the year ended 31 December 200—

INCOME			
Profit costs		76,422	
ADD closing Work in Progress		8,569	84,991
LESS EXPENSES			
Telephone and postage		1,300	
ADD provision		505	1,805
Council tax			2,950
Light and heat		1,550	
ADD provision		551	2,101
Salaries			25,270

Depreciation:			
Motor cars	2,060		
Fixtures and fittings	260	2,320	
Bad debts and provision		337	34,783
(£122 + £215 provision)			
NET PROFIT			50,208

J Milton: Balance Sheet as at 31 December 200—

FIXED ASSETS			
Premises		132,000	
Fixtures and fittings at cost	5,200		
LESS accumulated depreciation	1,560		
		3,640	
Motor cars at cost	20,600		
LESS accumulated depreciation	6,180		
		14,420	
			150,060
CURRENT ASSETS			
Closing Work in Progress		8,569	
Debtors	4,300		
LESS provision	215		
		4,085	
Cash at bank, office account		14,190	
Petty cash		123	
		26,967	
LESS CURRENT LIABILITIES			
Creditors		4,763	
Outstanding expenses		1,056	
		5,819	
NET CURRENT ASSETS			21,148
			171,208
LESS LONG-TERM LIABILITIES			—
TOTAL NET ASSETS			171,208
CAPITAL EMPLOYED			
Capital at start		140,000	
ADD net profit		50,208	
		190,208	
LESS drawings		19,000	
TOTAL DUE TO OWNER			171,208
Client account			
Cash at bank, client account		315,000	
Due to clients		315,000	

5 **C. Arnold: Profit and Loss account for the year ended 31 December 200—**

INCOME
Profit costs		78,021	
ADD closing Work in Progress		14,270	
		92,291	
LESS opening Work in Progress		16,582	75,709
Additional income			
Insurance commission received			369
			76,078
LESS EXPENSES			
Rent and rates	2,626		
LESS paid in advance	500	2,126	
Salaries	30,226		
PLUS outstanding	426	30,652	
General expenses		12,500	
Interest		735	
Bad and doubtful debts		3,344* [see note below]	
Depreciation: cars	4,000		
Fixtures and fittings	400	4,400	53,757
NET PROFIT			22,321

Note:
Bad debts	2,400
ADD this year's provision	2,600
	5,000
LESS last year's provision	1,656
	3,344

C. Arnold: Balance Sheet as at 31 December 200—

FIXED ASSETS			
Freehold premises		200,500	
Fixtures and fittings at cost	8,000		
LESS accumulated depreciation	1,600		
		6,400	
Motor cars at cost	20,000		
LESS accumulated depreciation	12,000		
		8,000	
			214,900
CURRENT ASSETS			
Closing Work in Progress		14,270	
Debtors	12,009		
LESS provision	2,600	9,409	
Petty cash		55	

Payment in advance			
Rates		500	
		24,234	
LESS CURRENT LIABILITIES			
Creditors	9,235		
Office bank account overdraft	4,552		
Outstanding expenses: salaries	426		
		14,213	
NET CURRENT ASSETS			10,021
			224,921
LESS LONG-TERM LIABILITIES			—
TOTAL NET ASSETS			224,921
CAPITAL EMPLOYED			
Capital at start	223,059		
ADD net profit	22,321		
		245,380	
LESS drawings		20,459	
TOTAL DUE TO OWNER			224,921
CLIENT ACCOUNT			
Cash at bank, client account	450,000		
LESS due to clients	450,000		

6

Partnership accounts

6.1 The accounts kept by a partnership—introduction

6.1.1 General

The accounts kept by a partnership are largely the same as those kept by a sole practitioner. The asset and income and expense accounts are the same and the clients' accounts are the same, as are the accounting procedures up to the preparation of final accounts. The main differences are as follows:

6.1.1.1 Profit and Loss account—Appropriation account

There is an extension to the Profit and Loss account, known as the Appropriation account, which will show how the profit is divided between the partners.

6.1.1.2 The Balance Sheet

In the Capital Employed section, the partners each have a separate capital account and a separate current account, which shows details of all the profit allocated to the partner, less drawings.

6.2 Final accounts

6.2.1 Profit and Loss account—the Appropriation account

Up to the point of calculating the firm's net profit, the Profit and Loss account of a partnership is the same as that of a sole practitioner. In a partnership the Profit and Loss account is extended to show the allocation of the net profit amongst the partners in the profit-sharing ratio provided for in the partnership agreement, after such items as salaries and interest on capital, also provided for in the partnership agreement, have been taken into account. The extension of the Profit and Loss account is called an Appropriation account. Note that partners' salaries in this context are merely a fixed prior allocaton of profit.

> **EXAMPLE**
>
> The firm has three partners A, B and C. The profit and loss account records a net profit for the year of £120,000. The partnership agreement provides that A is to receive interest on

capital of £2,000 and a salary of £8,000, C is to receive interest on capital of £1,000 and a salary of £2,000 and B is to receive a salary of £2,000. Profits are then shared in the ratio A2 : B2 : C1. The Appropriation account for A, B and C will appear as follows:

A, B & C: Appropriation account for the year ending

NET PROFIT   120,000

SALARIES:
A   8,000
B   2,000
C   2,000
                                                            12,000

INTEREST ON CAPITAL:
A   2,000
C   1,000   3,000

PROFIT SHARE:
A: 2/5ths   42,000
B: 2/5ths   42,000
C: 1/5th   21,000   105,000

                                                                           120,000

Note the following with regard to the Appropriation account:

(a) Net profit is carried down from the Profit and Loss account.

(b) Partners' entitlements to salary and interest on capital, for example, must be deducted first from the net profit.

(c) The resulting balance is shared amongst the partners in the profit-sharing ratio.

6.2.2 The Balance Sheet

The current account for each partner will show any salary, interest on capital and profit share that they are entitled to. This will form part of the Balance Sheet—see later.

To continue the above example, the current account for partner A would appear as follows:

Current account: A

Date	Details	DR	CR	Balance
	Appropriation: salary		8,000	8,000 CR
	Appropriation: interest on capital		2,000	10,000 CR
	Appropriation: profit share		42,000	52,000 CR

6.3 Drawings

A drawings account may be opened for each partner or alternatively drawings may be debited to the partners' current accounts when they are made.

6.3.1 Cash drawings

If a drawings account is used the following entries will be made to record the partners' cash drawings.

(a) DEBIT drawings account.
(b) CREDIT cash account.

EXAMPLE

On 31 March partner A draws £2,000, on 30 April A draws £2,000, on 10 May the firm pays A's home gas bill, £150.

Drawings account: A

Date	Details	DR	CR	Balance
31 Mar	Cash	2,000		2,000 DR
30 Apr	Cash	2,000		4,000 DR
10 May	Cash: home gas bill	150		4,150 DR

If the firm does not use a drawings account for the partners but debits drawings into the partners' current accounts, when the drawings are made, the above entries would have been recorded in A's current account.

6.3.2 End of the financial year

At the end of the financial year the partner's drawings account will be closed and the balance on the account will be transferred to the partner's current account.

6.3.3 Capital accounts

In a partnership the capital is introduced by more than one person and therefore a separate capital account is kept for each partner.

Note that the partners' profit entitlement and drawings will be shown separately on current accounts; see below.

EXAMPLE

A and B enter into partnership introducing £30,000 and £90,000 capital, respectively.

Capital account: A

Date	Details	DR	CR	Balance
	Balance			30,000 CR

Capital account: B

Date	Details	DR	CR	Balance
	Balance			90,000 CR

6.3.4 Current accounts

A current account is opened for each partner.

A partner's current account is credited with any sums which the partner is entitled to receive from the practice, for example, the profit share, interest on capital and salary.

A partner's current account is debited with any sums which the partner has taken out of the practice or which are owed to the practice, for example, drawings (transferred at the end of the financial year from the partner's drawings account).

If a partner's current account has a credit balance, then the firm owes money to the partner. If the current account has a debit balance, then the partner owes money to the firm, which is a current asset of the firm.

However by convention, the balances on the partners' current accounts will always be shown on the Capital Employed part of the Balance Sheet.

EXAMPLE

In the example in **6.3.3**, assume that on 30 June 200—, the end of the financial year for A and B's first year of practice, net profit is £86,000. Interest on capital is allowed to both partners at the rate of 5% per annum. A has made drawings of £20,000 and B has made drawings of £30,000. B is paid a salary of £5,000 per annum. A's share of the net profit is £25,000 and B's share is £50,000.

Current account: A

Date	Details	DR	CR	Balance
200—				
30 June	Profit share		25,000	25,000 CR
	Interest on capital		1,500	26,500 CR
	Drawings	20,000		6,500 CR

Thus at the end of the year the firm owes A £6,500.

Current account: B

Date	Details	DR	CR	Balance
200—				
30 June	Profit share		50,000	50,000 CR
	Salary		5,000	55,000 CR
	Interest on capital		4,500	59,500 CR
	Drawings	30,000		29,500 CR

Thus at the end of the year the firm owes B £29,500.

6.3.5 Balance Sheet

The balance sheet of a partnership is the same as that of a sole practitioner except:

(a) The capital accounts of the partners are shown separately. The capital accounts show capital at the start of the year.

(b) Net profit and drawings are *not* transferred to a partner's capital account and therefore are not shown as additions to and deductions from capital, respectively, as happens with a sole practitioner.

(c) The current accounts of the partners are shown on the liabilities part (capital employed) of the balance sheet. If there is a credit balance on the current accounts, this is added to the capital account balance. If there is a debit balance on the current accounts this is deducted from the capital account balance.

(d) It is not usual to show movements on partners' current accounts on the Balance Sheet itself. At the end of the Balance Sheet is a schedule showing the movement on the current accounts.

6.3.6 Example on partners' final accounts

Ginger, Tom and Arnold are in partnership, sharing profits and losses in the ratio 2 : 2 : 1. Each partner is entitled to interest on capital at 10% per annum and to salaries of £10,000 to Ginger and £7,000 to Arnold.

An abridged trial balance prepared from the partnership books shows the following position at 30 September 200—.

	DR	CR
Total assets	320,000	
Total liabilities		150,000
Profit for the year from the Profit and Loss account		140,000
Drawings		
Ginger	30,000	
Tom	25,000	
Arnold	25,000	
Capital accounts		
Ginger		50,000
Tom		40,000
Arnold		20,000
	400,000	400,000

From the above, prepare the profit and loss appropriation account for the year ended 30 September 200—, together with a balance sheet as at that date.

6.3.7 Answer to example on partners' final accounts

Profit and Loss and appropriation account for the year ended 30 September 200—

NET PROFIT		140,000
INTEREST ON CAPITAL:		
Ginger 10% on £50,000	5,000	
Tom 10% on £40,000	4,000	
Arnold 10% on £20,000	2,000	11,000
		129,000
SALARIES:		
Ginger	10,000	
Arnold	7,000	17,000
		112,000

SHARE OF PROFIT:
Ginger: 2/5ths	44,800	
Tom: 2/5ths	44,800	
Arnold: 1/5th	22,400	112,000

Ginger, Tom and Arnold: Balance Sheet as at 30 September 200—

ASSETS	320,000	
LESS liabilities	150,000	
TOTAL NET ASSETS		170,000
CAPITAL EMPLOYED		
Capital accounts:		
Ginger	50,000	
Tom	40,000	
Arnold	20,000	
	110,000	
Current accounts (see movements on current accounts):		
Ginger	29,800	
Tom	23,800	
Arnold	6,400	
	60,000	
TOTAL DUE TO PARTNERS		170,000

Movements on partners' current accounts

	Ginger	Tom	Arnold
Opening balance			
Salary	10,000	—	7,000
Interest on capital	5,000	4,000	2,000
Profit share	44,800	44,800	22,400
	59,800	48,800	31,400
LESS drawings	30,000	25,000	25,000
	29,800 CR	23,800 CR	6,400 CR

6.4 Partnership changes

The constitution of a partnership may change during the financial year as a result of a partner dying, retiring from the practice, a new partner joining the practice or because the partners decide to vary their profit sharing agreement.

When there is a partnership change during the year, the format of the Balance Sheet and the Profit and Loss account to the net profit stage will not change.

The format of the Appropriation account will change as there will be a split appropriation. This means that there will be one Appropriation account for the period before the change and one for the period after the change to the end of the financial year. Each

Appropriation account will reflect the terms of the partnership agreement in force for the period to which the Appropriation account relates. Unless you are told the net profit for the period before and after the change you will have to apportion the net profit for each period on a time basis.

The net profit, interest on drawings, interest on capital and salaries must be apportioned. For example, if there is a partnership change three months into the year, in the first Appropriation account, net profit, etc., for the year will be divided by four to reflect the fact that the Appropriation account relates to only one quarter of the year.

If a sole practitioner takes in a partner part way through the year, the profits for the time as a sole practitioner will belong wholly to the sole practitioner. There will be no salary, interest on capital, etc., in the first part of the Appropriation account as these are relevant only where there is a partnership. It therefore follows that provision for salaries, etc. in the partnership agreement can apply only to the second appropriation period.

EXAMPLE

A and B are in partnership. A's capital is £60,000 and B's is £40,000. They share the profits in the ratio 3 : 2. Their financial year runs from 1 January to 31 December. C joins the partnership on 1 July 200—. C is to receive a salary of £12,000 per annum and A and B interest on capital of 10% per annum. A, B and C are to share the profits in the ratio of 2 : 2 : 1.

Net profit for the year ended 31 December 200— is £140,000.

A, B & C: profit and loss account for the year ended 31 December 200—

NET PROFIT			140,000
Appropriation account 1 January to 30 June 200—			
PROFIT SHARE:			
A: 3/5ths	42,000		
B: 2/5ths	28,000		70,000
1 July to 31 December 200—			
INTEREST ON CAPITAL:			
A for half year on 60,000 at 10%	3,000		
B for half year on 40,000 at 10%	2,000	5,000	
SALARIES:			
C for half year at 12,000 p.a.		6,000	
PROFIT SHARE:			
A: 2/5ths	23,600		
B: 2/5ths	23,600		
C: 1/5th	11,800	59,000	70,000
			140,000

6.5 Check list

By the end of this chapter you should be able to:

1. appreciate that there will be an addition to the Profit and Loss account which will show how the profit is divided between the partners, known as the Appropriation account;
2. note the difference between the Balance Sheet of a partnership and that of a sole owner;
3. appreciate that on the Balance Sheet in the Capital Employed section the partners will have separate accounts, broken down into Capital accounts and Current accounts;

4. understand that the details on the Current accounts may be shown as a schedule to the Balance Sheet;
5. understand that partners may split the profit in different ways, providing for any partners' salaries and interest on capital as a prior allocation of the profit;
6. draw up an Appropriation account;
7. draw up details of movement on partners' Current accounts;
8. draw up a partnership Balance Sheet;
9. complete the self-test exercises at the end of the chapter.

6.6 Exercises on partnership final accounts

When you have completed these exercises in the time allocated you should move on to basic accounting concepts and trading accounts (Chapter 7).

1. Allow 15 to 20 minutes.

   Allan, Black and Clark are in partnership sharing profits as to Allan 50%, Black 25% and Clark 25%.

   Each partner is entitled to interest on capital of 5% and Clark is entitled to a partnership salary of £5,000 a year. The net profit at the end of the year is £250,000 and the partners' capital account balances are Allan £60,000, Black £40,000 and Clark £20,000.

   Draw up the Appropriation account for the partners.

2. Allow about 30 minutes.

   The Trial Balance of Javid and Khan at the end of the year 31 December 200— showed the following Capital and current account balances:

   Capital accounts
   Javid   40,000
   Khan   20,000

   Current accounts
   Javid   5,426
   Khan   3,040

   Net profit for the partnership at the end of the year was £110,000. Interest on capital is 6% a year. Khan has a salary of £2,000 a year and the profit share ratio is Javid 2: Khan 1. Drawings for the year were Javid £50,000 and Khan £35,000.

   Draw up the Appropriation account, the movement on Current accounts and the capital employed section of the Balance Sheet at the end of the year.

3. Allow 1 hour to 1 hour 20 minutes.

   The bookkeeper of the firm Bertram, Crawford and Norris, solicitors, draws up a trial balance in respect of the year ending 31 December 200—.

   Trial balance at 31 December 200—

	DR	CR
Profit costs less Work in Progress at start of year		544,060
General and administrative expenses	372,900	
Due to clients		943,560
Bad debts	4,900	
Capital accounts		
Bertram		130,000
Crawford		100,000
Norris		80,000

Current accounts		
Bertram		5,000
Crawford		4,000
Norris		6,000
Sundry creditors		8,100
Interest received		6,420
Freehold premises	320,000	
Library furniture & equipment at cost	42,000	
Accumulated depreciation on library		
Furniture & equipment		12,600
Motor cars	45,000	
Accumulated depreciation on motor cars		18,000
Due from clients	51,820	
Overdraft office account		3,000
Cash at bank client current account	493,560	
Cash at bank client deposit account	450,000	
Petty cash	560	
Drawings		
Bertram	30,000	
Crawford	25,000	
Norris	25,000	
	1,860,740	1,860,740

The partnership agreement provides that Crawford has a partnership salary of £5,000 per annum, interest on capital for the partners is 5% per annum and profits and losses are shared equally.

Work in progress as at 31 December 200— is £50,000. Payments in advance are £1,800 and outstanding expenses are £2,100. Provision for doubtful debts for the year to 31 December 200— is set at £1,200. Depreciation for the year on the library furniture and equipment is 10% of the cost price, and depreciation for the year on motor cars is 20% of the cost price.

Draw up the Profit and Loss and Appropriation account for the partners together with the Balance Sheet. Show full details of the movement on Current accounts.

4 Allow 1 hour to 1 hour 20 minutes.

Ash and Rowan are in partnership as solicitors, sharing profits and losses as to Ash two-thirds and Rowan one-third. Each partner is entitled to interest on capital in the firm at the rate of 5% per annum. Rowan is also entitled to a salary of £10,000 per annum. The following trial balance was prepared from the firm's accounts for the year ended 31 December 200—.

Trial balance at 31 December 200—

	DR	CR
Capital accounts		
Ash		50,000
Rowan		25,000
Current accounts		
Ash		3,450
Rowan		1,620
Lease at cost price	15,000	
Motor cars	30,000	
Furniture, library and equipment	22,000	

Partners' drawings		
Ash	23,500	
Rowan	28,000	
Administration and general expenses	118,520	
Profit costs		190,425
Interest received		2,900
Due to clients		425,380
Provision for doubtful debts b/d		560
Creditors		18,375
Cash at bank: clients' account:		
Deposit account	350,000	
Current account	75,380	
Petty cash	270	
Cash at bank: office account	12,840	
Work in Progress (1 January 2002)	34,200	
Due from clients	24,000	
Loan account: bank		10,000
Rent received		6,000
	733,710	733,710

Work in progress at 31 December 200— is valued at £38,000. This year's provision for doubtful debts is £800.

Depreciation on motor cars for the year ending 31 December 200— is £6,000. Depreciation on furniture, library and equipment is £4,800.

From the above information prepare a Profit and Loss and Appropriation account for the year ended 31 December 200— together with a Balance Sheet as at that date.

5 Allow 50 minutes to 1 hour.

Beth and Amy are in partnership as solicitors sharing profits and losses in the ratio 3:2. Each partner is entitled, under the partnership agreement, to interest on capital at the rate of 10% per annum and Amy is entitled, in addition, to a partnership salary of £12,000 per annum.

On 1 July 200—, Jo is admitted into the partnership, contributing £10,000 as her share of the capital in the firm. The new partnership agreement provides that, as from 1 July 200—, profits and losses will be shared between Beth, Amy and Jo in the ratio 2:2:1 respectively. Furthermore, partnership salaries of £20,000, £15,000 and £10,000 per annum will be allowed to Beth, Amy and Jo respectively. No interest is to be allowed on capital, and no interest is to be charged on partners' drawings.

An abridged trial balance, prepared from the partnership books, shows the following position as at 31 December 200—.

NET PROFIT for the year, before charging interest on capital, and other appropriations		120,000
Partners' drawings:		
Beth	30,700	
Amy	28,400	
Jo	11,000	
Partners' capital accounts:		
Beth		70,000
Amy		50,000
Jo		10,000

Sundry assets	194,700	
Sundry liabilities		14,800
	264,800	264,800
Amounts due to clients		894,568
Cash at bank: clients	894,568	
	1,159,368	1,159,368

From the above information, prepare the Profit and Loss and Appropriation account for the year ended 31 December 200—, together with a Balance Sheet as at that date. The allocation of profits between the partners is to be determined on a time basis. (Calculations to be made in months.) Detailed movements on partners' Current accounts should also be shown.

6 Allow 1 hour to 1 hour 20 minutes.

Hale and Hearty are in partnership as solicitors. Hale and Hearty receive interest on capital of 5% per annum and Hearty receives a salary of £2,000 per annum. The remaining profits are shared equally. Their financial year ends on 31 December. On 31 December 200— the Trial Balance is:

	DR	CR
Freehold premises	145,000	
Fixtures and fittings	15,000	
Accumulated depreciation on fixtures and fittings		3,000
Library	2,000	
Accumulated depreciation on library		500
Capital accounts:		
Hale		80,000
Hearty		75,000
Current accounts:		
Hale		2,500
Hearty		2,000
Drawings:		
Hale	24,000	
Hearty	24,500	
Profit		
Profit costs		78,000
Insurance commission received		600
Salaries	20,000	
Insurance paid	1,500	
Council tax	1,620	
Light and heat	1,400	
Stationery	900	
Travelling	400	
Creditors		820
Debtors	3,000	
Office bank account	3,000	
Petty cash	100	
Client bank account	465,000	
Client ledger account		465,000
	707,420	707,420

At 31 December 200— work in progress amounts to £5,000; there is a stock of stationery valued at £300. Depreciation is charged on fixtures and fittings and library at 10% on the cost price. There is an amount outstanding for electricity of £100.

Prepare final accounts for Hale and Hearty for the year ended 31 December 200—.

6.7 Suggested answers to exercises on partnership final accounts

1 Allan, Black and Clark appropriation account for the year ending   ....

NET PROFIT		250,000
LESS		
Salary Clark		5,000
		245,000
INTEREST ON CAPITAL		
Allan 5% on 60,000	3,000	
Black 5% on 40,000	2,000	
Clark 5% on 20,000	1,000	
		6,000
		239,000
PROFIT SHARE		
Allan 50%	119,500	
Black 25%	59,750	
Clark 25%	59,750	
		239,000

2 Appropriation account for Javid and Khan for the year ending 31 December 200—

NET PROFIT		110,000
INTEREST ON CAPITAL		
Javid 6% on 40,000	2,400	
Khan 6% on 20,000	1,200	
		3,600
		106,400
SALARY		
Khan		2,000
		104,400
PROFIT SHARE		
Javid	69,600	
Khan	34,800	
		104,400

Movement on current accounts

	Javid	Khan
Opening balance	5,426	3,040
Interest on capital	2,400	1,200
Salary		2,000
Profit share	69,600	34,800
Total	77,426	41,040

LESS Drawings	50,000	35,000
Balance	27,426	6,040

Javid and Khan Balance sheet as at 31 December 200—

CAPITAL EMPLOYED			
Capital accounts			
Javid	40,000		
Khan	20,000		
			60,000
Current accounts (see movement on current accounts)			
Javid	27,426		
Khan	6,040		
			33,466
TOTAL DUE TO PARTNERS			93,466

3 Bertram, Crawford and Norris

Profit and Loss and Appropriation account for the year ending 31 December 200—

INCOME			
Profit costs		544,060	
ADD Work in Progress at end of year		50,000	
Value of work done			594,060
ADDITIONAL INCOME			
ADD interest received		6,420	600,480
LESS EXPENSES			
General and admin. expenses	372,900		
Bad debts	4,900		
Provision for doubtful debts	1,200		
depreciation on cars	9,000		
depreciation on furniture, etc.	4,200		
ADD outstanding expenses	2,100		
	394,300		
LESS payments in advance	1,800		392,500
NET PROFIT			207,980
APPROPRIATION ACCOUNT			
Profit available			207,980
SALARY			
Crawford			5,000
INTEREST ON CAPITAL			
Bertram		6,500	
Crawford		5,000	
Norris		4,000	15,500
PROFIT SHARE			
Bertram		62,494	
Crawford		62,493	
Norris		62,493	187,480

Bertram, Crawford and Norris: Balance Sheet as at 31 December 200—

FIXED ASSETS			
Freehold premises		320,000	
Library, etc. cost price	42,000		
LESS depreciation	168,000		
		25,200	
Motor cars cost price	45,000		
LESS depreciation	27,000		
		18,000	
			363,200
CURRENT ASSETS			
Work in Progress		50,000	
Debtors (due from clients)	51,820		
LESS provision	1,200		
		50,620	
Petty cash		560	
Payments in advance		1,800	
		102,980	
LESS CURRENT LIABILITIES			
Sundry creditors		8,100	
Overdraft office account		3,000	
Outstanding expenses		2,100	
		13,200	
NET CURRENT ASSETS			89,780
			452,980
LESS LONG-TERM LIABILITES			—
TOTAL NET ASSETS			452,980
CAPITAL EMPLOYED			
Capital accounts:			
Bertram	130,000		
Crawford	100,000		
Norris	80,000		
		310,000	
Current accounts (see schedule movement on current accounts)			
Bertram	43,994		
Crawford	51,493		
Norris	47,493		
		142,980	
TOTAL DUE TO PARTNERS			452,980
CLIENT ACCOUNT			
Due to clients		943,560	
Cash at bank client			
current account	493,560		

Cash at bank client deposit account	450,000	
		943,560

Movements on partners' current accounts

	Bertram	Crawford	Norris
Opening Balance	5,000	4,000	6,000
Salary	—	5,000	—
Interest on capital	6,500	5,000	4,000
Profit share	62,494	62,493	62,493
	73,994	76,493	72,493
LESS drawings	30,000	25,000	25,000
	43,994	51,493	47,493

4 Ash and Rowan

Profit and Loss and Appropriation account for the year ended 31 December 200—

Profit costs		190,425	
ADD closing Work in Progress		38,000	
		228,425	
LESS opening Work in Progress		34,200	
Value of work done		194,225	
ADDITIONAL INCOME			
Interest received	2,900		
Rent received	6,000		
		8,900	
			203,125
LESS: EXPENSES			
Administrative and general expenses		118,520	
Provision for doubtful debts			
This year's provision	800		
LESS last year's	560	240	
Depreciation:			
Cars	6,000		
Furniture, etc.	4,800	10,800	129,560
NET PROFIT			73,565
APPROPRIATION			73,565
SALARIES:			
Rowan		10,000	
INTEREST ON CAPITAL:			
Ash	2,500		
Rowan	1,250	3,750	
PROFIT SHARE:			
Ash: 2/3rds		39,877	
Rowan: 1/3rd		19,938	

(round up or down to nearest pound to balance)

Note that last year's provision for doubtful debts brought down will reduce the expense this year.

Schedule to Balance Sheet.

Movement on partners' current accounts

	Ash	Rowan
Balance	3,450 CR	1,620 CR
Salary	—	10,000
Interest on capital	2,500	1,250
Profit share	39,877	19,938
	45,827	32,808
LESS drawings	23,500	28,000
	22,327 CR	4,808 CR

Ash and Rowan: Balance Sheet as at 31 December 200—

FIXED ASSETS			
Leasehold premises		15,000	
Furniture, library and equipment			
at cost	22,000		
LESS depreciation	4,800		
		17,200	
Motor cars		30,000	
LESS depreciation		6,000	
		24,000	
			56,200
CURRENT ASSETS			
Closing Work in Progress		38,000	
Debtors	24,000		
LESS provision	800		
		23,200	
Cash at bank office account		12,840	
Petty cash		270	
		74,310	
LESS CURRENT LIABILITIES			
Creditors		18,375	
NET CURRENT ASSETS			55,935
			112,135
LESS LONG-TERM LIABILITIES			
Bank loan			10,000
TOTAL NET ASSETS			102,135
CAPITAL EMPLOYED			
Capital accounts:			
Ash		50,000	
Rowan		25,000	
			75,000

Current accounts:
(see schedule to the Balance Sheet)

Ash	22,327		
Rowan	4,808		
		27,135	
TOTAL DUE TO PARTNERS			102,135

CLIENT ACCOUNT
Bank balance:

Deposit account	350,000		
Current account	75,380		
		425,380	
Due to clients		425,380	

5   Beth, Amy and Jo

Profit and Loss and Appropriation account for period 1 January 200— to 30 June 200—

NET PROFIT (for 6 months)		60,000
SALARY (for 6 months):		
Amy	6,000	
INTEREST ON CAPITAL (for 6 months):		
Beth	3,500	
Amy	2,500	
		12,000
PROFIT SHARE:		
Beth: 3/5ths	28,800	
Amy: 2/5ths	19,200	48,000

Profit and Loss and Appropriation account for period 1 July to 31 December 200—

NET PROFIT (for 6 months)		60,000
SALARIES (for 6 months):		
Beth	10,000	
Amy	7,500	
Jo	5,000	
		22,500
PROFIT SHARE:		
Beth: 2/5ths	15,000	
Amy: 2/5ths	15,000	
Jo: 1/5th	7,500	37,500

Schedule to Balance Sheet

Movement on partners' current accounts

	Beth	Amy	Jo
Salary	10,000	13,500	5,000
Interest on capital	3,500	2,500	—
Profit share	43,800	34,200	7,500
	57,300	50,200	12,500

Less balance	30,700	28,400	11,000
	26,600 CR	21,800 CR	1,500 CR

Beth, Amy and Jo: Balance Sheet as at 31 December 200—

ASSETS		194,700	
LESS LIABILITIES		14,800	
TOTAL NET ASSETS			179,900
CAPITAL EMPLOYED			
Capital accounts:			
Beth	70,000		
Amy	50,000		
Jo	10,000		
			130,000
Current accounts:			
Beth	26,600 CR		
Amy	21,800 CR		
Jo	1,500 CR		
			49,900
TOTAL DUE TO PARTNERS			179,900
CLIENT ACCOUNT			
Client bank balance		894,568	
Due to clients		894,568	

6 Hale and Hearty

Profit and Loss and Appropriation account for the year ended 31 December 200—

INCOME			
Profit costs		78,000	
ADD closing Work in Progress		5,000	
Value of work done			83,000
ADD insurance commission received		600	
			83,600
LESS EXPENSES			
Salaries		20,000	
Insurance paid		1,500	
Council tax		1,620	
Light and heat	1,400		
Plus outstanding expense	100	1,500	
Stationery	900		
LESS closing stock	300	600	
Travel expenses		400	
Depreciation:			
Fixtures and fittings	1,500		
Library	200	1,700	27,320
NET PROFIT			56,280

APPROPRIATION ACCOUNT

Salary:		
Hearty	2,000	2,000
Interest on capital:		
Hale	4,000	
Hearty	3,750	7,750
Profit share:		
Hale: 1/2	23,265	
Hearty: 1/2	23,265	46,530
		56,280

Hale and Hearty: Balance Sheet as at 31 December 200—

FIXED ASSETS			
Premises		145,000	
Fixtures and fittings	15,000		
LESS accumulated depreciation	4,500		
		10,500	
Library	2,000		
LESS accumulated depreciation	700		
		1,300	
			156,800
CURRENT ASSETS			
Closing work in progress	5,000		
Debtors	3,000		
Office bank account	3,000		
Petty cash	100		
Stock of stationery	300		
		11,400	
LESS CURRENT LIABILITIES			
Creditors	820		
Outstanding expenses	100		
		920	
NET CURRENT ASSETS			10,480
			167,280
LESS LONG-TERM LIABILITIES			—
TOTAL NET ASSETS			167,280
CAPITAL EMPLOYED			
Capital accounts:			
Hale	80,000		
Hearty	75,000		
			155,000
Current accounts: see movement on current accounts			
Hale	5,765		
Hearty	6,515		
			12,280

TOTAL DUE TO PARTNERS		167,280

CLIENT ACCOUNT

Client bank balance	465,000	
Due to clients	465,000	

Movement on partners' current accounts

	Hale	Hearty
Opening balance	2,500	2,000
Salary		2,000
Interest on capital	4,000	3,750
Profit share	23,265	23,265
	29,765	31,015
LESS drawings	24,000	24,500
	5,765	6,515

6.8 Test on partnership final accounts

Allow 1 hour to 1 hour 20 minutes to complete this test.

From the Trial Balance of Rip, Van and Winkle set out below draw up a Profit and Loss account and Appropriation account for the year ended 31 December 200—, together with a Balance Sheet as at that date.

	DR	CR
Current accounts:		
Rip		2,771
Van		3,055
Winkle	760	
Capital accounts:		
Rip		160,000
Van		120,000
Winkle		80,000
Drawings:		
Rip	25,000	
Van	25,000	
Winkle	25,000	
Creditors		5,923
Premises—cost price	300,000	
Office equipment—cost price	25,000	
Office furniture—cost price	30,000	
Motor cars—cost price	45,000	
Accumulated depreciation on office equipment		5,000
Accumulated depreciation on office furniture		6,000
Accumulated depreciation on motor cars		9,000
General expenses	415,000	

Cash at bank—office account	7,543	
Petty cash	96	
Profit costs		539,700
Interest received		7,150
Work in Progress as at 1 January 200—	35,000	
Cash at Bank Client account		
current account	176,000	
deposit account	490,000	
Amount due to clients		666,000
Due from clients	5,200	
	1,604,599	1,604,599

Note the following:

Expenses due and not yet paid during the year amount to £895, those expenses prepaid amount to £625. A bad debt has to be written off in the sum of £600, and provision for bad and doubtful debts amounts to £530. Work in progress as at 31 December 200— amounts to £38,800. Depreciation on office equipment and on office furniture is 10% per annum on the cost price, and depreciation on cars is 20% per annum on the cost price. Rip has a partnership salary of £5,000, and the partners allow interest on capital at 5% per annum. The profits are then shared equally between the partners.

6.9 Suggested answer to test on partnership final accounts

Rip, Van and Winkle

Profit and Loss and Appropriation account for the year ended 31 December 200—

INCOME		
Profit costs	539,700	
ADD Work in Progress at the end of the year 31 December 200—	38,800	
	578,500	
LESS Work in Progress at the start of the year 1 January 200—	35,000	
Value of work done	543,500	
ADD ADDITIONAL INCOME		
Interest received	7,150	
		550,650
LESS EXPENSES		
Admin. and general expenses	415,000	
Outstanding expenses	895	
Bad debt written off	600	
Provision for doubtful debts	530	
	417,025	
LESS prepaid	625	
	416,400	

ADD depreciation			
On office equipment		2,500	
On office furniture		3,000	
On motor cars		9,000	
		14,500	
			430,900
NET PROFIT			119,750

APPROPRIATION ACCOUNT

Profit available for distribution		119,750
SALARY		
Rip		5,000
INTEREST ON CAPITAL		
Rip	8,000	
Van	6,000	
Winkle	4,000	
		18,000
Profit share		
Rip	32,250	
Van	32,250	
Winkle	32,250	
		96,750

Rip, Van and Winkle: Balance Sheet as at 31 December 200—

FIXED ASSETS			
Premises cost price		300,000	
Office equipment cost price	25,000		
LESS total depreciation	7,500	17,500	
Office furniture cost price	30,000		
LESS total depreciation	9,000		
		21,000	
Motor cars cost price	45,000		
LESS total depreciation	18,000		
		27,000	
			365,500
CURRENT ASSETS			
Work in Progress		38,800	
Debtors (5,200 − 600)	4,600		
LESS provision	530		
		4,070	
Cash at Bank office		7,543	
Petty cash		96	
Pre-paid		625	
			51,134

LESS CURRENT LIABILITIES			
Creditors	5,923		
Outstanding expenses	895		
		6,818	
NET CURRENT ASSETS			44,316
			409,816
LESS LONG-TERM LIABILITIES			—
TOTAL			409,816
CAPITAL EMPLOYED			
CAPITAL ACCOUNTS			
Rip	160,000		
Van	120,000		
Winkle	80,000		
			360,000
CURRENT ACCOUNTS			
See schedule movement on current accounts			
Rip	23,021		
Van	16,305		
Winkle	10,490		
			49,816
TOTAL			409,816

Schedule movement on current accounts

	Rip	Van	Winkle
Opening balance	2,771	3,055	760 (DR)
Salary	5,000	—	—
Interest on capital	8,000	6,000	4,000
Profit share	32,250	32,250	32,250
	48,021	41,305	35,490
LESS drawings	25,000	25,000	25,000
	23,021	16,305	10,490

Basic accounting concepts and trading accounts

7.1 Introduction

This chapter includes accounting concepts which underpin accounts, and explains briefly accounting bases and policies. It then deals with basic trading accounts.

7.2 Financial accounting concepts

Accounting has certain rules, known as accounting concepts, which are applied in drawing up accounts and making adjustments. There are detailed accounting standards set out for accountants, earlier these were known as Statements of Standard Accounting Practice (SSAPs), later standards are known as Financial Reporting Standards (FRSs).

Any accounting methods used are supposed to give a true and fair view of a business, of its profit and loss and its value.

Fundamental accounting concepts are the assumptions on which accounts of businesses are drawn up. They include the following:

7.2.1 The business entity concept

This means that for accounting purposes a business is treated as a separate entity from its owner or owners, even though in law this may not be the case for a sole trader or a partnership. Thus when an owner puts money into the business this is recorded as the business having received the money and that the business owes that money to the owner (see capital accounts at **1.5.2**).

7.2.2 The money measurement concept

Accounts give information about a business, but only in money terms. They do not, for example, give information about the motivation of the workforce or how competent the managing director is.

7.2.3 The cost concept

This means that assets would be valued at cost price rather than by estimating their current value.

7.2.4 The going-concern concept

This is the assumption that the business will continue to operate in the future. Thus the Profit and Loss account and the Balance Sheet will be drawn up on the assumption that the business will continue at the same level and not be sold. For example, if a business ceases to operate, its assets may be worth considerably less on a closing down sale than if the business continues.

7.2.5 The accruals concept

This is the assumption that income and expenses should be matched and actually recorded in the period in which they are earned or incurred, rather than the period in which they are actually received or paid, e.g. adjustments for work in progress, payments in advance, outstanding expenses, etc. that we have seen previously (see **Chapter 2**). Thus if work has been carried out within a particular accounting period, then the amount earned in respect of that work should be shown as income. Or if a payment is made in advance it should not be treated as an expense of the period in which it has been paid, but should be shown as an expense in the next period.

7.2.6 The consistency concept

This means that there should be consistency in the accounting methods used for similar items, in the same accounting period and in later periods. If a firm changes the basis on which it values stock or work in progress then the profit figure may be different from the figure that would be obtained had stock or work in progress been valued in the same way. Thus if businesses wish to change the basis on which they value stock, or value assets, then they must mention the effect on the profit of the change in accounting method.

7.2.7 The concept of prudence

This is the principle that profit should not be overstated. Thus income should not be anticipated and should be recorded in the Profit and Loss account only when received in cash, or as assets (e.g. debtors) which can be converted readily into cash. However, provision should be made for all possible known or expected future losses.

7.2.8 The concept of materiality

This means that there is no need to make detailed accounting records of items which are regarded as not material. For example, small items purchased, e.g. biros used in the office, will be treated as part of the expenses in the period in which they are purchased, and there will be no need to record on the balance sheet at the end of the year that the firm has six biros. Firms will decide individually whether an item is material, e.g. for a large firm items costing less than £500 may be treated as not material, if the firm is smaller then it may treat items costing less than £50 as not material. All such items will be treated as expenses and any remaining items will not be shown on the balance sheet, i.e. there is no need to make adjustments for small amounts.

7.3 Accounting bases and policies

Accounting bases are methods which have been developed for applying the accounting concepts to accounting transactions and items. These will vary according to the type of business and business transaction. They can be used, for example, to decide the accounting periods in which income and expenses should be recognised in the profit and loss account, and to decide the amounts at which items are considered material for inclusion in the balance sheet.

Accounting policies are particular accounting bases which are considered by individual businesses to be most appropriate to their particular circumstances for the purpose of giving a true and fair view. Accounting policies used by a business should be disclosed by way of a note to the accounts, e.g. how depreciation is treated, or how work in progress or stock is valued.

7.4 Trading accounts

7.4.1 Introduction

We have previously looked at the accounts of solicitors, who derive their income from services, or work done (see **Chapters 1–3**). With a trader, goods will be purchased for resale, there will be an account to record the value of all purchases, and a separate account to record the value of all sales.

7.4.2 Trading account

When the trader draws up his final accounts, a trading account will be drawn up, showing the sales less purchases, to give the gross profit. This will be followed by the Profit and Loss account, showing income, the gross profit and other income not derived from trading, e.g. interest receivable, less expenses, administrative expenses, financial expenses, etc.

Trading account

Sales	£40,000
Less purchases	£15,000
Gross profit	£25,000

This is a simple form of trading account. Additional items to be taken into account might include sales returns: e.g. where goods have been returned to the business, the sales returns account would be debited and then the cash book or the customer's personal ledger card would be credited. The debit balance on the sales returns account will be deducted from the sales figure, to give net sales. For example:

Sales	£700,000
Less sales returns	£10,000
	£690,000

The purchases figure will have to be adjusted, to take account of any stock held by the trader at the start of the year, and any stock left at the end of the year, to give the actual cost of the goods sold.

EXAMPLE

A trader starts the year with £60,000 worth of goods (opening stock). During the year a further £300,000 worth of goods is purchased, and at the end of the year there is £40,000 worth of goods remaining.

The cost of goods sold is therefore:

Opening stock	60,000	
Plus purchases	300,000	
		360,000
Less closing stock		40,000
Cost of goods sold		320,000

The adjustment for stock will be shown on the Purchases account.

Purchases account

Date	Details	DR	CR	Balance
	Opening stock brought down from previous period	60,000		60,000 DR
	Purchases during the year	300,000		360,000 DR
	Closing stock		40,000	320,000 DR
	Transfer to profit and loss		320,000	—
	Opening stock b/d	40,000		40,000 DR

The Trading and Profit and Loss account would therefore appear as set out below:

Trading and Profit and Loss account for the year ending 31 December 200—

Sales	700,000	
Less returns	10,000	
		690,000
Less		
Cost of goods sold		
Opening stock	60,000	
Plus purchases	300,000	
	360,000	
Less closing stock	40,000	
Cost of goods sold		320,000
GROSS PROFIT		370,000
Less expenses		100,000
NET PROFIT		270,000

7.5 Check list

By the end of this chapter you should be able to:

1. understand the accounting concepts and their application to accounts, including adjustments made;
2. note accounting bases and policies;
3. understand and draw up a simple trading account;
4. note the structure of a Manufacturing account;
5. use the self-test exercises at the end of the chapter to achieve the above.

7.6 Practice exercises

When you have completed these excercises, move on to company accounts (Chapter 8).

1 Allow 10 to 15 minutes.
From the following figures extracted from the Trial Balance of Dell on 31 December, 2005 draw up a trading account for the period.

	DR	CR
Purchases	250,000	
Sales		600,000
Sales returns	30,500	
Stock on 1 January 2005	18,600	

Stock on 31 December 2005 is £10,400.

2 Allow 15 to 20 minutes.
Figures extracted from the Trial balance of Kirk are shown below. From these draw up a Trading and Profit and Loss account for Kirk for the period.

Kirk Trial Balance 31 December 200—

	DR	CR
Purchases	35,000	
Sales		99,850
Salaries	22,000	
Stock at 1 Jan	3,945	
General expenses	5,680	
Sales returns	4,500	
Light and heat	1,900	
Rent paid	10,000	

Stock on 31 December 200— is £5,625.

3 Allow 50 minutes to 1 hour.
The Trial Balance for Zodiac drawn up on 31 December 2005 is shown below:

	DR	CR
Loan		40,000
Drawings	55,000	
Capital		200,000
Stock on 1 January 2005	20,800	
Purchases	95,000	

General expenses	12,560	
Administrative expenses	5,490	
Sales		215,280
Sales returns	10,450	
Car cost price	24,000	
Freehold premises cost price	190,000	
Fixtures and fittings cost price	12,300	
Cash at bank	3,240	
Petty cash	520	
Salaries	30,000	
Debtors	8,900	
Creditors		12,980
	468,260	468,260

Closing stock on 31 December 2005 is £11,000. Depreciation of cars is 15% and on fixtures and fittings 10%. Draw up the Trading and Profit and Loss account and the Balance Sheet for Zodiac.

7.7 Suggested answers to practice exercises

1 Trading account for Dell for the year ending 31 December 2005

Sales			600,000
LESS returns			30,500
			569,500
LESS COST OF GOODS SOLD			
Opening stock	18,600		
Plus purchases	250,000		
		268,600	
LESS closing stock		10,400	
			258,200
Net profit			311,300

2 Kirk Trading and Profit and Loss account for the year ending 31 December 200—

Sales		99,850
LESS returns		4,500
		95,350
Less cost of goods sold		
Opening stock	3,945	
Plus Purchases	35,000	
	38,945	
LESS closing stock	5,625	
		33,320
GROSS PROFIT		62,030
LESS EXPENSES		
Salaries	22,000	
General expenses	5,680	

Light and heat	1,900	
Rent paid	10,000	
		39,580
NET PROFIT		22,450

3 Zodiac Trading and Profit and Loss account for the year ending 31 December 2005

Sales		215,280	
LESS returns		10,450	
		204,830	
LESS COST OF GOODS SOLD			
Opening stock	20,800		
Plus Purchases	95,000		
		115,800	
LESS closing stock		11,000	
			104,800
GROSS PROFIT			100,030
LESS EXPENSES			
General expenses	12,560		
Administrative expenses	5,490		
Salaries	30,000		
Depreciation on car	3,600		
Depreciation on fixtures and fittings	1,230		
			52,880
NET PROFIT			47,150

Zodiac Balance Sheet as at 31 December 2005

Fixed Assets			
Freehold premises cost price		190,000	
Car cost price	24,000		
LESS depreciation	3,600		
		20,400	
Fixtures and fittings	12,300		
LESS depreciation	1,230		
		11,070	
			221,470
CURRENT ASSETS			
Closing stock	11,000		
Debtors	8,900		
Cash at Bank	3,240		
Petty cash	520		
		23,660	
LESS CURRENT LIABILITIES			
Creditors		12,980	
NET CURRENT ASSETS			10,680
Total			232,150

LESS LONG-TERM LIABILITY		40,000
TOTAL NET ASSETS		192,150
CAPITAL EMPLOYED		
Capital	200,000	
ADD Net Profit	47,150	
	247,150	
LESS Drawings	55,000	
TOTAL DUE TO OWNER		192,150

8

Company accounts

8.1 Introduction

This chapter deals with the accounts of limited companies, in particular:

1. Entries on the accounts in respect of share capital and debentures.
2. Profit and Loss accounts—layout and treatment of taxation and dividends, retained profit and reserves.
3. The form of the Balance Sheet.
4. Practice exercises.

You may find the following web sites useful:
www.companieshouse.gov.uk
www.dti.gov.uk

8.2 Accounts of limited companies

At the time of writing, companies may be incorporated under the provisions of the Companies Acts 1985 and 1989. These include:

(a) a company limited by shares—a member's liability is limited to any part of the issued price of the member's shares not yet paid to the company;

(b) a company limited by guarantee—a member's liability is limited to the sum that the member undertook to contribute to the company in the event of its being wound up;

(c) an unlimited company with no limit on a member's liability.

We will look at companies limited by shares.

8.2.1 Share capital

The capital of a limited company is divided into shares which will have a nominal value, e.g., £1 each, or £5 or £10. When the company issues shares for cash, the entries are the same as the entries made when a sole proprietor or a partner introduces capital. The capital account will be known as the Share Capital account.

EXAMPLE

A company issues 60,000 £1 ordinary shares for £60,000 cash.

DEBIT the Cash Book.
CREDIT the Share Capital Account.

Cash book

Date	Details	DR	CR	Balance
	Share capital	60,000		60,000 DR

Share capital account
£1 ordinary shares

Date	Details	DR	CR	Balance
	Cash		60,000	60,000 CR

A company may issue the shares at par, i.e., sell the shares at their nominal value. Thus if the company above issued 60,000 shares at a nominal value of £1 for £1 each, then the entries would be as above.

The Balance Sheet would show:

FIXED ASSETS		XX
CURRENT ASSETS		
Cash	60,000	
CAPITAL EMPLOYED		
Share capital £1 ordinary shares	60,000	

8.2.2 Issuing shares at a premium

A company may, however, set a price which is higher than the nominal value, when it will issue the shares at a premium. For example, the company issues 60,000 £1 shares at £1.20 each, giving total cash of £72,000. The Cash book will be debited with the total amount received, broken down into the nominal value of £60,000 and the premium of £12,000. The Share Capital account will be credited with the £60,000 and the Share Premium account will be credited with the £12,000.

Cash book

Date	Details	DR	CR	Balance
	Share capital	60,000		60,000 DR
	Share premium	12,000		72,000 DR

Share capital account

Date	Details	DR	CR	Balance
	Cash		60,000	60,000 CR

Share premium account

Date	Details	DR	CR	Balance
	Cash		12,000	12,000 CR

The Balance Sheet would show:

FIXED ASSETS		XX
CURRENT ASSETS		
Cash		72,000
CAPITAL EMPLOYED		
Share capital £1 ordinary shares	60,000	
Share premium	12,000	
		72,000

Note that a company may not issue all the shares which it is authorised to sell. The shares that are sold are called the issued capital.

Different types of shares may be offered, e.g., ordinary, preference or deferred shares. There may also be voting and non-voting shares.

8.2.3 Preference shares

These will get an agreed percentage rate of dividend before the ordinary shareholders, i.e., they have priority. There may be different classes of preference shares, e.g:

8.2.3.1 Non-cumulative preference shares

These receive the dividend before the ordinary shareholders up to an agreed percentage. However, if the amount paid in a year is less than the maximum agreed percentage, the shareholder cannot claim the shortage in the next year or years.

8.2.3.2 Cumulative preference shares

In this case, if a full dividend is not received in a year, the arrears of dividend can be carried forward and paid together with the dividend due in the next year before the ordinary shareholders are entitled to receive any dividend.

8.2.3.3 Participating preference shares

In this case the shareholders may also have the right to participate in any remaining profits after the ordinary shareholders have received their dividend.

8.2.3.4 Redeemable preference shares

In such a case the shares will be repaid by the company at some time in the future.

This may sound complicated, but the accounting entries for the issue of all types of preference shares will be the same. A separate share capital account for each type of shares will be opened.

EXAMPLE

A company issues 50,000 ordinary shares at £1 each, and 10,000 7% preference shares at £1.

DEBIT the Cash Book for each.
CREDIT the relevant share account for each.

Cash book

Date	Details	DR	CR	Balance
	Ordinary shares	50,000		50,000 DR
	7% preference shares	10,000		60,000 DR

Ordinary share capital account

Date	Details	DR	CR	Balance
	Cash		50,000	50,000 CR

7% Preference Share Capital account

Date	Details	DR	CR	Balance
	Cash		10,000	10,000 CR

Note: the cash received from the share issue will be used in the business, e.g., to purchase assets.

8.2.4 Debentures

A debenture is a bond which acknowledges a loan to a company and which bears a fixed rate of interest. As this is really a type of loan to the company, the debenture holder is not a member of the company like a shareholder and the interest will be paid whether the company makes a profit or not. A debenture may be redeemable, i.e., repayable at or before a specified date, or irredeemable and thus only repayable when the company is liquidated.

When debentures are issued, then the entries will be similar to those shown on the issue of share capital.

EXAMPLE

A company issues debentures of £60,000 at fixed interest of 10%.

DEBIT the Cash Book.
CREDIT the Debenture stock account.

Cash book

Date	Details	DR	CR	Balance
	10% debentures	60,000		60,000 DR

10% Debenture stock

Date	Details	DR	CR	Balance
	Cash		60,000	60,000 CR

8.2.5 Issuing debentures at a discount

EXAMPLE

A company issues 12% (interest) debentures at a discount of 10%. The debentures have a nominal value of £40,000. With the discount of 10%, i.e., £4,000, the cash received will be £36,000. The 12% Debenture account will be credited with £40,000, broken down into the cash received and the amount of the discount. The Cash book will be debited with the cash received, and a Debenture discount account will be debited with the discount.

12% Debenture account

Date	Details	DR	CR	Balance
	Cash		36,000	36,000 CR
	Discount		4,000	40,000 CR

Cash book

Date	Details	DR	CR	Balance
	12% debenture	36,000		36,000 DR

Debenture discount account

Date	Details	DR	CR	Balance
	12% debenture	4,000		4,000 DR

When the company redeems the debentures, it will repay them at the full price, i.e., £40,000. This is shown by the credit balance on the Debenture account, i.e., the company owes £40,000. The debit balance on the Debenture Discount account shows the loss in issuing the debenture. If, e.g., the ordinary share capital of the company was £100,000 the Balance Sheet would show:

LONG-TERM LIABILITY
12% Debenture   40,000
CAPITAL EMPLOYED
Ordinary share capital   100,000

The debit balance on the Debenture Discount account will be shown as a deduction in the Capital Employed section until it has been written off.

LONG-TERM LIABILITY
12% debenture   40,000
CAPITAL EMPLOYED
Ordinary share capital   100,000
Reserves say (see **8.2.6**)   80,000
LESS debenture discount   4,000
                                                     76,000
                                                     176,000

8.3 Limited companies' Profit and Loss accounts

A company may draw up its own final accounts for internal use in any way it considers most suitable. However, when the accounts are sent to the Registrar of Companies or to a shareholder, the Companies Acts lay down the information that must be shown, and also how it should be shown, in line with European Community requirements.

There is a choice of layout, four forms for Profit and Loss account, and two forms for the Balance Sheet.

The (vertical form) Format 1 Profit and Loss account is set out below:

Profit and Loss account

1. Turnover
2. Cost of sales
3. Gross profit or loss
4. Distribution costs
5. Administrative expenses
6. Other operating income
7. Income from shares in group undertakings
8. Income from participating interests
9. Income from other fixed asset investments
10. Other interest receivable and similar income
11. Amounts written off investments
12. Interest payable and similar charges
13. Tax on profit or loss on ordinary activities
14. Profit or loss on ordinary activities after taxation
15. Exceptional income
16. Exceptional charges
17. Exceptional profit or loss
18. Tax on Exceptional profit or loss
19. Other taxes not shown under the above items
20. Profit or loss for the financial year

A company's Profit and Loss account is similar to that of a sole trader or a partnership. However, there will be some differences.

Salaries paid to directors will be shown as an expense of the company (like wages of employees). Contrast this with a salary paid to a partner, which was shown as an allocation of profit in the Appropriation account. The Appropriation account shows how the net profit will be used. After the net profit has been calculated, tax will have to be considered, and provided for. Once this has been done then dividends should be provided for, and then any surplus profit may be retained or transferred to reserves.

8.3.1 Appropriation of profit—taxation

Corporation tax is NOT an expense of the company but is regarded as an appropriation of profit.

For large companies corporation tax is paid by quarterly equal instalments. The instalments are paid on the basis of anticipated current year liabilities for tax. Medium and small companies do not have to pay their corporation tax by instalments.

Large companies are those with taxable profits over £1.5 million a year. Medium-size companies are those with taxable profits between £0.3 million and £1.5 million a year. Small companies are those with taxable profits up to £0.3 million a year. The rate of corporation tax at present is 19% for small companies, a marginal relief rate for medium size companies, and 30% for large companies.

For convenience, in the following examples rates have been taken that are easy to calculate.

To provide for taxation, the Appropriation account will be debited (remember that this forms part of the double-entry system) and a Taxation account will be credited.

EXAMPLE

The net profit of a company is £200,000. Assuming the rate of corporation tax to be 19% the tax would be £38,000.

DEBIT the Profit and Loss Appropriation account.
CREDIT the Taxation Account.

Profit and Loss account
Net profit   200,000
Less corporation tax (debit)   38,000
                                    ———————
                                    162,000

Taxation account

Date	Details	DR	CR	Balance
	Profit and loss account		38,000	38,000 CR

These entries do not involve any payment or transfer of cash. The net profit is merely appropriated, and the credit balance on the taxation account shows that £38,000 is due to the Inland Revenue. Until the tax is paid this will be shown as a current liability on the Balance Sheet. When the tax is actually paid, the cash book will be credited, and the taxation account debited. Continuing the above example:

Cash book

Date	Details	DR	CR	Balance
	Balance say			150,000 DR
	Taxation—Inland Revenue		38,000	112,000 DR

Taxation account

Date	Details	DR	CR	Balance
	Balance			38,000 CR
	Cash	38,000		Nil

8.3.2 Deferred taxation

This is to take account of the fact that the figure for profits shown on the company's profit and loss account may not be the same as the figure for profits on which tax is payable. The reasons for this include:

(a) the difference between the figures used for depreciation by the company each year and the figures for capital allowances allowed by the Inland Revenue;

(b) that the Inland Revenue may not allow all the figures that have been shown as expenses on the Profit and Loss account.

Where there is a difference between the figures used for depreciation and the capital allowances, this will lead to timing differences, as the capital allowances allowed by the Inland Revenue may fall into different periods from the depreciation figures used by the company, even though in the end the amount overall may be the same.

So that a true picture can be given to, e.g., shareholders, deferred taxation is used to adjust the tax shown on the Appropriation account. The tax will be adjusted to show the tax on the profit based on depreciation used by the company, rather than based on the capital allowances allowed by the Inland Revenue.

Where the taxation payable for the year is lower than it would be based on the company's own figures then:

DEBIT the Profit and Loss Appropriation account.
CREDIT the Deferred Taxation account.

The credit balance will be shown as a separate item on the Balance Sheet under provisions for liabilities and charges.

Where the taxation payable is higher than it would be based on the company's calculation of profit then the entries would be:

CREDIT the Profit and Loss Appropriation account.
DEBIT Deferred Taxation account.

EXAMPLE

Year 1

Profit based on the company's calculations:		£200,000
Tax payable based on taxable profit of £160,000 at 19%	30,400	
Deferred taxation	7,600	38,000
Balance retained profit		162,000

Taxation account

	DR	CR	Balance
		30,400	30,400 CR

Deferred Taxation account

	DR	CR	Balance
		7,600	7,600 CR

The Balance Sheet would show:
Creditors due within one year
  taxation   30,400
Provisions for liabilities and charges
Deferred taxation   7,600

Year 2
Profit based on company's
  calculations   £200,000
Less tax based on taxable profit of
  £240,000 at 19%   − 45,600
Add deferred tax adjustment   + 7,600
                                                            38,000
Balance retained profit   162,000

Taxation account

	DR	CR	Balance
		45,600	45,600 CR

Deferred Taxation account

	DR	CR	Balance
Brought down			7,600 CR
Year 2	7,600		nil

The Balance Sheet would show:
Creditors due within one
  year taxation   £45,600
Provisions for liabilities and charges
Deferred taxation   —

8.3.3 Dividends

The directors of a company will propose that part of the net profit be distributed to the shareholders, usually expressed as a percentage of the nominal value of the shares.

8.3.3.1 Appropriation of dividend

DEBIT the Appropriation account.
CREDIT the Dividend account.

EXAMPLE

A company declares a dividend of 10% in respect of ordinary shares with a nominal value of £100,000, being £10,000. Net profit after tax is £97,200, The directors will not allocate all the profit remaining after taxation, as:

(a) Profit will need to be retained to run the business, or for expansion.

(b) Net profit will not necessarily be represented by cash at the bank.

Profit and Loss account

Net profit	120,000
Less corporation tax (debit)	22,800
	97,200
Less dividend	10,000
	87,200

Dividend account

Date	Details	DR	CR	Balance
	Profit and Loss account		10,000	10,000 CR

The amount shown on the dividend account shows the amount due for the dividend. This will be shown as a current liability on the balance sheet. The size of the dividend will be agreed at the annual general meeting of the company, when the accounts are agreed. The dividend can then be paid. Continuing the above example:

8.3.3.2 Payment of dividend

CREDIT the Cash Book.
DEBIT the Dividend Account.

Cash book

Date	Details	DR	CR	Balance
	Balance say			25,000 DR
	Dividend		10,000	15,000 DR

Dividend account

Date	Details	DR	CR	Balance
	Balance			10,000 CR
	Cash	10,000		Nil

8.3.3.3 Payment of interim dividend

If the company has paid an interim dividend before the end of the year, the entries to record the payment of the interim dividend will be the same as the payment of the dividend above. The interim dividend will be shown in the appropriation section of the profit and loss account, in the same way that the end of year dividend was shown.

EXAMPLE

During the year a company pays an interim dividend of £10,000. At the end of the year the net profit after taxation is £80,000. A final dividend of £15,000 is recommended by the directors.

1. Payment of the interim dividend during the year.
   CREDIT Cash Book.
   DEBIT Dividend Account.

Cash book

Date	Details	DR	CR	Balance
	Balance say			48,000 DR
	Interim dividend		10,000	38,000 DR

Dividend account

Date	Details	DR	CR	Balance
	Cash—interim dividend	10,000		10,000 DR

2. Final dividend at end of year

   Profit and Loss account
   Net profit after taxation   80,000
   Less dividend
      interim   10,000
      final   15,000
           25,000
           55,000

Dividend account

Date	Details	DR	CR	Balance
	Balance (interim dividend)			10,000 DR
	Profit and Loss account			
	Interim dividend		10,000	Nil
	Final dividend		15,000	15,000 CR

The £15,000 credit balance on the dividend account will be shown on the Balance Sheet as a current liability, being the amount due to the shareholders. When the final dividend is paid the entries will be as shown previously.

8.3.4 Appropriation—retained profit and reserves

After providing for taxation and dividends, the balance of the net profit is retained on the Appropriation account, or it may be transferred to a reserve account. Either way it will be shown as a reserve on the Balance Sheet, in the capital employed section (like the net profit due to a sole proprietor).

Net profit is not necessarily represented by cash—it is represented by an increase in recorded net assets. Thus 'retention of profit' or 'reserves' are merely retaining in the business the assets which are attributable to profit.

The balance of net profit will be transferred to a reserve account if it is to be retained for a specific purpose, e.g., replacement of fixed assets, or redemption (repayment) of debentures. The entries to record a transfer to a reserve account are:

DEBIT the Appropriation account.
CREDIT the Reserve account.

EXAMPLE

Net profit after taxation is £40,000. A dividend of £10,000 is declared. Of the remaining £30,000, £16,000 is transferred to a reserve account.

Net profit after taxation	£40,000
Less dividend	£10,000
	£30,000
Transferred to reserve	£16,000
	£14,000

Note: both the balance of £14,000 and the reserve of £16,000 will be shown on the balance sheet as part of the capital employed.

Capital employed		
Share capital		100,000 (say)
Reserves		
Special reserve	16,000	
Profit and Loss	14,000	
		30,000
		130,000

As mentioned in **3.4.1.2**, this is the same principle as in the Balance Sheet of a sole proprietor, where the net profit would be shown added to their capital.

The share capital and reserves shown above are known as the shareholders' equity, or the ordinary shareholders' funds. These will be represented by the assets of the company, shown in the Employment of Capital section of the Balance Sheet.

In the event of the company being wound up the shareholders would be entitled to the return of their capital, plus a share in the surplus assets of the company, represented by the reserves.

8.3.5 Provisions, reserves and liabilities

A provision, as we have seen in **5.1.3**, may be debited to the Profit and Loss account, or it may be debited to the Appropriation account of a company. A provision may be created in respect of a known liability which exists at the date of the Balance Sheet where the amount cannot be determined with substantial accuracy. The provision may, for example, be for (estimated) doubtful debts, or depreciation, which would be debited to the Profit and Loss section. Provision may also be made for estimated taxation, or a dividend, which would be debited to the Appropriation section.

Provisions are in contrast to liabilities, which are amounts owed and which can be determined with substantial accuracy, e.g., rent due. Provisions may also be contrasted with reserves, which can only be debited to the Appropriation section, and which do not relate to any liability or loss which is known to exist at the time of the Balance Sheet.

Definitions of these are contained in the Companies Act 1985, sch. 9, para. 32.

8.3.6 Capital and revenue reserves

8.3.6.1 Revenue reserves

These are reserves transferred from the Profit and Loss appropriation account (i.e., retained profit) which can be general, or for some particular purpose, e.g., a foreign exchange reserve account, to meet any possible losses through devaluation of a foreign currency. General revenue reserve accounts may be used in future years, should profit be insufficient for dividends, when the reserve may be used for the payment of dividends, provided that cash is available. (If this was done then the revenue reserve account would be debited and the Profit and Loss appropriation account would be credited.)

General reserve accounts may also be used to increase the capital required with inflation as the amount of working capital required by the company will increase. When we looked at final accounts in **Chapter 2**, we saw on the Balance Sheet a figure for net current assets, or working capital—this means the portion of capital invested in the business which is left to run the business after providing the fixed assets.

8.3.6.2 Capital reserves

These are not available for distribution by way of dividend under the Companies Acts.

Capital reserves which cannot be used for the declaration of dividends payable in cash are:

(a) capital redemption reserves;

(b) a share premium account;

(c) a revaluation reserve.

Capital redemption reserves include a preference shares redemption reserve, which can be used to redeem redeemable preference shares, or, e.g., a debenture redemption reserve, which can be used to redeem debentures on the date specified. A company may transfer a certain amount of net profit each year to a redemption reserve account.

A share premium account is needed when the company issues shares at a premium—the additional amount over the nominal value of the shares is shown in the share premium account.

A revaluation reserve is used when a company revalues its assets. If the value of the assets is increased, then there must be a corresponding increase in the capital employed section of the balance sheet. The asset account is to be debited and the revaluation reserve account is to be credited. This cannot be used to pay a dividend as it merely represents the increase in value of the assets.

8.3.7 Capitalisation of reserves: bonus issue of shares

Although reserves may not be available for distribution by way of dividend, they may be capitalised by issuing bonus or free shares to shareholders.

EXAMPLE

A company has an issued share capital of £40,000,000 £1 ordinary shares and general reserves of £15,000,000. It makes a bonus issue of one share for every four shares held. The bonus issue will therefore be £10,000,000.

Before the bonus issue the Balance Sheet would show:

	000
Capital employed	
Share capital	40,000
General reserves	15,000
	55,000

After the bonus issue the Balance Sheet will show:

	000
Capital employed	
Share capital	50,000
General reserves	5,000
	55,000

The entries on the accounts would be:

Share capital account

Date	Details	DR	CR	Balance
		000	000	000
	Balance			40,000 CR
	General reserve		10,000	50,000 CR

General reserve account

Date	Details	DR	CR	Balance
		000	000	000
	Balance			15,000 CR
	Share capital	10,000		5,000 CR

Although each shareholder will own more shares, these will be worth less individually, as the shares are still represented by the same amount of assets. Any dividend payable in respect of the shares may be at a lower percentage, as the same net profit will have to be apportioned between the shares.

8.3.8 Sinking funds

As mentioned in **8.2.4**, retained net profit is not equivalent to cash, it merely represents an increase in assets. If cash is required then it will be necessary, at the same time as profit is transferred to a reserve, to transfer the required amount of cash, or easily realisable assets, to a sinking fund (or reserve fund) which can then be used when needed.

EXAMPLE

A company transfers £200,000 to debenture redemption reserve from net profit after taxation and dividends of £500,000. It also transfers £200,000 from the cash at the bank to a deposit account, to be used as a reserve fund for debenture redemption.

Profit and Loss Appropriation account
Net profit after tax and dividend £500,000
Transfer to debenture redemption reserve £200,000
£300,000

Debenture redemption reserve account

Date	Details	DR	CR	Balance
	Profit and loss		200,000	200,000 CR

Cash book

Date	Details	DR	CR	Balance
	Balance say			350,000 DR
	Debenture redemption reserve (sinking) fund		200,000	150,000 DR

Debenture redemption reserve (sinking) fund account

Date	Details	DR	CR	Balance
	Cash	200,000		200,000 DR

The Balance Sheet would show:

FIXED ASSETS
Debenture redemption 200,000
reserve (sinking fund)
NET CURRENT ASSETS
CAPITAL EMPLOYED
Share capital XX
Debenture redemption reserve 200,000

8.4 The form of the Balance Sheet

There are two formats, the vertical form and the horizontal form. The vertical format is set out below:

Balance Sheet: format 1—the vertical

A CALLED UP SHARE CAPITAL NOT PAID*
B FIXED ASSETS
I Intangible assets
   1 Development costs
   2 Concessions, patents, licences, trademarks and similar rights and assets
   3 Goodwill
   4 Payments on account

cont.

- II Tangible assets
    1. Land and buildings
    2. Plant and machinery
    3. Fixtures, fittings, tools and equipment
    4. Payments on account and assets in course of construction
- III Investments
    1. Shares in group undertakings
    2. Loans to group undertakings
    3. Participating interests
    4. Loans to undertakings in which the company has a participating interest
    5. Other investments other than loans
    6. Other loans
    7. Own shares
- C CURRENT ASSETS
- I Stocks
    1. Raw materials and consumables
    2. Work in progress
    3. Finished goods and goods for resale
    4. Payments on account
- II Debtors
    1. Trade debtors
    2. Amounts owed by group undertakings
    3. Amounts owed by undertakings in which the company has a participating interest
    4. Other debtors
    5. Called up share capital not paid*
    6. Prepayments and accrued income**
- III Investments
    1. Shares in group undertakings
    2. Own shares
    3. Other investments
- IV Cash at bank and in hand
- D PREPAYMENTS AND ACCRUED INCOME**
- E CREDITORS: AMOUNTS FALLING DUE WITHIN ONE YEAR
    1. Debenture loans
    2. Bank loans and overdrafts
    3. Payments received on account
    4. Trade creditors
    5. Bills of exchange payable
    6. Amounts owed to group undertakings
    7. Amounts owed to undertakings in which the company has a participating interest
    8. Other creditors including taxation and social security
    9. Accruals and deferred income***
- F NET CURRENT ASSETS (LIABILITIES)
- G TOTAL ASSETS LESS CURRENT LIABILITIES
- H CREDITORS: AMOUNTS FALLING DUE AFTER MORE THAN ONE YEAR
    1. Debenture loans
    2. Bank loans and overdrafts
    3. Payments received on account
    4. Trade creditors
    5. Bills of exchange payable
    6. Amounts owed to group undertakings
    7. Amounts owed to related undertakings in which the company has a participating interest
    8. Other creditors including taxation and social security
    9. Accruals and deferred income***
- I PROVISIONS FOR LIABILITIES AND CHARGES
    1. Pensions and similar obligations
    2. Taxation, including deferred taxation
    3. Other provisions

cont.

> J   ACCRUALS AND DEFERRED INCOME***
> K CAPITAL AND RESERVES
>   I   Called up share capital
>   II Share premium account
>   III Revaluation reserve
>   IV Other reserves
>   1 Capital redemption reserve
>   2 Reserve for own shares
>   3 Reserves provided for by the articles of association
>   4 Other reserves
>   V PROFIT AND LOSS ACCOUNT
> * ** *** These items may be shown in either of the two positions indicated.

Items preceded by letters or Roman numerals must be disclosed on the face of the Balance Sheet, e.g., B fixed assets, KI called up share capital, but those with ordinary Arabic numbers, e.g., 1,2,3, may be combined where they are not material or the combination aids assessment of the company's affairs. Where they are combined the details of each item should be shown in the notes to the accounts.

8.4.1 Public companies and the Stock Exchange

Shares of most public companies are dealt with on the Stock Exchange. Private companies cannot issue their shares to the public; their shares cannot be bought and sold on the Stock Exchange. Sale and purchase of shares on the Stock Exchange will have no effect on the accounting entries made in the company's books. However, the price of the shares on the Stock Exchange will affect, e.g., the price at which any new shares are to be issued.

8.4.2 Example Balance Sheet

What follows is an example of a balance sheet using the format required by the Companies Acts.

Balance Sheet as at—

	'000	'000	'000
FIXED ASSETS			
Intangible assets			
Goodwill		10,000	
Tangible assets			
Premises	200,000		
Machinery	80,000		
Motor cars	40,000		
		320,000	
			330,000
CURRENT ASSETS			
Stock	30,000		
Debtors	26,000		
Cash at bank	20,000		
		76,000	

LESS CREDITORS		
Amounts falling due within one year		
Proposed dividend	10,000	
Creditors	18,000	
Corporation tax due	9,000	
	37,000	
		39,000
TOTAL ASSETS LESS CURRENT LIABILITIES		369,000
CREDITORS		
Amounts falling due after more than one year		90,000
TOTAL		279,000
CAPITAL AND RESERVES		
Authorised and issued fully paid ordinary £1 shares	240,000	
Share premium account	13,000	
General reserve	15,000	
Profit and Loss account	11,000	
TOTAL		279,000

8.5 Check list

By the end of this chapter you should be able to:

1. appreciate that shares can be issued as the capital of a company;
2. appreciate that a company can also be funded by loans and debentures;
3. appreciate the structure of a company's Profit and Loss account;
4. understand that taxation is not an expense of a company, but will be an appropriation of profit;
5. understand that dividends will be an appropriation of profit and the treatment of interim dividends;
6. note the treatment of retained profit and reserves;
7. note the reports and records required under the Companies Acts and a form of a company's Balance Sheet;
8. complete some of the practice exercises at the end of the chapter.

8.6 Practice exercises

The following exercises will aid your understanding of company accounts. When you have completed these exercises move on to group companies and consolidated accounts (Chapter 9).

1 Allow 5 to 10 minutes.

Explain what would be shown on a company's Balance Sheet after it has issued for cash 100,000 £1 ordinary shares at a price of £3.00 per share.

2 Allow 5 to 10 minutes.
A company estimates its taxation liability at the end of the year to be £40,000. Explain where this would be recorded on the company's final accounts.

3 Allow 10 minutes.
Look at the following abbreviated company's Balance Sheet. Would the directors be able to authorise payment of a cash dividend to shareholders totalling £30,000?

Fixed assets			800,000
Current assets			
Stock	45,000		
Debtors	32,000		
Cash at bank	15,000		
		92,000	
Current liabilities			
Taxation	12,000		
Creditors	26,000		
		38,000	
Net current assets			54,000
			854,000
Capital employed			
Share Capital	700,000		
Reserves	154,000		
			£854,000

4 Allow about 1 hour for this exercise.
From the following trial balance of Randall Limited drawn up on 31 March 200—, draw up the Trading and Profit and Loss account and the Balance Sheet for the year ending 31 March 200—.

Trial Balance	DR	CR
Ordinary share capital		120,000
10% preference share capital		25,000
Debentures		20,000
Buildings	150,000	
Equipment	45,000	
Motor cars	20,000	
Accumulated depreciation: equipment		5,000
Accumulated depreciation: motor cars		10,000
Stock at start of year	19,000	
Sales		375,000
Purchases	149,000	
Wages	40,000	
Directors' remuneration	70,000	
Motor expenses	6,000	
Rates insurance	3,000	
General expenses	19,000	
Debenture interest payable	2,000	
Debtors	29,000	
Creditors		18,000
Cash at bank	26,000	

Interim ordinary dividend paid	10,000	
General reserve		15,000
	588,000	588,000

Additional information required to complete the accounts:
- stock at the end of the year is £21,000;
- depreciation on equipment is £2,000, and on motor cars is £5,000;
- taxation is estimated at £20,000;
- the preference share dividend is £2,500; and
- the final dividend for the ordinary shareholders is £2,000.

5. Allow about 1 hour for this exercise.

   From the Trial Balance of Down and Out Limited shown below, draw up a Trading and Profit and Loss account and a Balance Sheet, in the format required under the Companies Acts.

   Trial Balance as at 31 December 200—

	DR '000	CR '000
Ordinary share capital £1 shares fully paid		160,000
12% debentures repayable in 2006		40,000
Goodwill at cost	20,000	
Buildings	150,000	
Fixtures and fittings	40,000	
Motor cars	25,000	
Accumulated depreciation: fixtures and fittings		8,000
Accumulated depreciation: motor cars		10,000
Stock as at 1 January 200—	23,000	
Sales		179,000
Purchases	70,000	
Salaries/wages	33,000	
Directors' fees	39,000	
Motor expenses	2,500	
Council tax	2,300	
General expenses	11,400	
Debenture interest	6,000	
Debtors	26,500	
Creditors		19,900
Cash at bank	13,200	
General reserve		15,000
Share premium account		16,000
Interim ordinary dividend paid	3,000	
Profit and Loss account 1 Jan 200—		17,000
	464,900	464,900

   The following should be taken into account:

	'000
stock at the end of the year	26,000
depreciation on cars for the year	5,000
depreciation on fixtures	4,000
proposed final dividend	2,000
provision for corporation tax due	2,640

8.7 Suggested answers to practice exercises

1 The Balance Sheet would show a current asset of cash of £300,000 and in the Capital Employed section share capital £1 ordinary shares at £100,000 and share premium at £200,000.

2 The taxation would be shown as a deduction from net profit in the Appropriation section. It would also be shown as a liability in current liabilities on the Balance Sheet.

3 Although the company has net current assets of £54,000 it only has £15,000 cash, it is likely this will be needed to pay creditors etc. If stock could be sold and debtors paid then the company may be able to consider a cash distribution. Note that reserves in the Capital Employed section are not cash, nor are they necessarily represented by cash. Reserves show the total due to shareholders, and only reflect any increase in assets.

4 **Randall Limited: Trading and Profit and Loss account for the year ending 31 March 200—**

Sales			375,000
LESS cost of goods sold			
Opening stock	19,000		
ADD purchases	149,000		
	168,000		
LESS closing stock	21,000		
			147,000
Gross profit			228,000
LESS expenses			
Wages	40,000		
Motor expenses	6,000		
Directors' remuneration	70,000		
Rates and insurance	3,000		
General expenses	19,000		
Debenture interest payable	2,000		
Depreciation on equipment	2,000		
Depreciation on cars	5,000		
			147,000
Profit before taxation			81,000
Taxation			20,000
Profit after taxation			61,000
LESS appropriation			
Preference share dividend		2,500	
Ordinary share dividend			
Interim paid	10,000		
Final dividend	2,000		
		12,000	
			14,500
Reserves (retained profit)			46,500

Randall Limited: Balance Sheet as at 31 March 200—

FIXED ASSETS			
Buildings			150,000
Equipment	45,000		
LESS depreciation	7,000		
		38,000	
Motor cars	20,000		
LESS depreciation	15,000		
		5,000	
			193,000
CURRENT ASSETS			
Stock	21,000		
Debtors	29,000		
Cash at bank	26,000		
		76,000	
LESS CURRENT LIABILITIES			
Creditors	18,000		
Preference share dividend	2,500		
Final dividend	2,000		
Taxation	20,000		
		42,500	
NET CURRENT ASSETS			33,500
TOTAL ASSETS LESS CURRENT LIABILITIES			226,500
LESS Debentures			20,000
			206,500
CAPITAL AND RESERVES			
Ordinary share capital		120,000	
Preference shares		25,000	
		145,000	
Reserves	15,000		
This year	46,500		
		61,500	
			206,500

5 **Down and Out Limited: Trading and Profit and Loss account for the year ending 31 December 200—**

	'000	'000	'000
Sales			179,000
LESS cost of goods sold			
opening stock	23,000		
plus purchases	70,000		
	93,000		
LESS closing stock	26,000		
			67,000
Gross profit			112,000

LESS expenses			
Salaries	33,000		
Directors' fees	39,000		
Motor expenses	2,500		
Council tax	2,300		
General expenses	11,400		
Debenture interest	6,000		
Depreciation on fixtures	4,000		
Depreciation on cars	5,000		
			103,200
Profit for the year			8,800
LESS provision for corporation tax			2,640
Profit after tax			6,160
ADD retained profit from last year			17,000
			23,160
LESS dividends			
Interim dividend paid	3,000		
Final dividend proposed	2,000		
			5,000
Retained profit carried forward to next year			18,160

Down and Out Limited: Balance Sheet as at 31 December 200—

FIXED ASSETS	'000	'000	'000
Intangible assets			
Goodwill			20,000
Tangible assets			
Premises		150,000	
Fixtures costs	40,000		
LESS depreciation	12,000		
		28,000	
Cars cost	25,000		
LESS depreciation	15,000		
		10,000	
			188,000
			208,000
CURRENT ASSETS:			
Stock		26,000	
Debtors		26,500	
Cash at bank		13,200	
		65,700	
Creditors: amounts falling due within one year			
Creditors	19,900		
Proposed dividend	2,000		
Taxation due	2,640		
		24,540	

NET CURRENT ASSETS		41,160
Total assets less current liabilities		249,160
LESS LONG-TERM LIABILITIES		
Debentures		40,000
TOTAL		209,160
CAPITAL AND RESERVES		
Share capital £1 ordinary shares	160,000	
Share premium	16,000	
General reserve	15,000	
Profit and Loss account	18,160	
TOTAL		209,160

9

Group companies and consolidated accounts

9.1 Introduction

This chapter deals with companies and their subsidiaries and the requirements for consolidated accounts, which aggregate the Profit and Loss accounts and Balance Sheets of the companies and their subsidiaries.

Separate companies operating independently will have separate accounting records and financial statements. Where one company controls another then this is regarded as a group, with a controlling, or parent, company which is called the parent undertaking, and the subsidiary company, called the subsidiary undertaking. Although the companies are still separate legal entities with separate financial records, the idea is that the shareholders of the parent company should be given some information about the subsidiary company. This information is provided by consolidated accounts for the group, being a consolidated Profit and Loss account and a consolidated Balance Sheet. These are created by aggregating the separate Profit and Loss accounts and Balance Sheets of the parent and subsidiary undertaking and are produced *in addition* to the separate final accounts for each company.

9.1.1 What is a parent undertaking?

An undertaking is a parent undertaking in relation to another undertaking, a subsidiary, if:

(a) it holds a majority of the voting rights in the undertaking; or

(b) it is a member of the undertaking and has the right to appoint or remove a majority of its board of directors; or

(c) it has the right to exercise a dominant influence over the undertaking;
   (i) by virtue of provisions contained in the undertaking's memorandum or articles; or
   (ii) by virtue of a control contract; or

(d) it is a member of the undertaking and controls alone, pursuant to an agreement with other shareholders or members, a majority of the voting rights in the undertaking.

An undertaking is also a parent undertaking in relation to another undertaking, a subsidiary undertaking, if it has a participating interest in the undertaking, and:

(a) it actually exercises a dominant influence over it; or

(b) it and the subsidiary undertaking are managed on a unified basis.

The above is really based on a company's ability to exercise control over another company. A group will thus exist whenever legal entities which are independent of each other are under central management, regardless of the share ownership. This legislation implements the EC Seventh Directive. It should be noted that certain partnerships and joint ventures can also come within the consolidation requirement.

9.2 The consolidated Balance Sheet

9.2.1 Merging the Balance Sheets

The Balance Sheets of each company will be merged. The issued capital shown will be that of the parent company only, represented by the assets of the two companies. Merging does not mean that the two Balance Sheets are added together: the inter company shares should be cancelled out first, and then the assets of the two companies will be added together. Inter company shares mean those shares in the subsidiary undertaking owned by the parent undertaking shown in its Balance Sheet, and the subsidiary company's capital and reserves which represent those shares shown in the subsidiary undertaking's Balance Sheet.

EXAMPLE

Company P Ltd owns the whole share capital of company S Ltd and the two separate Balance Sheets show:

	P Ltd	(parent company)
	'000	
Fixed assets	25,000	
Shares in B Ltd		
(at cost)	15,000	inter company shares (investment in subsidiary)
Net current assets	10,000	
	50,000	
Share capital	50,000	
	50,000	

	S Ltd	(subsidiary company)
	'000	
Fixed assets	10,000	
Net current assets	5,000	
	15,000	
Share capital	15,000	(representing the above)
	15,000	

The inter company shares are to be cancelled out, i.e., the shares held in S Ltd by P Ltd are to be taken out from P Ltd's Balance Sheet and the share capital representing this must be taken out from S Ltd's Balance Sheet.

	P Ltd	(parent company)
	'000	
Fixed assets	25,000	
Net current assets	10,000	
	35,000	
Share capital	50,000	
	50,000	

	S Ltd	(subsidiary company)
	'000	
Fixed assets	10,000	
Net current assets	5,000	
	15,000	

Next, the assets of S Ltd must be added into P Ltd's Balance Sheet to make the consolidated account for P Ltd and S Ltd.

P Ltd and S Ltd: Consolidated Group Balance Sheet

	'000	'000
Fixed assets: P Ltd		25,000
S Ltd		10,000
		35,000
Net current assets: P Ltd	10,000	
S Ltd	5,000	
		15,000
Total		50,000
Share capital		50,000

If the subsidiary undertaking has reserves, then the share capital and the reserves (shareholder's funds) in the subsidiary undertaking must be excluded.

EXAMPLE

P Ltd has purchased all the shares in S Ltd. The two Balance Sheets are as follows:

	P Ltd	(parent company)
	'000	
Fixed assets	40,000	
Shares in S Ltd (at cost)	30,000	investment in subsidiary
Net current assets	10,000	
	80,000	
Share capital	60,000	
Reserves	20,000	
	80,000	

	S Ltd	(subsidiary company)
	'000	
Fixed assets	25,000	
Net current assets	5,000	
		30,000
Share capital	20,000	
Reserves	10,000	(representing the above)
		30,000

The inter-company shares and reserves (in S) must be cancelled out and then the assets of both companies added together.

P Ltd and S Ltd: Consolidated Balance Sheet

	'000	'000
Fixed assets: P Ltd	40,000	
S Ltd	25,000	
		65,000
Net current assets: P Ltd	10,000	
S Ltd	5,000	
		15,000
		80,000
Share capital	60,000	
Reserves	20,000	
		80,000

In the above two examples, P Ltd, the acquiring company, paid the book value of the assets owned by S Ltd. However, the acquiring company may pay more, or less, than the book value of the assets of the subsidiary undertaking.

9.2.2 Acquiring shares for more than the book value of the assets

EXAMPLE

P Ltd purchases the shares and reserves of S Ltd for £100,000,000. The balance sheet value of these are £90,000,000. The excess paid of £10,000,000 is known as goodwill, which will be included in the consolidated Balance Sheet.

The Balance Sheets before consolidation will look like this:

	P Ltd	(parent company)
	'000	
Fixed assets	200,000	
Shares in S Ltd		
(at cost)	100,000*	less £90,000,000 (book value of investment
Net current assets	30,000	in S Ltd)
	330,000	
Share capital	250,000	
Reserves	80,000	
	330,000	

	S Ltd	(subsidiary company)
	'000	
Fixed assets	80,000	
Net current assets	10,000	
	90,000	
Share capital	75,000	
Reserves	15,000	
	90,000*	(representing the above inter company shares)

The book value of the investment in S Ltd and the share capital and reserves of S Ltd totalling £90,000,000 must be cancelled out from the shares in S Ltd shown on P Ltd's Balance Sheet.

This will leave £10,000,000 on P Ltd's Balance Sheet in respect of the shares in S Ltd, which will be called goodwill, being the additional payment in respect of the shares.

The assets of the two companies are then to be added together as before.

P Ltd and S Ltd: Consolidated Balance Sheet

	'000	'000
Goodwill re S Ltd shares		10,000
Fixed assets: P Ltd		200,000
S Ltd		80,000
		280,000
Net current assets: P Ltd	30,000	
S Ltd	10,000	
		40,000
		330,000
Share capital		250,000
Reserves		80,000
		330,000

9.2.3 Acquiring shares for less than the book value of the assets

EXAMPLE

Company P Ltd acquires all the share capital and reserves of S Ltd for £100,000,000 when the balance sheet value of these is £120,000,000. P Ltd has therefore made a 'profit' in respect of the purchase. This is due to the shareholders of P Ltd, but it cannot be distributed to them. A capital reserve account will be opened in respect of the profit of £20,000,000.

The Balance Sheets before consolidation will look like this:

	P Ltd	(parent company)
	'000	'000
Fixed assets	200,000	
Shares in S Ltd		
(at cost)	100,000	(less value of S Ltd £120,000,000)*
Net current assets	150,000	
		450,000
Share capital	400,000	
Reserves	50,000	
		450,000
	S Ltd	(subsidiary company)
Fixed assets	85,000	
Net current assets	35,000	
		120,000
Share capital	110,000	
Reserves	10,000	
		120,000* (representing the above)

When the total value of S Ltd, i.e., £120,000,000, is removed from P Ltd's Balance Sheet, this would result in a minus figure of £20,000,000 in the assets. This is a credit balance which should be shown as a capital reserve in the share capital and reserves section.

	P Ltd '000	(parent company) '000
Fixed assets	200,000	

(Shares in S Ltd—£20,000,000 now a credit—move to the share capital and reserves section)

Net current assets	150,000	

The consolidated balance sheet will appear as follows:

P Ltd and S Ltd: Consolidated Balance Sheet

	'000	'000
Fixed assets: P Ltd	200,000	
S Ltd	85,000	
		285,000
Net current assets: P Ltd	150,000	
S Ltd	35,000	
		185,000
		470,000
Share capital	400,000	
Capital reserve (re shares in S Ltd)	20,000	
Other reserves	50,000	
		470,000

9.3 The consolidated Profit and Loss account

9.3.1 Merging the Profit and Loss accounts

These can be fairly complicated. The sales, cost of sales and expenses will be merged and the net profits, taxation, and transfers to reserves will be merged, but the dividend payable to the parent undertaking (inter company dividend) will be excluded. In order to keep things simple, the following example will just show the net profit onwards.

EXAMPLE

The Profit and Loss accounts of P Ltd and S Ltd are as follows:

	P Ltd (parent)	
	'000	'000
Net profit		50,000
Add dividend from S Ltd		10,000
		60,000
Taxation, say		15,000
Profit after tax		45,000
Dividend (to P Ltd's shareholders)		15,000
Retained profit (reserves)		30,000

	S Ltd (subsidiary)	
	'000	'000
Net profit		40,000
Taxation		12,000
Profit after tax		28,000
Dividend to P Ltd		10,000
Retained profit (reserves)		18,000

P Ltd and S Ltd: consolidated Profit and Loss account

	'000	'000
Net profit: P Ltd	50,000	
S Ltd	40,000	
		90,000
Taxation: P Ltd	15,000	
S Ltd	12,000	
		27,000
		63,000
Dividend		15,000
Reserves: P Ltd	30,000	
S Ltd	18,000	
		48,000

9.3.1.1 Effect on the consolidated Balance Sheet

The share capital of P Ltd will be shown, together with the increased reserves of P Ltd and the increase in reserves of S Ltd. This will be represented by the increased assets of P Ltd and S Ltd.

EXAMPLE

Consolidated Balance Sheet before the Profit and Loss accounts

	'000	'000
Fixed assets: P Ltd	100,000	
S Ltd	60,000	
		160,000
Net current assets: P Ltd	65,000	
S Ltd	25,000	
		90,000
		250,000
Share capital	200,000	
Reserves	50,000	
		250,000

Consolidated Balance Sheet after the Profit and Loss accounts

	'000	'000
Fixed assets: P Ltd	100,000	
S Ltd	60,000	
		160,000

Net current assets: P Ltd	95,000	
S Ltd	43,000	
		138,000
TOTAL		298,000
Share capital		200,000
Reserves: P Ltd	80,000	
S Ltd	18,000	
		98,000
TOTAL		298,000

9.4 Where a company holds a majority interest in the subsidiary

In these circumstances consolidated final accounts will still be required.

9.4.1 The Balance Sheet

This will show the whole of the subsidiary's assets and liabilities. The minority shareholders' interest will be shown as liabilities.

EXAMPLE

Company P Ltd has acquired 80% of the issued share capital of S Ltd: the Balance Sheets show:

P Ltd (parent company)

	'000	'000
Fixed assets	200,000	
80% of shares (reserves) in S Ltd at cost	80,000	
Net current assets	70,000	
		350,000
Share capital	300,000	
Reserves	50,000	
		350,000

S Ltd (subsidiary company)

	'000	'000
Fixed assets	60,000	
Net current assets	40,000	
		100,000
Share capital	80,000	
Reserves	20,000	
		100,000

To consolidate the accounts the inter company shares figure must be excluded, i.e., £80,000,000. This is attributable to the share capital and reserves of S Ltd, i.e., it is made up of:

	'000
80% of £80,000,000 share capital of S Ltd	64,000
80% of reserves of £20,000,000 of S Ltd	16,000
	80,000

Thus the amount of share capital and reserves attributable to the minority shareholders will be:

	'000
Share capital	80,000
Less 80%	64,000
20%	16,000
Reserves	20,000
Less 80%	16,000
20%	4,000

The consolidated Balance Sheet will show:

	'000	'000
Fixed assets: P Ltd	200,000	
S Ltd	60,000	
		260,000
Net current assets: P Ltd	70,000	
S Ltd	40,000	
		110,000
Total assets less current liabilities		370,000
Less Interest of minority shareholders		
in S Ltd capital	16,000	
reserves	4,000	20,000
		350,000
Share capital	300,000	
Reserves	50,000	
		350,000

9.4.2 The Profit and Loss account where a company holds a majority of shares

That part of the subsidiary's net profit after tax which belongs to the minority shareholders in respect of dividend and reserves will be deducted first, before appropriations are made for dividend and reserves.

EXAMPLE

Company P Ltd holds 80% of the share capital of S Ltd.
The Profit and Loss accounts for P Ltd and S Ltd are as follows:

P Ltd (parent company)

	'000	'000
Net profit		90,000
Dividend from S Ltd		8,000
		98,000
Taxation, say		27,000
		71,000
Dividend		20,000
Reserves		51,000

	S Ltd (subsidiary company)	
	'000	'000
Net profit		40,000
Taxation		12,000
		28,000
Dividend: P Ltd	8,000	
Others	2,000	
		10,000
Reserves: P Ltd	14,400	
Others	3,600	
		18,000

Consolidated Profit and Loss account for P Ltd and S Ltd

	'000	'000
Net profit: P Ltd	90,000	
S Ltd	40,000	
		130,000
Taxation: P Ltd	27,000	
S Ltd	12,000	
		39,000
		91,000
Less minority interest		
Dividend	2,000	
Reserve	3,600	
		5,600
		85,400
Dividend		20,000
Reserves: P Ltd	51,000	
S Ltd	14,400	
		65,400

9.5 Check list

By the end of this chapter you should be able to:

1. understand how the Balance Sheets of each company are merged;
2. understand how the Profit and Loss accounts of each company are merged;
3. understand the structure of a consolidated Profit and Loss account and a consolidated Balance Sheet;
4. complete some of the exercises at the end of the chapter.

9.6 Practice exercises

When you have completed these exercises, move on to interpretation of accounts and accounting ratios (Chapter 10).

1 Ball Limited owns all the shares in Chain Limited. The summarised Profit and Loss accounts and Balance Sheets for Ball and Chain drawn up on 30 September 200— are shown below. The Balance Sheets take into account retained profit (reserves) shown on the Profit and Loss account. Draw up the consolidated Profit and Loss account and the consolidated Balance Sheet for Ball Limited and Chain Limited.

Ball Limited: Profit and Loss account for the year ending 30 September 200—

	'000	'000
Net profit	100,000	
ADD dividend from Chain Limited	12,000	
	112,000	
LESS taxation, say	30,000	
Profit after tax	82,000	
Dividend to Ball Limited's shareholders	20,000	
Reserves	62,000	

Chain Limited: Profit and Loss account for the year ending 30 September 200—

	'000	'000
Net profit	44,000	
LESS taxation	13,200	
Profit after tax	30,800	
Dividend to Ball Limited	12,000	
Reserves	18,800	

Ball Limited: Balance Sheet as at 30 September 200—

	'000	'000
Fixed assets		300,000
Shares in Chain Limited at cost		89,000
Net current assets		192,000
TOTAL		581,000
Share capital		500,000
Reserves	19,000	
	62,000	
		81,000
TOTAL		581,000

Chain Limited: Balance Sheet as at 30 September 200—

	'000	'000
Fixed assets		65,000
Net current assets		42,800
TOTAL		107,800
Share capital		80,000
Reserves	9,000	
This year's	18,800	
		27,800
TOTAL		107,800

2 Ash Limited has 80% of the share capital of Willow Limited. The summary balance sheets of the two companies are as follows:

Ash Limited: Balance Sheet as at 30 November 200—

	'000	'000
Fixed assets		320,000
Shares in Willow Limited at cost		160,000
Net current assets		120,000
		600,000
Share capital		500,000
Reserves		100,000
		600,000

Willow Limited: Balance Sheet as at 30 November 200—

	'000	'000
Fixed assets		150,000
Net current assets		50,000
		200,000
Share capital		180,000
Reserves		20,000
		200,000

Draw up the consolidated balance sheet for the two companies.

9.7 Suggested answers to practice exercises

1 Ball Limited

Consolidated Profit and Loss account for Ball Limited and Chain Limited for the year ending 30 September 200—

	'000	'000
Net profit: Ball Limited	100,000	
Chain Limited	44,000	
		144,000
LESS taxation: Ball Limited	30,000	
Chain Limited	13,200	
		43,200
		100,800
Dividend to Ball Limited shareholders		20,000
Reserves: Ball Limited	62,000	
Chain Limited	18,800	
		80,800

Consolidated Balance Sheet for Ball Limited and Chain Limited as at 30 September 200—

	'000	'000
Fixed assets: Ball Limited	300,000	
Chain Limited	65,000	
		365,000
Net current assets: Ball Limited	192,000	
Chain Limited	42,800	
		234,800
		599,800
Share capital		500,000
Reserves: Ball Limited	19,000	
plus this year's	62,000	
	81,000	
Chain: increase in reserve	18,800	
		99,800
TOTAL		599,800

2 **Ash Limited**

Consolidated Balance Sheet for Ash Limited and Willow Limited as at 30 November 200—

	'000	'000
Fixed assets: Ash Limited	320,000	
Willow Limited	150,000	
		470,000
Net current assets: Ash Limited	120,000	
Willow Limited	50,000	
		170,000
Total assets less current liabilities		640,000
LESS interest of minority shareholders		
(being 20% of share capital	36,000	
20% of reserves)	4,000	
		40,000
TOTAL		600,000
Share capital	500,000	
Reserves	100,000	
TOTAL		600,000

10

Interpretation of accounts and accounting ratios

10.1 Introduction

This chapter deals with the following:

1. Use of accounts by different people.
2. Limitations of accounts and other factors to take into account.
3. Trends in accounts.
4. Accounting ratios with examples.
5. An exercise using ratios.

10.2 Use of accounts

Accounts may be used by many different people, e.g., by the management of a business, by employees, by investors in the business, by shareholders, by long-term lenders or trade creditors or by the Government for taxation and statistics. Each of these may be looking for different things in the accounts. A creditor, for example, would want to make sure that the debt could be repaid, whereas a shareholder in the business may be looking for increasing profit, so that dividends will be higher, or may be looking for capital appreciation.

The interpretation of accounts can help to assess how a business is performing at present and can also enable inferences to be made about its future performance. The current level of profit may be compared with other similar businesses to see if it is satisfactory, and whether it can be improved. By looking at the accounts of a business over a number of years trends may be seen. A business may have sufficient assets to cover liabilities, but if these are tied up in fixed assets, or stock which is not selling, or work in progress, or debtors who are unlikely to pay, it may not be able to pay its current liabilities.

You may wonder whether you need to know about interpretation of accounts at all. Why not leave it to the accountants? One good reason is that, as a sole practitioner or as a partner, the accounts will explain the profit due to you. It is not a good idea to leave the understanding of accounts to your accountants or to one or two of the other partners. You will not be able to make informed decisions about the business where necessary, for example, whether to retain staff, or take on more staff, or change the type of work done by the firm. Understanding accounts will also be necessary where you are dealing with commercial work; even where accountants are involved, you should have at least some idea of the advice given. You may be asked to give advice on proposed investments suggested by a stockbroker for a client or, for example, a trust in which you are a trustee.

Note that there may be financial services implications here. There are few areas of work today where an understanding of accounts will not be needed.

10.3 Check factors outside the accounts

To interpret accounts, ratio analysis may be used, as ratios can be used to compare performances from year to year and to compare different companies. Take care, however, as reading the accounts and looking at ratios on their own will not provide sufficient information about a company; other information should be sought as well. A company may have been doing very well, but may have just lost its managing director, or industrial action may be threatened by its workforce. The business may possibly have been involved in an area which has now expanded to saturation point, and the market may no longer be there. A business should be compared with others of a similar type, i.e., dealing with the same services or products and of a similar size. If profits are disappointing there may be a recession generally. Are the markets for the business still there? Is there increased competition, e.g., from abroad?

10.4 General areas to look at

When accounts are looked at, absolute changes may be found, e.g., is this year's profit more than last year's, have the expenses of the business gone up? Relative changes should also be found, e.g., what are the expenses of the business as a percentage of the turnover or sales? What is the profit as a percentage of the sales? How much profit has been generated from the capital employed (i.e., total assets less current liabilities)? The business may have invested heavily in fixed assets, but profit may have gone up by only a modest amount.

10.4.1 Accounts for past years

In interpreting accounts, the accounts for the last few years should be looked at, as these should establish general trends. Note that the figures shown on the accounts may not always be accurate. The business may be overstating the value of its assets. Examples may include stock or work in progress. If stock is valued at cost price, rather than its sale price, this may sound reasonable, but the stock may not have been sold for some time, and it may be necessary to sell the stock at a lower price than that shown on the Balance Sheet. How work in progress is valued should be checked—is this based on an accurate time recording system, or does it involve some guesswork? Other assets shown may be falling in value, e.g., office furniture, office equipment, and it is important that sufficient provision for depreciation has been made. On the other hand, if the business has freehold premises shown at cost price then the present value should be checked, as it may be much higher.

The figure for debtors (an asset) may be high, but if this is in respect of one or two debtors who are in trouble themselves, the debts may not be paid. Check that sufficient provision has been made for bad debts and doubtful debts.

There may also be changes in circumstances. A company may have just employed a new managing director who has a reputation as a troubleshooter, able to improve companies with poor performance. Thus in future years profit may go up dramatically.

It is also always worth reading the information supplied by a company and the notes attached to the accounts.

There are two main areas that will be looked at in any analysis:

(a) the solvency or liquidity of the business;
(b) the profitability of the business.

10.5 Trends

Figures over the years may be compared, e.g., the profit over the last five years may show a general trend up, even though there may be the odd year when profit has fallen. Has the turnover increased? Have expenses increased?

10.6 Ratios

These will be calculated from a set of accounts for a year, but can then be compared with other years.

10.6.1 Liquidity ratios

Liquidity means the ability of a business to pay its short-term debts. This is not the same as solvency, which means the ability of the business to pay all its liabilities. A firm may have sufficient assets to pay all its liabilities, but will still not be able to pay off short-term liabilities because it has insufficient cash or easily realisable assets.

10.6.1.1 The current assets ratio

$$\frac{\text{Current assets}}{\text{Current liabilities}}$$

This compares current assets with current liabilities. There should normally be enough current assets to cover current liabilities. The comparison is between assets which should be converted into cash in approximately 12 months; with liabilities which will be due for payment within the same 12 months. What is a satisfactory figure will vary with the type of business or with the reputation of the business. For example:

$$\frac{\text{Current assets}}{\text{Current liabilities}} \quad \frac{'000}{20,000} = 2:1$$

This would be a satisfactory ratio.
For example:

$$\frac{\text{Current assets}}{\text{Current liabilities}} \quad \frac{30,000}{20,000} = 1.5:1$$

Again this may be an acceptable ratio.

A very high figure may not mean that the business is safe and it is essential to look behind the figures. The company may have overvalued its current assets, e.g., the stock (or work in progress). Generally, if the ratio is less than 1 : 1, there may be a problem.

Where, however, the company has a bank overdraft and the bank is prepared to allow the overdraft to continue long term, this may then be treated as a long-term liability instead of a short-term liability and thus can be left out of the ratio. This will clearly improve the ratio.

10.6.1.2 The acid test

This ratio uses only cash or assets which can be converted quickly into cash, thus stock or work in progress will be excluded from the figure for current assets.

$$\frac{\text{Current assets less stock (or work in progress)}}{\text{Current liabilities}}$$

If this is 1:1 or better then the company will have sufficient liquid assets to meet its current liabilities: this is provided that the creditors are paid and debtors pay at approximately the same time. Sometimes an even stricter test is used, that of measuring cash as against current liabilities. If debtors have been included in the ratio then, to check how fast debts will be paid, another ratio can be used; see **10.5.2**.

10.6.2 The average collection period—trade debtors to sales ratio

To find the length of time in days that debtors will pay debts, the following formula is used:

$$\frac{\text{Trade debtors}}{\text{Sales}} \times 365 \quad \text{or for solicitors' use} \quad \frac{\text{Debtors}}{\text{Profit costs}} \times 365$$

EXAMPLE

Sales are £200,000 for the year and trade debtors are £10,000.

$$\frac{£10,000}{£200,000} \times 365 = 18.25 \text{ days}$$

If, e.g., sales are £200,000 for the year and trade debtors are £40,000:

$$\frac{£40,000}{£200,000} \times 365 = 73 \text{ days}$$

The ratio may not accurately reflect the length of time allowed to debtors. If, for example, sales had been strong just before the balance sheet was drawn up, this may give a high debtors figure, which would distort the ratio, making it appear that the length of credit given was much longer, as in the second example.

If the length of time allowed for debtors to pay is too long, then steps should be taken to tighten up debt collection. It is usual for a business to allow a specified length of time for debtors to pay the amount due before action is taken by the business. This time should be compared with the actual time which the debtors are taking. Whether the time has increased from previous years will need to be checked, as will the times for other similar businesses. It may also be advisable to check the individual debts to see how long each one has been outstanding. Some of them may be irrecoverable.

To check how quickly the business pays its creditors, a similar ratio is used; see **10.5.3**.

10.6.3 The average payment period—trade creditors to purchases ratio

$$\frac{\text{Trade creditors}}{\text{Purchases}} \times 365$$

If purchases for the year are £90,000 and trade creditors are £20,000:

$$\frac{£20,000}{£90,000} \times 365 = 81.1 \text{ days}$$

Again this should be compared with previous years, with similar businesses, and the length of time that creditors allow for payment. Note that a business may deliberately delay payment of creditors for as long as reasonably possible. Large companies in particular may do this as they have stronger bargaining power than their smaller creditors. If the period has dramatically increased, it may be that the business is having difficulty in paying its bills. However, a large figure for creditors may just be due to an increase in purchases just before the date of the balance sheet, and this may have been in anticipation of increased sales, or to buy in before prices are increased.

10.6.4 Shortage of working capital

Working capital or net current assets is that portion of capital left to run the business after providing for fixed assets. A business needs to pay out money to run the business, e.g., paying salaries and other expenses, or buying goods or services, before receiving payment itself for the goods or services it provides. How much will be needed will vary. It may be that credit is given on purchases: if this is a longer period than the time in which the business collects its own debts, then not as much working capital will be required. The amount of working capital will need to increase if there is inflation, as expenses will increase. If the business wishes to expand then again more working capital will be required. Reserve funds based on retained profit (sec 5.2.8) can be used to finance the increased requirement. If this is not possible then the business will have to raise funds by issuing more shares, or borrowing.

If a business runs short of working capital then it will have insufficient funds to meet its short-term liabilities, and may not be able to take advantage of, e.g., discounts for prompt payment. It may also have to offer discounts itself to customers for prompt payment.

Indications of a shortage of working capital may be found from using the following ratios:

10.6.4.1 The working capital ratio

$$\frac{\text{Net current assets (working capital)}}{\text{Sales (or use profit costs for solicitors)}}$$

EXAMPLE

A company has net current assets of £20,000 and sales are £200,000. The working capital ratio is:

$$\frac{20,000}{200,000} = 0.1 : 1$$

If net current assets were still £20,000 and sales were £400,000 then the ratio would be 0.05 : 1, clearly a lower ratio.

10.6.4.2 The ratio between debtors and creditors

$$\frac{\text{Debtors}}{\text{Creditors}}$$

If this ratio falls then again it may be a sign of overtrading. There may also be a shortage of cash. If the company is unable to find more capital to finance working capital, through borrowing or from the shareholders, then it may have to sell fixed assets, and lease instead, although there may be disadvantages in doing this.

Alternatively the business may be able to reduce the requirement for working capital, by ensuring that stock or work in progress is kept to a minimum and that debtors pay quickly, thereby releasing cash to use in the business.

If the company has over-expanded, i.e., sales have increased too fast, it may be necessary to halt the expansion.

10.6.5 Profitability ratios

10.6.5.1 Return on capital employed

This is the most important ratio in relation to profitability, for those who invest in the business it shows the rate of return on the capital used in the business. If net assets of the business are £2,000,000 and the profit is £20,000 then the return is only 1%, which is too low; as an investment the money would be better used elsewhere.

The ratio is:

$$\frac{\text{Operating profit (before interest and tax)}}{\text{Capital employed (total assets less current liabilities)}} \times 100\%$$

$$\frac{£20,000}{£2,000,000} \times 100\% = 1\%$$

The figure taken for profit is before tax and interest. If the figure was taken after interest on debentures, loans and overdrafts, the return on assets would be understated. Any interest received should also be excluded from the calculation, to ensure that the profit shown is that made by operations.

A problem with this particular ratio is that the capital employed is measured at the date of the balance sheet. This may be misleading if, for example, the company has recently increased its capital to fund expansion, by purchasing fixed assets, which have not yet created any increased profit. The figure for capital employed could be taken from the balance sheet at the end of the year, or at the start of the year, or an average of the figure at the start of the year and the figure at the end of the year.

Even if the return is satisfactory, it should be looked at with caution. The true value of the assets on the balance sheet should be checked. They may have been undervalued, e.g., premises may have been shown at cost price.

The ratio may also be adjusted in respect of a bank overdraft. If this is effectively long-term lending, it should be included in the figure for capital employed, i.e., added back.

$$\frac{\text{Operating profit (before taxation and interest)}}{\text{Total assets less current liabilities} + \text{overdraft}} \times 100\%$$

10.6.5.2 The gross profit percentage

$$\frac{\text{Gross profit}}{\text{Sales}} \times 100\%$$

This shows the profitability of the sales. Even if sales have increased, this does not necessarily mean that the gross profit has increased.

EXAMPLE

Year 1

$$\frac{30{,}000}{125{,}000} \times 100\% = 24\%$$

EXAMPLE

Year 2

$$\frac{40{,}000}{200{,}000} \times 100\% = 20\%$$

Although the sales and the gross profit have increased in year 2, it should be noted that the gross profit percentage is lower. If the gross profit percentage has fallen this may be because:

(a) the cost of goods sold has increased, but that selling prices have not been increased by an equivalent amount;

(b) sale prices have been reduced in order to sell more goods;

(c) if different types of goods have been sold, profit margins on some goods may be greater than on other goods.

10.6.5.3 Net profit percentage

$$\frac{\text{Operating or trading profit before interest and tax}}{\text{Sales}} \times 100\%$$

or for solicitors' use $\dfrac{\text{Net profit}}{\text{Profit costs}} \times 100\%$

Both this ratio and the ratio in **10.5.5.2** will vary, depending on the type of business being carried out. As with all ratios they should be compared with similar businesses. Some businesses operate with a very low profit margin, relying on a large turnover.

If the gross profit ratio has remained the same, but the net profit ratio has fallen, then the expenses must have increased.

Each type of expense can be compared with the sales figure, for the current year and previous years, to find whether the increase is general or limited to a particular area.

EXAMPLE

$$\frac{\text{Marketing costs}}{\text{Sales}} \times 100\%$$

$$\frac{\text{Administrative expenses}}{\text{Sales}} \times 100\%$$

10.6.6 Efficiency ratio—rate of stock turnover

The faster stock is turned over, or sold, the more profit will be made, provided the gross profit percentage stays the same. There are two ratios which may be used to find stock turnover:

(a) either divide stocks by sales:

$$\frac{\text{Stocks}}{\text{Sales}} \text{ (based on the selling price)}$$

EXAMPLE

If stock was £80,000 and sales were £700,000 the ratio would be:

$$\frac{80,000}{700,000} = 0.114 \text{ or every 41.7 days}$$

(b) or probably the better ratio, divide cost of goods sold by average stock:

$$\frac{\text{Cost of goods sold (sales at cost price)}}{\text{Average stock (at cost)}}$$

As you will not have the detailed accounts of the business to find average stock, use the average of the opening and closing stock:

EXAMPLE

If opening stock was £50,000 and closing stock was £80,000 then the average would be:

$$\frac{50,000 + 80,000}{2} = 65,000$$

If the cost of goods sold was £450,000 then the stock turnover would be:

$$\frac{450,000}{65,000} = 6.92 \text{ times per year, i.e., stock is turned over 6.92 times per year, or every 52.75 days}$$

The rate of stock turnover will vary, depending on the type of stock being carried. Although a fast rate of stock turnover should lead to increased profit, the business must be careful to have enough stock at any given time to meet demand.

If the rate of stock turnover has fallen then the business should check whether it is carrying too much stock, or whether sales have decreased generally.

After analysing the profitability of the business, it may be that profitability is satisfactory, or it may be considered that there is room for improvement. The business may attempt to reduce expenses, or increase prices or sales, to improve profitability. Increasing prices may not be the best solution, as customers may decide to go somewhere cheaper.

If sales are to be increased the business will have to work more efficiently, or expect its workforce to work harder. It may be that the business decides to reduce its workforce but expects them to retain the same level of sales. Increased sales will be possible only if the market for those goods is there.

10.6.7 Capital gearing ratios

Gearing relates to the capital structure of the company, the relationship between the capital provided by shareholders and the capital provided by borrowing. A high-geared company is one which has a high proportion of borrowing. A company with low gearing has most of its funds provided by the ordinary shareholder. The ratios used may be calculated in different ways.

10.6.7.1 A commonly used ratio

$$\frac{\text{Preference shares} + \text{long-term loans}}{\text{All shareholders funds} + \text{long-term loans}} \times 100\%$$

EXAMPLE 1

A company has share capital and long-term borrowings as follows:

Ordinary share capital	100
Reserves	50
7% preference shares	10
12% debentures	30
	190

$$\frac{10 + 30}{190} \times 100 = 21.05\%$$

EXAMPLE 2

A company has share capital and long-term borrowings as follows:

Ordinary share capital	80
Reserves	20
Preference shares	10
Debentures	40
	150

$$\frac{10 + 40}{150} \times 100 = 33.33\%$$

The second company is a higher geared company than the first company.

If a company is highly geared, then any change in the profits will affect the shareholders more than in a low-geared company, as the interest on the borrowing will have to be paid before any dividend is available to the ordinary shareholders. The company will be susceptible to changes in interest rates, e.g., if these increase substantially. The borrowing will also have to be repaid at some stage. If the company requires additional capital to expand the business it may be better to do this through increasing the share capital.

10.6.7.2 An alternative ratio

Another ratio is the ratio of borrowings to shareholders' funds.

EXAMPLE

If borrowing is £200,000 and shareholders' funds are £500,000 then the ratio will be:

Borrowing:	200,000
Shareholders' funds	500,000
Gearing	2 : 5

10.6.8 Investment ratios

An investor will be concerned with the profitability of a business, and whether the investment will give a good return.

10.6.8.1 The return on capital employed ratio

This ratio, shown previously, can be used.

$$\frac{\text{Net profit (before interest and tax)}}{\text{Capital employed}} \times 100\%$$

10.6.8.2 Return on ordinary shareholders' interest

The return on capital employed shows only the return before tax and interest. An ordinary shareholder will want to know what the return is after payment of interest and tax, and after payment of any preference shares dividends.

$$\frac{\text{Net profit after interest, tax and preference share dividend}}{\text{Ordinary shareholders' interest (ordinary share capital plus any reserves attributable to them)}} \times 100\%$$

10.6.8.3 Earnings per share

This will show the return per single share, in money.

$$\frac{\text{Net profit after interest, tax and preference share dividend}}{\text{Number of ordinary shares}}$$

This is an important ratio and FRS14 requires limited companies to show the earnings per share in the published accounts.

However, this figure will not be the amount that the shareholder receives per share—the amount received will be the dividend declared by the directors. As we have seen in **8.2.6**, part of the profit will often be transferred to reserves and, although these belong to the shareholders, they may not be available for distribution.

10.6.8.4 Dividend yield

This is the annual return by way of dividend based on an investment of £100 in the shares at the current price. If, e.g., the shares cost £2.00 each, then 50 shares could be purchased for £100. If the dividend was 10p per share, then the total would be £5.00, giving a dividend yield of 5%.

10.6.8.5 Dividend cover

$$\frac{\text{Earnings per share}}{\text{Dividend per share}}$$

This shows the proportion of earnings distributed against the proportion retained by way of reserves.

EXAMPLE

If net profit after tax and any preference share dividend was £8,000,000 and the number of ordinary shares was 4,000,000, then the earnings per share would be £2.00. If the dividend was £2,000,000, then the dividend per share would be 50p.

$$\frac{2.00}{.50} = 4 \text{ times}$$

An alternative way of showing this would be:

$$\frac{\text{Net profit after tax and preference share dividend}}{\text{Dividend to ordinary shareholders}}$$

Continuing the above example:

$$\frac{8,000,000}{2,000,000} = 4 \text{ times}$$

This shows that the dividend is covered four times by the profit earned, after tax and the preference share dividend. The higher this is, the more the company is reinvesting its profits in the business.

The amount retained will not only increase the underlying value of the shares but ensure that dividends can be paid if in any future year there is insufficient net profit available.

10.6.8.6 Price earnings ratio (PE ratio)

Once the earnings per share has been calculated, the actual earnings based on the present market price of the share (where applicable), rather than the value at which the share was issued, can be calculated.

$$\frac{\text{Market price per share}}{\text{Earnings per share}}$$

E.g. $\dfrac{£2.00}{.20} = 10$

This means that the investor has to pay £2.00 to get the benefit of earnings of 20p per annum—10 times the year's earnings have been paid, or 10 years' purchase of earnings.

When the market is convinced that the future earnings of a company are going to increase, the market price of the shares may go up. The price earnings ratio will therefore be higher. If the market is convinced that future earnings are not going to be as good, then the price of the shares may go down, and the PE ratio will be lower. However, PE ratios will vary depending on the type of business being carried out.

If a takeover bid is rumoured in respect of the company then the value of the shares may well go up, which will lead to a high PE ratio.

If a PE ratio for a company is higher than other companies in a similar business, it may be that the company is highly regarded, or possibly that the shares are overvalued. A lower PE ratio may mean that the company is not highly regarded, or possibly that the shares are undervalued.

10.7 Example

Dilley Tante Limited: Profit and Loss accounts for the year ending

	31 Dec 2002	31 Dec 2003
	'000	'000
Sales	800,000	1,200,000
LESS cost of sales	500,000	700,000
Gross profit	300,000	500,000
LESS expenses	132,000	240,000
Loan interest	8,000	40,000
Profit before tax	160,000	220,000
Taxation say	40,000	55,000
Profit after tax	120,000	165,000
Dividends	30,000	40,000
Retained profit	90,000	125,000

Dilley Tante Limited: Balance Sheet as at 31 December

	2002	2003
Fixed assets		
	'000	'000
Tangible assets	810,000	960,000
Current assets		
Stock	80,000	175,000
Debtors	50,000	110,000
Cash	10,000	5,000
	140,000	290,000
Creditors:		
Amounts falling due within one year	80,000	80,000
Net current assets	60,000	210,000
Total assets less current liabilities	870,000	1,170,000
Creditors:		
Amounts falling due after more than one year		
Loans and other borrowings	50,000	225,000
	820,000	945,000

	2002	2003
Capital and reserves		
Called up share capital		
Ordinary £1 shares	600,000	600,000
Profit and loss account		
Retained profit	220,000	345,000
	820,000	945,000

Ratios   2002   2003

Liquidity

Current ratio

$$\frac{\text{Current assets}}{\text{Current liabilities}}$$

	2002 ('000)	2003 ('000)
Current assets	140,000	290,000
Current liabilities	80,000	80,000
	= 1.75 to 1	= 3.625 to 1

The liquidity ratio or the acid test

$$\frac{\text{Current assets less stock}}{\text{Current liabilities}}$$

	2002	2003
	60,000	115,000
	80,000	80,000
	= 0.75 to 1	= 1.438 to 1

The average collection period—debtors to sales ratio

$$\frac{\text{Debtors}}{\text{Sales}} \times 365$$

	2002	2003
	$\frac{50,000}{800,000} \times 365$	$\frac{110,000}{1,200,000} \times 365$
	= 22.8 days	= 33.46 days

The average payment period—creditors to purchases ratio

$$\frac{\text{Creditors}}{\text{Purchases}} \times 365$$

	2002	2003
	$\frac{80,000}{500,000} \times 365$	$\frac{80,000}{700,000} \times 365$

Note: No purchases figure shown
Cost of sales taken as an approximation = 58.4 days   = 41.7 days

The working capital ratio

$$\frac{\text{Net current assets (working capital)}}{\text{Sales}}$$

	2002	2003
	60,000	210,000
	800,000	1,200,000
	= 0.075 to 1	= 0.175 to 1

The ratio between debtors and creditors

$$\frac{\text{Debtors}}{\text{Creditors}}$$

	2002	2003
	50,000	110,000
	80,000	80,000
	= 0.625 to 1	= 1.375 to 1

Return on capital employed

$$\frac{\text{Operating profit (before tax and interest)}}{\text{Capital employed (total assets less current liabilities)}} \times 100\%$$

$$\frac{168{,}000}{870{,}000} \times 100\% \quad \frac{260{,}000}{1{,}170{,}000} \times 100\%$$

$$= 19.31\% \quad\quad\quad = 22.22\%$$

The gross profit percentage

$$\frac{\text{Gross profit}}{\text{Sales}} \quad\quad \frac{300{,}000}{800{,}000} \times 100\% \quad \frac{500{,}000}{1{,}200{,}000} \times 100\%$$

$$= 37.5\% \quad\quad\quad = 41.67\%$$

The net profit percentage

$$\frac{\text{Operating or trading profit before interest and tax}}{\text{Sales}} \times 100\%$$

$$\frac{168{,}000}{800{,}000} \times 100\% \quad \frac{260{,}000}{1{,}200{,}000} \times 100\%$$

$$= 21\% \quad\quad\quad = 21.67\%$$

Rate of stock turnover

$$\frac{\text{Stocks}}{\text{Sales}} \quad\quad \frac{80{,}000}{800{,}000} \quad\quad \frac{175{,}000}{1{,}200{,}000}$$

0.1 36.5 days   0.146 53.29 days

Capital gearing

$$\frac{\text{Preference shares + lone-term liabilities}}{\text{Capital employed}} \times 100\%$$

$$\frac{50{,}000 \times 100\%}{870{,}000} \quad \frac{225{,}000 \times 100\%}{1{,}170{,}000}$$

$$= 0.057 \text{ to } 1 \quad = 0.192 \text{ to } 1$$

or   5.7%   19.2%

Return on ordinary shareholders' interest

$$\frac{\text{Net profit after interest, tax and preference share dividend}}{\text{Ordinary shareholders' interest}} \times 100\%$$

$$\frac{120{,}000}{820{,}000} \times 100\% \quad \frac{165{,}000}{945{,}000} \times 100\%$$

$$= 14.63\% \quad\quad\quad = 17.46\%$$

Earnings per share

$$\frac{\text{Net profit after interest, tax and preference share dividend}}{\text{Number of ordinary shares}}$$

$$\frac{120{,}000}{600{,}000} \quad\quad \frac{165{,}000}{600{,}000}$$

$$= 20\text{p} \quad\quad = 27.5\text{p}$$

Dividend cover

$\dfrac{\text{Net profit after tax, etc.}}{\text{Dividend to ordinary shareholders}}$	$\dfrac{120{,}000}{30{,}000}$ = 4 times	$\dfrac{165{,}000}{40{,}000}$ = 4.125 times

Comment

Liquidity: the current ratio was acceptable in 2002 at 1.75 to 1. In 2003 it increased to 3.625 to 1 as current assets, particularly stock and debtors, have increased dramatically, but creditors have remained the same. Clearly sales have increased, but the rate of stock turnover has reduced from 36.5 days to 53.29 days. This should be checked; also debtors should be checked to make sure that these will pay. Funding has come from increased long-term borrowing, now £225,000,000 instead of £50,000,000. Presumably the company has decided to increase turnover. The liquidity or acid test again shows an improvement from a rather weak 0.75 to 1 to an acceptable 1.438 to 1.

Given the high debtors figure, the average collection period has increased from 22.8 days to 33.46 days. This should be looked at with care and possibly steps taken to ensure that debtors pay within a set time.

The average payment period shown is an approximation; seemingly this has improved from 58.4 days to 41.7 days.

The working capital ratio has again improved, showing more working capital as mentioned above. The ratio of debtors to creditors has increased.

Return on capital employed has improved from 19.31% to 22.22%. There is also an improvement in the gross profit percentage. However, the net profit percentage has not improved much, i.e., from 21% to 21.67%. Expenses have increased, in particular the loan interest on the increased borrowing.

As mentioned previously, the rate of stock turnover has slowed and this should be looked at.

Given the increased long-term borrowing the gearing is now higher at 19.2% instead of the very low 5.7%. However, this is still not a high-geared company.

The return on ordinary shareholders' interest has improved as have earnings per share. Dividend cover remains approximately the same.

Clearly a decision was made to increase borrowing to invest in the company. Perhaps a further year is needed to consolidate.

10.8 Check list

By the end of this chapter you should to be able to:

1. appreciate that accounts can be looked at for different purposes;
2. appreciate the limitations in looking at accounts without checking other factors;
3. understand the types of ratios that can be used and their uses;
4. complete a short exercise using some accounting ratios.

10.9 Exercise

When you have completed this exercise, you will have covered the entire business accounts section.

Allow about 45 minutes for this exercise.

Below are shown the accounts of Perry and Mason for the year ending 30 November 200—

Perry and Mason: Profit and Loss account for the year ending 30 November 200—

Income				
Profit costs		300,000		
ADD Work in Progress at 30 Nov 200—		50,000		
		350,000		
LESS Work in Progress at start of year		40,000		
Work done			310,000	
Interest received			4,000	
			314,000	
Less expenses				
General and administrative expenses including staff wages		210,000		
ADD outstanding expenses		920		
		210,920		
LESS payments in advance		1,040		
		209,880		
Travelling expenses		1,000		
Depreciation: library, furniture and equipment		7,000		
			217,880	
Net profit			96,120	
Appropriation account				
Interest on capital at 5%	Perry	8,500		
	Mason	6,000		
			14,500	
Profit share	Perry	40,810		
	Mason	40,810		
			81,620	
				96,120

Perry and Mason: Balance Sheet as at 30 November 200—

FIXED ASSETS		
Freehold premises		240,000
Library furniture and equipment	35,000	
Less depreciation	14,000	
		21,000

			261,000
CURRENT ASSETS			
Work in Progress	50,000		
Debtors	60,000		
Petty cash	360		
Payments in advance	1,040		
		111,400	
LESS CURRENT LIABILITIES			
Creditors	10,000		
Outstanding expenses	920		
Bank overdraft	35,000		
		45,920	
NET CURRENT ASSETS			65,480
			326,480
LESS LONG-TERM LIABILITIES			—
			326,480
CAPITAL EMPLOYED			
Capital accounts:			
Perry	170,000		
Mason	120,000		
			290,000
Current accounts: see movement on current accounts:			
Perry	22,310		
Mason	14,170		
			36,480
			326,480
Client account			
Cash at the bank client account			
Current account	190,510		
Deposit account	266,380		
		456,890	
Amount due to clients		456,890	

Movement on current accounts

	Perry	Mason
Interest on capital	8,500	6,000
Profit share	40,810	40,810
	49,310	46,810
LESS drawings	27,000	32,640
	22,310	14,170

From these calculate:

(a) the current ratio;

(b) the acid test;

(c) the net profit percentage;

(d) the average collection period;

(e) the return on capital employed.

Comment on these ratios and on the accounts themselves. How relevant is the return on capital employed ratio? What suggestions would you have for the partners, who are concerned at the overdraft and would like to draw out more cash if possible. What further information would you ask for?

10.10 Suggested answer to exercise

The current ratio

$$\frac{\text{Current assets}}{\text{Current liabilities}} \qquad \frac{111{,}400}{45{,}920} = 2.43 \text{ to } 1$$

The acid test

$$\frac{\text{Current assets less work in progress}}{\text{Current liabilities}} \qquad \frac{61{,}400}{45{,}920} = 1.34 \text{ to } 1$$

The net profit percentage

$$\frac{\text{Net profit}}{\text{Profit costs}} \qquad \frac{96{,}120}{300{,}000} \times 100 = 32.04\%$$

The average collection period

$$\frac{\text{Debtors}}{\text{Profit costs}} \qquad \frac{60{,}000}{300{,}000} \times 365 = 73 \text{ days}$$

The return on capital employed

$$\frac{\text{Net profit}}{\text{Capital employed}} \times 100 \qquad \frac{96{,}120}{326{,}480} \times 100 = 29.44\%$$

The current ratio measures the short-term financial position of the firm. Here clearly there are sufficient current assets to cover current liabilities, a ratio of 2.43 to 1 is good. The acid test is also satisfactory at 1.34 to 1. However, the figures for work in progress and debtors are high; there is no cash at the bank. The value of work in progress should be checked, and bills should be sent out. Debtors should also be checked. There may be some debtors that have been outstanding for a long time, some of these may be irrecoverable, and provision for doubtful debts should be checked. Debtors should be chased, and much tighter control exerted over the length of time that they are taking to pay—see the average collection period of 73 days. However, if a large number of bills were sent out just before the balance sheet was drawn up this would distort the period calculated.

The net profit percentage at 32.04% may be reasonable, but previous years should be checked, and comparison made, if possible, with similar firms.

The return on capital employed is not very useful in a partnership, as account must be taken of the partners' work—notional salaries could be taken to give a more accurate ratio. The partners have provided for interest on capital as part of the appropriation of profit.

Note that the profit is not cash, and the partners must solve the cash flow problem. Provided that the work in progress figure is realistic, and that the bulk of the debtors are able to pay, this should be possible—see above. It is also possible that the bank is happy to continue financing the firm by way of an overdraft, when the overdraft could be treated as long-term lending. However, given the work in progress and debtors, this would not seem to be necessary, and the firm will save interest charges, etc. if they manage to convert these assets into cash.

As mentioned above, previous years' accounts would be helpful to establish any trends. Is the firm checking bad debts, provision, etc.? What are other similar firms doing? The value of the premises should be checked—is this the correct value, or has it increased or decreased? Should the partners consider sale/leaseback or do they regard this as investment for the future? Any new partner coming in would have to fund this, if, e.g., one of the existing partners left. How old are the partners? Possibly check expenses; can these be reduced?

11

Basic solicitors' accounts

11.1 Introduction

This chapter deals with the following:

1. The basic principles of the Solicitors' Accounts Rules 1998 (SAR).
2. The need to keep client and office money separate.
3. A form of account showing office and client account.
4. The definition of client money and the rules relating to receipt and payment out.
5. The definition of controlled trust money and the rules applicable.
6. The definition of office money.
7. Basic accounting entries in respect of office and client money.
8. Accounting entries in respect of delivery of a bill to the client.
9. Treatment of agreed fees as defined under the SAR.
10. Record keeping and powers of the Law Society to ensure compliance.
11. Practice exercises.

You will need your copy of the Solicitors' Accounts Rules 1998. You may also find the Law Society's web site www.lawsociety.org.uk useful.

11.2 The Solicitors' Accounts Rules 1998 (SAR)

11.2.1 Using the rules

It is essential that you become familiar with the rules and refer to them when working on exercises. As the rules are meant to be read in the light of the notes to the rules, these are as important as the rules.

11.2.2 Basic principles, Rule 1

This rule gives the principles which underpin the SAR.
Solicitors must:

(a) comply with the requirements of practice rule 1 re the solicitor's integrity, the duty to act in the client's best interests, and the good repute of the solicitor and the profession;

(b) keep clients' money separate from office money (belonging to the solicitor or the practice);

(c) keep clients' money safely in a bank or building society account identifiable as a client account (except where the rules specifically provide otherwise);

(d) use each client's money for that client's matters only;

(e) use controlled trust money for the purposes of that trust only;

(f) establish and maintain proper accounting systems, and proper internal controls over those systems, to ensure compliance with the rules;

(g) keep proper accounting records to show accurately the position with regard to the money held for each client and each controlled trust;

(h) account for interest on other people's money in accordance with the rules;

(i) cooperate with the Law Society in checking compliance with the rules; and

(j) deliver annual accountant's reports as required by the rules.

11.2.3 Keeping clients' and office money separate

Solicitors must keep money belonging to clients (clients' money) separate from their own money (office money). This means having at least two separate accounts at the bank or building society, the Client bank account and the Office bank account.

A Client account must be in the name of the solicitor, the solicitors' firm, or solicitors' company, and must contain the word 'Client'. SAR Rule 14.

The solicitor must therefore have two cash accounts in the ledger system: the Office cash account and the Client cash account. For convenience these two are shown side by side, as follows:

Cash account

Date	Details	Office account			Client account		
		DR	CR	Balance	DR	CR	Balance

Each client ledger card will also show that there are two accounts:

Smith: re conveyancing

Date	Details	Office account			Client account		
		DR	CR	Balance	DR	CR	Balance

Although the money for all clients will, as a general rule, be kept in one bank account, the solicitor must record separately in respect of each client the money which is being held for that client. This means that the solicitor must not use money belonging to one client for the purposes of another client, nor may the solicitor transfer the money of one client from that client's ledger account to the ledger account of another client except as provided for in the rules (see **12.1.3**).

11.2.4 The definition of clients' money, Rule 13

Whenever a solicitor receives or pays money on behalf of a client, the solicitor must decide whether it is clients' or office money. The rules define clients' money as money held or received by a solicitor for a client. This includes money held as agent, bailee, stakeholder or as the donee of a power of attorney, or as a liquidator, trustee in bankruptcy or Court of Protection receiver.

11.2.4.1 Solicitors not to operate banking facilities

Note that the Solicitors' Disciplinary Tribunal stated in the case of Wood and Burdett that it is not a proper part of a solicitor's everyday business or practice to operate a banking facility for third parties, whether they are clients of the firm or not.

Solicitors should also bear in mind that there are criminal sanctions against assisting money launderers. See Rule 15 note (ix).

11.2.5 Payments into client account

Where a solicitor receives clients' money, the solicitor must normally pay it into a client bank account without delay. This means on the day the money is received or, if not possible, on the next working day, Rule 15.

11.2.5.1 Money received from client on account of costs and disbursements, Rules 13 and 19

Money paid generally on account of costs and disbursements is clients' money and must be paid into the client account.

11.2.5.2 Money which may be paid into client account, Rule 15

The following 'non-client' money may be paid into a client account:

(a) controlled trust money (see **11.2.7**);

(b) the solicitor's own money required to open or maintain the account;

(c) an advance from the solicitor to fund a payment needed on behalf of a client or controlled trust in excess of funds held for that client or controlled trust. Note that the sum becomes client money or controlled trust money on payment into the account;

(d) money to replace that withdrawn in breach of the rules;

(e) a sum in lieu of interest paid into client account;

(f) cheques which the solicitor would be entitled to 'split' but does not (i.e., mixed office/client money).

11.2.5.3 Receipt of mixed office/client money, Rules 19 and 20

Where money is received which is part office and part client money, this can be:

(1) split, part paid into office account, and part into client account;

(2) all paid into client account and then the office money transferred to office account within 14 days;

(3) if the mixed money consists of office money and unpaid professional disbursements only (for example unpaid counsel's fees) then the money can be paid into the office account, and within 2 working days the unpaid disbursement must either be paid or the unpaid amount transferred to client account.

There are also special rules relating to the treatment of monies received from the Legal Aid Board and payments from a third party in respect of legal aid work (see **11.2.6**).

11.2.5.4 Money which must be withheld from client account, Rule 16

(a) Money should not be paid into a client account if the client has asked for it not to be paid into a client account. (Such a request from the client should be in writing, or confirmed in writing by the solicitor.)

(b) Where a solicitor agrees to hold a cheque 'to the order' of a third party, the cheque should not be paid into a client account until it is released by the third party, as until that point it does not become the client's money.

11.2.5.5 Money which may be withheld from client account, Rule 17

A solicitor need not pay clients' money in to client account if received:

(a) in cash, which is, without delay, paid in cash, in the ordinary course of business, to the client or on the client's behalf to a third party; or

(b) as a cheque or banker's draft which is endorsed over in the ordinary course of business to the client or on the client's behalf to a third party; or

(c) which is paid into a separate bank account or building society account opened in the name of the client or a third party named in writing by the client or acknowledged in writing by the solicitor.

Note: if a solicitor negotiates cash or endorses a cheque made out to him, then the solicitor has handled clients' money and must make entries in the account to show the receipt and payment of clients' money. However many cheques are now non-endorsable.

If a solicitor receives a cheque made out to a third party which the solicitor passes on to that third party, then the solicitor has not handled clients' money and should not record a receipt and payment of clients' money in the accounts. It is, however, advisable to record the fact that the cheque has been received and passed on. This can be done by a file note and/or an entry on the client's ledger account by way of memorandum.

11.2.6 Receipts from the Legal Services Commission, Rule 21

An advance payment from the LSC in anticipation of work to be carried out, although client money, may be placed in office account provided the LSC instructs in writing that this may be done.

A payment for costs, interim or final, may be paid into office account, even though it may include client money re advance payments for fees of disbursements or money for unpaid professional disbursements, provided all money for payment of disbursements is transferred to client account or the disbursements paid within 14 days of receipt.

Regular payments from the LSC are office money and must be paid into office account. Within 28 days of submitting a report to the LSC notifying completion a solicitor must either:

pay any unpaid professional disbursements; or

transfer to a client account a sum equivalent to the amount of the unpaid professional disbursements.

11.2.7 Withdrawals from a client account, Rule 22

The following, in particular, should be noted with regard to the withdrawal of money from a client account:

(a) Clients' money can be used to make payments only if enough money is held in client account for the particular client on whose behalf it is desired to make the payment, Rule 22(5).

(b) If insufficient money is held in client account for the particular client the solicitor may either:
   (i) pay the disbursement out of office account (the solicitor may then transfer the balance held on client account, to office account); or
   (ii) draw two cheques, one on client account for the balance held and one on office account for the remainder.

   Note also that the solicitor may advance money to fund a payment on behalf of a client in excess of funds held for that client.

(c) **Client money** can be withdrawn if:
   (i) properly required for a payment to or on behalf of the client;
   (ii) properly required for payment of a disbursement on behalf of the client;
   (iii) properly required in full or partial reimbursement of money spent by the solicitor on behalf of the client. Money is spent by the solicitor at the time when the solicitor dispatches a cheque unless the cheque is to be held to the solicitor's order. Money is also spent by the use of a credit account, for example, search fees or taxi fares.
   (iv) transferred to another client account;
   (v) withdrawn on the client's instructions provided the instructions are for the client's convenience and are given in writing or confirmed by the solicitor in writing;
   (vi) a refund to the solicitor of an advance no longer required to fund a payment on behalf of a client;
   (vii) money which has been paid into the account in breach of the rules (e.g., money paid into the wrong separate designated client account or interest wrongly credited to a general client account);
   (viii) money withdrawn from the account on the written authorisation of the Law Society.

Office money can be withdrawn from client account if it is:
   (i) money which had properly been paid in to open or maintain the account;
   (ii) money properly required for payment of the solicitors' costs, where a bill of costs or other written notification of the costs incurred has been given to the client. Once the solicitor has done this the money must be transferred out of client account within 14 days.
   (iii) the whole or part of payment re legal aid payment paid in;
   (iv) part of a mixed office/client payment previously paid in.

Note that similar rules apply to controlled trust money.

Note it is possible to draw against an uncleared cheque under the rules.

However, a solicitor should use discretion in drawing against an uncleared cheque. If the cheque is not met then other client's money will have been used to make the payment in breach of the rules and the breach must be remedied. A solicitor may be able to avoid a breach of the rules by instructing the bank or building society to charge all unpaid credits to the solicitor's office or personal account.

11.2.8 Controlled trusts

11.2.8.1 Definition

A solicitor may hold money as a 'controlled trustee'. A solicitor will be a controlled trustee if a sole trustee or the only other trustees are his or her partners or employees. If a solicitor is a trustee with an outside third party then the solicitor is not a controlled trustee.

11.2.8.2 Rules

Normally controlled trust money should be paid without delay into a client account under Rule 15. This is subject to the same exceptions as client money, for example, cash received and without delay paid in cash in the execution of the trust to a beneficiary or third party (see **11.2.5.5** previously) and, in accordance with the trustee's powers, it may be paid into or retained in an account of the trustee which is not a client account (e.g., a building society share account or an account outside England and Wales) or properly retained in cash in the performance of the trustee's duties.

11.2.8.3 Interest on controlled trust money

The general law requires a solicitor to act in the best interests of a controlled trust and not to benefit personally from it. Note that the rules as to interest on client money do not apply to controlled trust money. A solicitor must obtain the best reasonably obtainable rate of interest for the controlled trust money and must account to the relevant controlled trust for all the interest earned, whether the controlled trust money is held in a separate designated client account or in a general client account.

To ensure that all interest is accounted for, solicitors may set up a general client account just for controlled trust money or can set up a designated account for each controlled trust.

When controlled trust money is held in a general client account, interest will be credited to the office account in the normal way, but all interest must be promptly allocated to each controlled trust—either by transfer to the general client account or to separate designated client accounts for the particular trust or by payment to each trust in some other way.

11.2.8.4 Indirect benefit

Solicitors must also consider whether they have received any indirect benefit from controlled trust money at the expense of the controlled trust. For example, the bank might charge a reduced overdraft rate on office account by reference to the total funds (including controlled trust money) held by the solicitors on client account in return for paying a lower rate of interest on those funds. The solicitor may have to do more for the trust than merely account for such interest earned in these circumstances.

Note that if controlled trust money is invested in the purchase of assets other than money, e.g., stocks and shares, it is no longer controlled trust money, but it will become controlled trust money again when the investments are later sold.

11.2.8.5 Delegation to outside manager

There is a special provision that controlled trustees may delegate to an outside manager the day-to-day keeping of accounts of the business or property portfolio of an estate or trust, provided the manager keeps and retains appropriate accounting records which are available for inspection by the Law Society.

11.2.8.6 Solicitor co-trustee with outsiders

Contrast the above with the position where the solicitor is trustee with others outside the firm and is not a controlled trustee. In such circumstances monies held will be normal client account money and the normal rules will apply, including the rules as to interest payable.

11.2.9 Note also the following under the SAR 1998

Liquidators, trustees in bankruptcy and Court of Protection receivers are now included in the rules, limited to record-keeping requirements, and subject to monitoring and inspection by the Law Society and reporting accountants, to protect the clients and the profession from claims on the Solicitors' Indemnity and Compensation Funds.

Solicitors operating a client's account, e.g., under a power of attorney, should receive all statements and passbooks and retain these, as they will be subject to monitoring and inspection by the Law Society and reporting accountants.

11.2.10 The definition of office money, Rule 13

This is money that belongs to the solicitor or to the practice. It includes:

(a) money held or received in connection with running the practice, e.g. PAYE or VAT on the firm's fees;

(b) interest on general client accounts (but see the rules related to interest on controlled trust money);

(c) payments received in respect of:
   (i) fees due to the practice re bill or written notification of costs incurred;
   (ii) money paid for or towards an agreed fee;
   (iii) disbursements already paid by the practice;
   (iv) disbursements incurred but not yet paid by the practice, but excluding unpaid professional disbursements.

11.2.10.1 Partners' money is office money

Money belonging to a principal solicitor or one of his partners cannot be treated as clients' money and must always be paid into office account. For example, if the firm acts for one of the partners in the purchase of a house in his sole name, free of mortgage, and the partner hands a cheque for the deposit to the firm's cashier, the cheque must be paid into office account. Note the following, however:

(a) If the firm is acting for a partner and that partner's spouse (who is not a partner), any moneys received will be held on behalf of both as trustees and must be treated as clients' money.

(b) If the firm is acting for a partner in the purchase of a property with the aid of a mortgage, the mortgage advance is clients' money.

(c) If the firm is acting for an assistant solicitor, a consultant or a non-solicitor employee, or in the case of a recognised body, a director, they will be regarded as clients even if dealing with the matter personally.

11.3 Basic entries

You should refer back to Chapter 1 for basic double-entry bookkeeping and entries on accounts. For solicitors, the office and client accounts are totally separate. An entry in the client column of one account must have its corresponding double entry in the client column of another account. The same obviously applies also to office account entries.

11.3.1 Receipt of office moneys

The firm must pay money owed to it into office account. The entries to record this are:

(a) CREDIT client's ledger account—office column.

(b) DEBIT Cash account—office column.

EXAMPLE

On 1 February the solicitor receives £100 in respect of payments already paid (called disbursements) out of office account for his client, Black.

Black

Date	Details	Office account			Client account		
		DR	CR	Balance	DR	CR	Balance
1 Feb	Balance due from your Cash		100	100 DR —			

Cash account

Date	Details	Office account			Client account		
		DR	CR	Balance	DR	CR	Balance
1 Feb	Black	100		100 DR			

11.3.2 Payments of office money

The firm must pay disbursements out of office account if there is insufficient money in client account for that particular client, unless the solicitor decides to transfer office money to client account (see **11.2.4.2**). The entries to record a payment of office monies are:

(a) DEBIT client's ledger account—office column.

(b) CREDIT Cash account—office column.

EXAMPLE

Brown's solicitors are acting on his behalf with regard to a personal injury claim. They are not holding any money on Brown's behalf and pay £400 to counsel for an opinion on liability on 1 March.

Brown: re personal injury action

Date	Details	Office account			Client account		
		DR	CR	Balance	DR	CR	Balance
1 Mar	Cash: counsel	400		400 DR			

Cash account

Date	Details	Office account			Client account		
		DR	CR	Balance	DR	CR	Balance
1 Mar	Brown—counsel		400	400 CR			

The client's ledger account should generally show a debit balance or a nil balance on office account. A credit balance may indicate a breach of the Solicitors' Accounts Rules. Exceptions to this include agreed fees (see **11.2.10**) mixed monies, including unpaid professional disbursements, and interest (see **15.2.2**).

If there is money held in client account but not enough to pay the particular disbursements, so that the whole payment is made out of office account, the solicitor may transfer the money held in client account to office account once the disbursement has been paid. As an alternative, two cheques could be drawn to pay the disbursement, one on client account for the amount held and the remainder on office account. In practice this is rarely done.

11.3.3 Receipt of clients' money

Once it has been decided that money received is clients' money it must be paid into client account promptly. The entries are:

(a) CREDIT client's ledger account—client column.

(b) DEBIT Cash account—client column.

EXAMPLE

On 1 April the firm receives a cheque for £10,000 from the Bramchester Building Society to be used as a deposit on the purchase of Blackacre by the firm's client, White.

White: re purchase of Blackacre

Date	Details	Office account			Client account		
		DR	CR	Balance	DR	CR	Balance
1 Apr	Cash: Bramchester Building Society					10,000	10,000 CR

Cash account

Date	Details	Office account			Client account		
		DR	CR	Balance	DR	CR	Balance
1 Apr	White: Bramchester Building Society				10,000		10,000 DR

If money is received from a third party on behalf of a client, as in the preceding example, the receipt is recorded in the ledger account of the client on whose behalf the money is received. An account is not opened for the third party.

Remember the solicitor must not pay the following into client account:

(a) the solicitor's own or a partner's money (except as allowed by the rules);

(b) money received to pay profit costs after a bill has been delivered;

(c) money the client asks him or her not to pay into client account.

Solicitors may receive cash on behalf of a client and are permitted to pay this over to the client. However they must still record the receipt and payment out of client money on the accounts.

11.3.4 Payment out of clients' money

Before making a payment out of client account, the solicitor should check:

(a) that sufficient money is held in client account for the client on whose behalf the payment is being made;

(b) that the payment is permissible within the Solicitors' Accounts Rules 1998.

The bookkeeping entries are:

(a) DEBIT the client's ledger account—client column.

(b) CREDIT the Cash account—client column.

EXAMPLE

On 7 April the firm pays the £2,000 deposit received from the Bramchester Building Society for White, to Fleets the seller's solicitors.

White: re purchase of Blackacre

Date	Details	Office account			Client account		
		DR	CR	Balance	DR	CR	Balance
1 Apr	Cash: Bramchester Building Society					10,000	10,000 CR
7 Apr	Cash: Fleets re deposit				10,000		—

Cash account

Date	Details	Office account			Client account		
		DR	CR	Balance	DR	CR	Balance
1 Apr	White: Bramchester Building Society				10,000		10,000 DR
7 Apr	White: Fleets re deposit					10,000	—

11.3.5 Cheques made payable to third parties

You may be required to show that you appreciate that when you hand over to a third party a cheque made payable to the third party, you have not handled clients' money. You can do this by making no entry at all in the accounts. Alternatively, you can make what is known as a memorandum entry. If you do this, remember; no entry is made in the cash account at all, no balance column entry is made in the client's ledger account and the details column should show clearly that the entry is by way of memorandum only.

EXAMPLE

You act for Charles to recover a debt owed to him by Janis. On 1 February Janis sends you a cheque for £250 made payable to Charles.

Charles: re debt collection

Date	Details	Office account			Client account		
		DR	CR	Balance	DR	CR	Balance
1 Feb	Cheque received from Janis payable to Charles memorandum entry only				[250	250]	

11.4 Payments out of petty cash—office account

Small disbursements paid on behalf of clients, for example, commissioner's fees, may be paid in cash rather than by cheque.

The solicitor maintains a petty cash float by drawing money out of office account at the bank. Any petty cash payments must therefore always be made from the office account.

To record dealings with petty cash, a petty cash account is used, or a petty cash book if the ledger system is operated.

To record the transfer of money from the office bank account as a float to the petty cash account the following entries are made:

(a) CREDIT the Cash account in the office column.

(b) DEBIT the Petty Cash account (office account).

EXAMPLE

On 10 January a solicitor draws £500 out of office account for petty cash.

Cash account

Date	Details	Office account			Client account		
		DR	CR	Balance	DR	CR	Balance
	Balance say			2,000 DR			
10 Jan	Petty cash		500	1,500 DR			

Only office money can be held in petty cash, therefore only office account columns are necessary.

Petty cash account (office account only)

Date	Details	DR	CR	Balance
10 Jan	Cash float	500		500 DR

As payments made out of petty cash are always office account payments, even if there is money in client account, a petty cash payment must always be recorded as coming out of office account.

To record the payment of a petty cash disbursement on a client's behalf the following entries are made in the accounts:

(a) DEBIT the client's ledger account in the office column.

(b) CREDIT the Petty Cash account (office).

EXAMPLE

On 15 January the firm pays £40 out of petty cash for local advertisements in the administration of Kate's estate.

Kate deceased: administration of estate

Date	Details	Office account			Client account		
		DR	CR	Balance	DR	CR	Balance
15 Jan	Petty cash: local advertisements	40		40 DR			

Petty cash account (office account)

Date	Details	DR	CR	Balance
10 Jan	Cash float	500		500 DR
15 Jan	Kate deceased		40	460 DR

11.5 Profit costs and VAT

11.5.1 Delivery of bills of costs

When a solicitor delivers a bill of costs to the client, a central record or file of copies of bills must be kept. This is in addition to the entries shown below. (See Rule 32(8)).

When a bill of costs is delivered to a client the following entries are made in the accounts:

(a) DEBIT client ledger account office column with profit costs and VAT (on separate lines)— charging the client.

(b) CREDIT the Profit Costs account with profit costs.

(c) CREDIT the HM Revenue and Customs account (HMRC) with VAT.

The Profit Costs account and HMRC accounts only record dealings with office money and therefore only have office columns.

EXAMPLE

On 15 June 2002 the firm delivers a bill of costs to Beryl, for whom it has acted in divorce proceedings, for £100 plus £17.50 VAT.

Beryl: re divorce

Date	Details	Office account			Client account		
		DR	CR	Balance	DR	CR	Balance
15 June	Profit costs	100					
	VAT	17.50		117.50 DR			

Profit costs account

Date	Details	Office account		
		DR	CR	Balance
15 June	Beryl		100	100 CR

HMRC account VAT

Date	Details	Office account		
		DR	CR	Balance
15 June	Beryl		17.50	17.50 CR

Entries are made to record the delivery of the bill of costs on the date of delivery regardless of the date of payment. When payment of the bill is made entries are made in the accounts to record a receipt of office money.

EXAMPLE

Beryl pays her bill on 1 July

Date	Details	Office account			Client account		
		DR	CR	Balance	DR	CR	Balance
15 June	Profit costs	100		100 DR			
	VAT	17.50		117.50 DR			
1 July	Cash you		117.50	—			

Note: DEBIT the Cash account—office column, £117.50.

11.5.2 Agreed fees, Rule 19(5)

A solicitor and client may agree a fee for work which the solicitor has done or is to do on the client's behalf. When the solicitor receives the agreed fee it must be paid into office account even though a bill of costs is not delivered until a later date. The agreed fee must be evidenced in writing. It is not necessary to draw a bill when a fee is agreed.

EXAMPLE

On 10 July the firm receives £94 from Jill in respect of a fee agreed at the beginning of the month for work done by the firm on Jill's behalf in connection with a tenancy dispute. A bill is delivered on receipt of the fee.

Jill: re housing

Date	Details	Office account			Client account		
		DR	CR	Balance	DR	CR	Balance
10 July	Cash you		94	94 CR			
	Profit costs (agreed fee)	80		14 CR			
	VAT	14		—			

Note:

(a) It would be a breach of the Solicitors' Accounts Rules to pay money, expressly paid in respect of an agreed fee, into client account.

(b) The tax point for VAT arises when the fee is received, not when a bill is subsequently delivered (see **13.3.1**).

11.6 Record keeping and compliance

11.6.1 Solicitors' duty to keep accounts

A solicitor has a duty to keep accounts to record transactions involving clients' money. The accounts and all bank statements must be preserved for a minimum period of six years

(r. 32(9) of the Solicitors' Accounts Rules 1998). Where a computerised system is used the solicitor must ensure that a hard copy can be produced reasonably quickly and that it remains capable of reproduction for at least six years.

In addition, all paid cheques and copies of authorities for withdrawal of money from a client account must be retained for at least two years. To avoid the practical problems associated with storage, there is provision in the rules for the solicitor to obtain written confirmation from the bank that it will retain cheques for the required two-year period.

Under Rule 35, solicitors who hold client money or controlled trust money during an accounting period must have their client accounts inspected by an accountant 'qualified' within the meaning of the rules, and must submit an accountant's report to the Law Society for that accounting period within six months of the end of the accounting period.

The Law Society has the power to appoint an accountant to investigate a solicitor's practice.

11.6.2 Powers of the Law Society to secure compliance

Section 34 of the Solicitors Act 1974 requires solicitors to deliver an annual accountant's report to the Law Society. If solicitors fail to deliver such a report or fail to comply with the Solicitors' Accounts Rules 1998, a complaint may be made to the Solicitors' Disciplinary Tribunal by the Law Society.

Under Rule 34 of the Solicitors' Accounts Rules 1998, solicitors must produce to any person appointed by the Law Society records necessary to enable preparation of a report on compliance with the Rules. Any report made by the person appointed may be sent to the Crown Prosecution Service or the Serious Fraud Office and/or used in proceedings before the Solicitors' Disciplinary Tribunal.

11.7 Check list

By the end of this chapter you should be able to:

1. identify office and client money;
2. understand when client money may be withdrawn from client account;
3. identify controlled trust money and appreciate the position in respect of interest and possible indirect benefit;
4. understand and be able to draw up basic entries in respect of the receipt and payment of office and client money;
5. appreciate that petty cash must be office money;
6. understand and be able to draw up entries on the relevant accounts in respect of the delivery of a bill of costs to the client;
7. understand that agreed fees as defined under the SAR should be paid into office account;
8. know the accounts record keeping requirements for solicitors and the powers of the Law Society to secure compliance;
9. complete the self-test exercises at the end of the chapter.

11.8 Practice exercises

Treat each of the first six questions separately, and assume in each example the cash account starts with nil balances on office and client account.

Allow 5 minutes each for exercises 1 to 3.

1. On 1 January the firm receives an agreed fee of £470 from their client Abraham. Show the entries that would be made on the client ledger account for Abraham and on the firm's cash book.
2. On 2 February the firm receives a cheque for £270,000 in respect of the sale of a property on behalf of a partner, Quasim. Show the entries required on the relevant accounts for the receipt.
3. On 3 March the firm pays out £40 being a court fee, on behalf of their client Silver. Silver has not yet made any payment on account of costs and disbursements. Show the relevant entries.

Allow 5 to 10 minutes each for exercises 4 and 5.

4. On 4 April the firm receives a cheque for £300 on general account of costs and disbursements from their client Manikai in respect of property transactions. The firm then pays a search fee of £120 on behalf of the client. Show the relevant entries on the accounts.
5. On 5 May the firm pays an expert £500 from office account on behalf of their client Humbert. On 10 May Humbert pays the firm £500 in respect of the disbursement paid. Show the relevant entries on the accounts.
6. Allow 10 to 15 minutes.

    On 6 June the firm pays out an expert's fee of £200 on behalf of their client Campbell from office account. On 9 June the firm sends a bill to Campbell for £160 plus VAT. On 15 June Campbell pays the total due to the firm. Show the relevant entries on the accounts.

When you have completed these exercises you should have an understanding of basic entries on solicitors accounts and can move on to transfers and mixed money (Chapter 12).

11.9 Answers to practice exercises

1 Abraham—general matters

Date	Details	Office account			Client account		
		DR	CR	Bal	DR	CR	Bal
1 Jan	Cash—you—agreed fee		470	470 CR			

Cash account

Date	Details	Office account			Client account		
		DR	CR	Bal	DR	CR	Bal
1 Jan	Abraham agreed fee	470		470 DR			

Note that as the date of receipt of the agreed fee is the tax point for VAT purposes then it would be advisable to send out a VAT invoice and record the fee and VAT on the account (see **11.5.2** and Chapter 13 on VAT).

2 Quasim—sale of property

Date	Details	Office account			Client account		
		DR	CR	Bal	DR	CR	Bal
2 Feb	Cash—sale proceeds		270,000	270,000 CR			

Cash account

Date	Details	Office account			Client account		
		DR	CR	Bal	DR	CR	Bal
2 Feb	Quasim—sale proceeds	270,000		270,000 DR			

Note that this money must be paid into office account as the partner is solely entitled to the money. See SAR rule 13 note (xii).

3 Silver—litigation

Date	Details	Office account			Client account		
		DR	CR	Bal	Dr	CR	Bal
3 Mar	Cash—court fee	40		40 DR			

Cash account

Date	Details	Office account			Client account		
		DR	CR	Bal	DR	CR	Bal
3 Mar	Silver—court fee		40	40 CR			

4 Manikai—property sale and purchase

Date	Details	Office account			Client account		
		DR	CR	Bal	DR	CR	Bal
4 Apr	Cash—you on account of costs & disbursements Cash—search fee				120	300	300 CR 180 CR

Cash account

Date	Details	Office account			Client account		
		DR	CR	Bal	DR	CR	Bal
4 Apr	Manikai—on account of costs Manikai—search fee				300	120	300 DR 180 DR

5 Humbert—general matters

Date	Details	Office account			Client account		
		DR	CR	Bal	DR	CR	Bal
5 May	Cash—expert	500		500 DR			
10 May	Cash—you payment of disbursement		500	—			

Cash account

Date	Details	Office account			Client account		
		DR	CR	Bal	DR	CR	Bal
5 May	Humbert—expert		500	500 CR			
10 May	Humbert—payment of disbursement	500		—			

6 Campbell—general matters

Date	Details	Office account			Client account		
		DR	CR	Bal	DR	CR	Bal
6 June	Cash—expert	200		200 DR			
9 June	Profit Costs—bill	160		360 DR			
	Customs & Excise VAT	28		388 DR			
15 June	Cash—you—balance due		388	—			

Cash account

Date	Details	Office account			Client account		
		DR	CR	Bal	DR	CR	Bal
6 June	Campbell—expert		200	200 CR			
9 June	Campbell—balance due	388		188 DR			

Profit costs account

Date	Details	Office account		
		DR	CR	Bal
9 June	Campbell—bill		160	160 CR

HM Revenue and Customs VAT account

Date	Details	Office account		
		DR	CR	Bal
9 June	Campbell—bill		28	28CR

Note the balances at the end of each account at the end of the transaction. Campbell's account is clear; he no longer owes the firm any money. The firm is holding £188 on the Cash book, which represents £160 for the firm's profit costs and £28 for Customs and Excise. It has been repaid the £200 it paid out.

Transfers and mixed money

12.1 Introduction

This chapter deals with the following:

1. Transfers from client to office account.
2. Transfers from office to client account.
3. Transfers between client accounts.
4. Methods of dealing with the receipt of mixed office and client money.

12.2 Transfers

12.2.1 Transfers from client to office account

A transfer may be made from client to office account if it is permissible, within the Solicitors' Accounts Rules 1998, to withdraw money from client account, Rule 22 (see **11.2.7**).

A solicitor may wish to transfer money from client to office account if:

(a) disbursements have been paid out of office account on the client's behalf;

(b) a bill of costs has been delivered to the client and the solicitor needs to obtain payment of costs by transferring money held in client account;

(c) a cheque for mixed office/client money has been paid into client account.

The bookkeeping entries to record a transfer from client to office account are:

(1) the entries to record a payment out of clients' money (see **11.3.4**);

(2) the entries to record a receipt of office money (see **11.3.1**).

EXAMPLE

On 2 September 2006 the firm delivered a bill of costs to its client Green, showing profit costs of £200 and VAT £35. The firm is holding £500 in client account for Green. On 5 September the firm transfers £235 from client to office account.

Green

Date	Details	Office account			Client account		
		DR	CR	Balance	DR	CR	Balance
2006							
	Balance						500 CR
2 Sept	Profit costs	200					
	VAT	35		235 DR			
5 Sept	Cash: transfer		235[2] IN	—	235[1] OUT		265 CR

Cash account

Date	Details	Office account			Client account		
		DR	CR	Balance	DR	CR	Balance
2006							
	Green				500		500 DR
5 Sept	Cash: transfer	235[2] IN		235 DR		235[1] OUT	265 DR

Note:

(1) Payment of client's money.

(2) Receipt of office money.

12.2.2 Transfer from office account to client account

A solicitor must make an immediate transfer from office account to client account if he or she has breached the Solicitors' Accounts Rules 1998 by overdrawing on client account, for example, by drawing against an uncleared cheque which is later dishonoured. (See Rule 7).

The bookkeeping entries to record a transfer of money from office account to client account are as follows:

(1) entries to record a payment of office money (see **11.3.2**);

(2) entries to record a receipt of clients' money (see **11.3.3**).

EXAMPLE

Brown has a credit balance on client account of £50. On 20 October her solicitor inadvertently pays counsel's fee of £70 out of client account. She makes an immediate transfer from office to client account to correct the breach, as she has taken £20 of other clients' money.

Brown

Date	Details	Office account			Client account		
		DR	CR	Balance	DR	CR	Balance
	Balance						50 CR
20 Oct	Cash: counsel				70		20 DR
	Cash: transfer	20[1] OUT		20 DR		20[2] IN	—

Cash account

Date	Details	Office account			Client account		
		DR	CR	Balance	DR	CR	Balance
20 Oct	Balance				50		50 DR
	Cash: counsel: Brown					70	20 CR
	Cash: transfer: Brown OUT		20[1]	20 CR	20[2] IN		—

Note:
(1) Entries to record payment of office money.
(2) Entries to record receipt of clients' money.

12.2.3 Transfers between client accounts, Rule 22(1)(d)

Money is not moved from one bank account to another and therefore NO entries are made in the Cash account.

A transfer can be made from one client ledger account to another client ledger account if:

(a) it is permissible within the rules to withdraw money from the account of client A;

(b) it is permissible within the rules to pay money into the account of client B.

When a transfer is made from one client ledger account to another, a separate record must be made. This may be, for example, in a journal if the ledger system is used, or on a transfer sheet if a card system is used. (Rule 32(2) SAR).

The bookkeeping entries to record transfers between client accounts are as follows:

(a) DEBIT the ledger account of the client from whose account the transfer is being made. (Make a separate record.)

(b) CREDIT the ledger account of the client to whose account the transfer is being made. (Make a separate record.)

EXAMPLE

The firm is holding £10,000 in client account for its client Burns. The firm also acts for Burns's son-in-law, Race, with regard to his house purchase. Burns is making a gift to Race of the deposit of £8,000 and asks the firm to pay Race's deposit on 7 April out of the money held for him.

Burns

Date	Details	Office account			Client account		
		DR	CR	Balance	DR	CR	Balance
	Balance						10,000 CR
7 Apr	Race: Transfer sheet				8,000		2,000 CR

Race

Date	Details	Office account			Client account		
		DR	CR	Balance	DR	CR	Balance
7 Apr	Burns: transfer sheet					8,000	8,000 CR
	Cash: deposit paid				8,000		—

Note: a transfer may be made from the client account of one client to the office account of another or vice versa. For example, if one client has agreed to moneys being taken from his or her client account to discharge another client's liability for costs. If this is done the four entries used to make a transfer from client to office account or vice versa must be shown (see **12.2.1** and **12.2.2**).

EXAMPLE

The firm acts for the executors of Alexander. It also acts for Olivia, Alexander's daughter and the sole beneficiary. There is a balance of £12,000 on Alexander's account. The firm has acted for Olivia in her divorce proceedings and a bill has been delivered to Olivia for £1,000 plus VAT. The executors agree to this being paid out of the estate.

Executors of Alexander deceased

Date	Details	Office account			Client account		
		DR	CR	Balance	DR	CR	Balance
	Balance						12,000 CR
	Cash transfer—Olivia				1,175 OUT(1)		10,825 CR

Olivia: re divorce

Date	Details	Office account			Client account		
		DR	CR	Balance	DR	CR	Balance
	Profit costs	1,000					
	VAT	175		1,175 DR			
	Cash—Alexander		1,175 IN(2)	—			

Cash account

Date	Details	Office account			Client account		
		DR	CR	Balance	DR	CR	Balance
	Balance						12,000 DR
	Alexander— transfer to Olivia	1,175 IN(2)		1,175 DR		1,175 OUT(1)	10,825 DR

Note that the Solicitors' Accounts Rules 1998 restrict inter-client transfers in respect of private loans. Rule 30(2) states that no sum in respect of a private loan shall be paid out of funds held on account of the lender, either:

(a) directly to the borrower; or

(b) by means of a payment from one client account to another or by a paper transfer from the ledger of the lender to that of the borrower

without the prior written authority of **both** clients.

A private loan on standard terms is defined as meaning a loan other than one provided by an institution which provides loans in the normal course of its activities. The solicitor should keep a register of the authorities for transactions of this type.

12.2.4 Mixed office/client money

When a solicitor receives mixed office/client money the alternatives are stated in Rule 20 SAR:

(a) pay the cheque into client account and then make a transfer from client to office account of the office money within 14 days of receipt; or

(b) split the cheque by paying the client's money into client account and the office money into office account.

(c) If the payment consists of office money and client money in the form of unpaid professional disbursements the entire sum may be paid into office account and by the end of the second working day following receipt either the unpaid professional disbursement should be paid or the relevant sum transferred to client account. See Rule 19(1)(b) SAR.

There are also special rules relating to the treatment of monies received from the Legal Services Commission and payment from a third party in respect of legal aid work (see Rule 21).

EXAMPLE

Pink sends a cheque for £250 to his solicitor on 1 March. The cheque represents £200 owed by Pink to a creditor and £50 costs owed to the solicitor in respect of which a bill was delivered to Pink on 1 February.

(a) If the cheque is split the entries in Pink's account will be:

Pink account

Date	Details	Office account			Client account		
		DR	CR	Balance	DR	CR	Balance
1 Mar	Balance Cash: you—split cheque		50	50 DR —		200	200 CR

Cash account

Date	Details	Office account			Client account		
		DR	CR	Balance	DR	CR	Balance
1 Mar	Pink—split cheque	50		50 DR	200		200 DR

(b) If the cheque is not split, the entries in Pink's account will be:

Pink account

Date	Details	Office account			Client account		
		DR	CR	Balance	DR	CR	Balance
	Balance			50 DR			
	Cash: you—mixed money					250	250 CR

The cash account would be debited with £250. When the £50 in respect of costs is transferred to office account, entries will be made in Pink's account and the cash account to record a transfer from client to office account (see **12.2.1**).

12.3 Check list

By the end of this chapter you should be able to:

1. understand when transfers from client to office account are permitted under the SAR and draw up the entries to record a transfer from client to office account on the relevant accounts;
2. understand the limited circumstances when a transfer from office account to client account will be made and draw up the entries to record a transfer from office account to client account on the relevant accounts;
3. understand when transfers can be made between client accounts and that these will not be recorded on the cash account but on the relevant client ledger accounts with a separate record of the transfer and draw up the entries required on the accounts in respect of a transfer between client accounts;
4. understand the options available in respect of the receipt of mixed office and client money and draw up the entries required;
5. complete the self-test exercises at the end of the chapter.

12.4 Exercises on basic ledger entries

In the following questions draw up the clients' ledger accounts to record the transactions.

1. Allow 5 to 10 minutes.
   Pay counsel's fee £188 on behalf of Nigel. Deliver a bill for £120 plus £21 VAT and disbursement. Receive payment from Nigel.
2. Allow 5 to 10 minutes.
   You act for Mary. Pay search fee £10 by cash. Pay for office copy entries by cheque £15. Receive £100 from Mary in respect of disbursements.
3. Allow 10 minutes.
   Lynn pays you £75 on account. Pay £5 out of petty cash on Lynn's behalf for inspection of deeds. Deliver a bill of costs for £100 plus VAT. Receive payment of balance from Lynn and close her account.
4. Allow 5 to 10 minutes.
   Receive £235 from John in respect of an agreed fee for conveyancing work, which includes VAT.
5. Allow 5 to 10 minutes.
   Margaret's account shows a balance in hand of £500. Margaret asks you to transfer £300 to Daphne, another client of the firm.

Allow 5 to 10 minutes each for exercises 6 and 7.

6 Keith asks you to pay a premium of £75 on his behalf to the Star Insurance Co. for whom you act. He pays £75 to you one week later, by agreement.

7 You act for Alan, pay counsel's fee £94 including VAT £14. Deliver a bill of costs to Alan for £120 plus VAT. Receive moneys due from Alan.

8 Allow about 10 minutes.

You act for Carol: 1 September pay counsel's fee £235 including VAT £35; 19 September receive £450 from Carol; 23 September pay disbursement £47 and deliver a bill of costs £120 plus VAT £21. Transfer sum due from client to office account. Pay balance due to Carol.

9 Allow about 10 minutes.

The firm's client, Smith, asks the firm to carry out a number of transactions whilst he is abroad. Smith promises to send a cheque for £800 to cover expenditure. The following events take place with regard to Smith's account.

1 June	Pay £30 to enquiry agent.
4 June	Pay counsel's fee £115.
8 June	Receive Smith's cheque for £600. The cheque is to be split between office and client account.
9 June	Send a bill of costs to Smith for £360 plus £63 VAT. Transfer costs and pay Smith the balance due to him.

Prepare Smith's account to record the above transactions.

10 Allow 20 to 25 minutes.

Your firm is acting for John Brown who is purchasing a house for £90,000. The following events occur:

4 September	Pay search fee £80.
20 September	Receive cheque for £9,000 from client for deposit.
21 September	Contracts exchanged—pay deposit of £9,000 to seller's solicitor.
29 September	Pay search fee £4.
9 October	Deliver a bill for £200 plus VAT.
13 October	Receive a cheque from client for £81,319, the balance of the purchase money and costs.
14 October	Complete purchase—pay £81,000 to seller's solicitors. Transfer amount due to office account.

Prepare the client ledger card for John Brown and the Cash account to record the above transactions.

11 Allow 20 to 30 minutes.

Your firm is acting for the executors of Olive White in the administration of her estate. The following events occur:

5 October	Pay probate fees of £80.
31 October	Receive £1,000 from the Longlife Insurance Company in respect of a policy which the deceased held with them.
	Pay £535 to the executors' bank to repay a loan.
5 November	Receive £2,000 from the deceased's building society account.
6 November	Receive £400 from sale of household contents.
	Pay legacy of £1,500.
10 November	Deliver a bill of costs £240 plus VAT.
11 November	Pay residuary beneficiary £1,003.
	Transfer £362 from client to office account.

Prepare the ledger account for the executors of Olive White and the cash account to record the above.

12.5 Suggested answers to exercises on basic ledger entries

1 Nigel

Date	Details	Office account			Client account		
		DR	CR	Balance	DR	CR	Balance
	Cash: counsel's fee	188		188 DR			
	Profit costs	120					
	VAT	21		329 DR			
	Cash: you		329	—			

The cheque from Nigel must be paid into office account. See Rule 13 Note (xi) (c) (A) and (B).

2 Mary

Date	Details	Office account			Client account		
		DR	CR	Balance	DR	CR	Balance
	Petty cash: search fee	10		10 DR			
	Cash: office copies	15		25 DR			
	Cash: you—split cheque		25	—		75	75 CR

Note that you could pay £100 into client account and then transfer £25 to office account. See Rule 20.

3 Lynn

Date	Details	Office account			Client account		
		DR	CR	Balance	DR	CR	Balance
	Cash: you					75	75 CR
	Petty cash: inspection fee	5		5 DR			
	Profit costs	100					
	VAT	17.50		122.50 DR			
	Cash: you		47.50	75 DR			
	Cash: transfer: profit costs		75	—	75		—

Petty cash must be drawn from office account. The balance due is office money. See Rule 13 Note (xi).

4 John

Date	Details	Office account			Client account		
		DR	CR	Balance	DR	CR	Balance
	Profit costs (agreed fee)	200					
	VAT	35		235 DR			
	Cash: you		235	—			

Note: a bill will be drawn up when the agreed fee is received, as the receipt of the agreed fee is the tax point for VAT, and the agreed fee must be paid into office account. See Rule 13 Note (xi) (D).

5 Margaret

Date	Details	Office account			Client account		
		DR	CR	Balance	DR	CR	Balance
	Balance						500 CR
	Daphne: transfer (transfer sheet)				300		200 CR

Daphne

Date	Details	Office account			Client account		
		DR	CR	Balance	DR	CR	Balance
	Margaret: transfer (transfer sheet)					300	300 CR

See Rule 22(1) (d).

6 Keith

Date	Details	Office account			Client account		
		DR	CR	Balance	DR	CR	Balance
	Cash: transfer premium to Star Insurance Co.	75		75 DR			
	Cash—you		75				

Star Insurance Co.

Date	Details	Office account			Client account		
		DR	CR	Balance	DR	CR	Balance
	Cash—Keith: transfer premium					75	75 CR

The transfer had to be from office account to client account and when Keith pays, this is office money. See Rule 22 Note (xi) (c) (B).

7 Alan

Date	Details	Office account			Client account		
		DR	CR	Balance	DR	CR	Balance
	Cash: counsel's fee	94		94 DR			
	Profit costs	120					
	VAT	21		235 DR			
	Cash—you		235	—			

8 Carol

Date	Details	Office account			Client account		
		DR	CR	Balance	DR	CR	Balance
1 Sept	Cash: counsel's fee	235		235 DR			
19 Sept	Cash—you					450	450 CR
23 Sept	Cash: disbursement				47		403 CR
23 Sept	Profit costs	120					
	VAT	21		376 DR			
	Cash: transfer: profit costs		376	—	376		27 CR
	Cash—you				27		—

For counsel's fee see also 13.4.6.1. The £450 is mixed office/client money. See Rule 20.

9 Smith

Date	Details	Office account			Client account		
		DR	CR	Balance	DR	CR	Balance
1 June	Cash—enquiry agent	30		30 DR			
4 June	Cash—counsel	115		145 DR			
8 June	Cash—you (split cheque)	145	—			455	455 CR
9 June	Profit costs	360		360 DR			
	VAT	63		423 DR			
	Cash: transfer: profit costs		423	—	423		32 CR
	Cash—you				32		—

10 John Brown: matter—conveyancing

Date	Details	Office account			Client account		
		DR	CR	Balance	DR	CR	Balance
4 Sept	Cash: search fee	80		80 DR			
20 Sept	Cash—you					9,000	9,000 CR
21 Sept	Cash: deposit				9,000		—
29 Sept	Cash: search fee	4		84 DR			
9 Oct	Profit costs	200		284 DR			
	VAT	35		319 DR			
13 Oct	Cash—you					81,319	81,319
14 Oct	Cash: completion				81,000		319 CR
	Cash: transfer profit costs		319	—	319		—

Cash account

Date	Details	Office account			Client account		
		DR	CR	Balance	DR	CR	Balance
4 Sept	Brown: search fee		80	80 CR			
20 Sept	Brown				9,000		9,000 DR
21 Sept	Brown: deposit					9,000	—
29 Sept	Brown: search fee		4	84 CR			
13 Oct	Brown				81,319		81,319 DR
14 Oct	Brown: completion					81,000	319 DR
	Brown: transfer profit costs	319		235 DR		319	—

11 Executors of Olive White deceased

Date	Details	Office account			Client account		
		DR	CR	Balance	DR	CR	Balance
5 Oct	Cash: probate fees	80		80 DR			
31 Oct	Cash: Longlife Insurance Co.					1,000	1,000 CR
	Cash: bank loan				535		465 CR
5 Nov	Cash: Building Society					2,000	2,465 CR
6 Nov	Cash: sale of household contents					400	2,865 CR
	Cash: legacy				1,500		1,365 CR
10 Nov	Profit costs	240		320 DR			
	VAT	42		362 DR			
	Cash: residuary Beneficiary				1,003		362 CR
	Cash: transfer profit costs		362	—	362		—

Cash account

Date	Details	Office account			Client account		
		DR	CR	Balance	DR	CR	Balance
5 Oct	Olive White: probate fee		80	80 CR			
31 Oct	Olive White: Longlife Insurance Co.				1,000		1,000 DR
	Olive White: Bank loan					535	465 DR
5 Nov	Olive White: Building Society				2,000		2,465 DR
	Olive White: re household contents				400		2,865 DR
	Olive White: legacy					1,500	1,365 DR
11 Nov	Olive White: legacy					1,003	362 DR
	Olive White: transfer profit costs	362		282 DR		362	—

Value added tax

13.1 Introduction

This chapter contains the following:

1. VAT—a brief overview.
2. Registering for VAT.
3. Accounting to HM Revenue and Customs for VAT, including input tax and output tax.
4. How to deal with disbursements paid on behalf of clients, the agency and principal methods.
5. VAT relief for bad debts.
6. Self-test exercises.

13.2 VAT—a brief overview

Value added tax (VAT) is an indirect tax, charged on goods or services rather than on income/gains. It is charged on supplies of goods or services made in the UK (or Isle of Man) by a taxable person in the course of a business. Some supplies are exempt from VAT. For those that are not exempt there are three rates of tax:

1. the standard rate of 17.5%;
2. the reduced rate of 5% (e.g. for domestic fuel);
3. the zero rate.

Solicitors will charge VAT, where applicable, at the standard rate of 17.5%.

Businesses required to be registered for VAT must account to HM Revenue and Customs (HMRC) for the VAT they charge their clients/customers, less the VAT they pay in the course of their business. The tax charged is known as output tax, being the tax on goods or services going OUT of the business. The tax paid is known as input tax, being the tax paid on goods or services coming IN to the business.

13.3 Registering for VAT

Solicitors whose taxable supplies exceed the VAT threshold set under the Valued Added Tax Act 1994 (currently £61,000) must register for VAT purposes. This threshold is changed from time to time to take account of inflation. In practice most solicitors will register for VAT.

13.4 Accounting to HM Revenue and Customs for VAT

Solicitors will account to HMRC for the balance on the HMRC (VAT) account, which will be:

        Tax charged on services or goods going out of the firm   OUTPUT TAX
Less Tax paid on goods or services coming in to the firm   INPUT TAX
                        Giving   TAX PAYABLE

Tax is normally paid to Customs and Excise quarterly. Within one month of the end of the quarter, a firm must send a completed return form and payment to HMRC. However there are provisions for small and medium sized firms to account yearly.

13.4.1 Tax points

The tax point determines the date on which the solicitor's firm must account to HMRC. Normally VAT becomes payable when a bill of costs is sent to the client, whether the client pays the bill or not. Note that if the firm receives payment in respect of an agreed fee before a bill has been sent, then this becomes the tax point for VAT. The firm will therefore usually record the bill and VAT immediately on receipt of the agreed fee.

13.4.2 Tax invoices

Solicitors must provide a tax invoice to clients who are themselves registered for VAT. In practice solicitors will usually supply invoices to all their clients. For an example of a tax invoice see the end of the example at **13.4.6.2**.

13.4.3 Account used

A VAT (HMRC) account will be required. This must be on OFFICE account, and it is a personal account with HMRC, showing the amount due to (or from) HMRC. The debit column will record all tax paid, the credit column will record all tax charged.

Normally, at the end of each quarter the firm will account to HMRC for the tax charged less the tax paid. Note that VAT is NOT an expense.

EXAMPLE

VAT (HMRC) account   Office account

	DR	CR	Balance
	Tax paid	Tax charged	

When VAT due is paid to HRMC then:

DEBIT HMRC account OFFICE account.
CREDIT Cash Book OFFICE account.

13.4.4 Recording VAT on payments made by the firm (input tax)

When solicitors pay VAT on supplies made to the firm the following entries will be made in the accounts:
CREDIT the Cash account OFFICE account with the net (tax-exclusive) amount and the VAT separately.

DEBIT the relevant real or expense account with the net (tax-exclusive) amount.
DEBIT the HMRC (VAT) account with the VAT paid.

EXAMPLE

The firm buys a computer on 1 March and pays £800 plus VAT £140.

Cash account

Date	Details	Office account		
		DR	CR	Balance
1 Mar	Balance (say)			2,000 DR
	Office computer		800	1,200 DR
	HMRC VAT		140	1,060 DR

Office computer account

Date	Details	Office account		
		DR	CR	Bal
1 Mar	Cash	800		800 DR

HMRC (VAT) account

Date	Details	Office account		
		DR Tax paid	CR tax charged	Bal
1 Mar	Cash	140		140 DR

Note that the debit balance on HMRC will offset any tax charged later.

13.4.5 Recording VAT on billing the client (output tax)

As you have seen in Chapter 11 (**11.5**), when the firm bills the client for work done, then VAT will be charged on the bill. As a reminder, the entries are as follows:

EXAMPLE

On 20 September the firm delivers a bill of costs to their client Farrell in respect of litigation for £800 plus VAT £140.

Farrell: re litigation

Date	Details	Office account			Client account		
		DR	CR	BAL	DR	CR	BAL
20 Sept	Profit costs	800		800 DR			
	VAT HMRC	140		940 DR			

Profit costs account

Date	Details	Office account		
		DR	CR	Balance
20 Sept	Farrell		800	800 CR

HMRC VAT account

Date	Details	Office account		
		DR	CR	Balance
		Input tax Paid	output tax charged	
20 Sept	Farrell		140	140 CR

Note that the credit balance on the HMRC account is the amount due to HMRC in respect of the tax charged, as this is a personal account.

13.4.6 Making payments out on behalf of a client (disbursements)

If a solicitor makes a payment on behalf of a client which includes VAT then how this is treated on the accounts will depend on who the invoice is made out to.

13.4.6.1 Invoice made out to the client (Agency method)

If the invoice is made out to the client, then the solicitor is just making a payment on behalf of the client and is not involved with the VAT. Thus the solicitor will merely make a payment of the TOTAL amount, including the VAT, in the normal way. The VAT (HMRC) account is not used. The solicitor may use office account or client account, if funds are available. This is known as the agency method for VAT. Thus:

DEBIT the client ledger account in the normal way with the TOTAL including VAT.
CREDIT the cash account in the normal way with the TOTAL including VAT.

With this method it is the client who will be able to offset the VAT paid against any VAT charged, if the client is a taxable person.

EXAMPLE

The firm receives an invoice from estate agents addressed to their client Breen, for their fees £6,000 plus VAT £1,050. The firm is holding £10,000 on client account for Breen and pays the amount due from client account.

Client ledger account for Breen

Date	Details	Office account			Client account		
		DR	CR	Bal	DR	CR	Bal
	Balance on account						10,000 CR
	Cash paid estate agents inc. VAT				7,050		2,950 CR

Cash account

Date	Details	Office account			Client account		
		DR	CR	Bal	DR	CR	Bal
	Breen—balance						10,000 DR
	Breen paid estate agents inc. VAT					7,050	2,950 DR

Note that there is an agreement with HMRC that Counsels' fee notes addressed to the firm can be amended and treated as addressed to the client, If so, the payment will be made using the agency method.

13.4.6.2 Invoice made out to the firm (Principal method)

Stage 1

Payment of disbursement

If the invoice is made out to the firm, then the firm's VAT (HMRC) account will be used to record the VAT paid as input tax (see **13.4.4**) above. Because of this the payment must always be made out of OFFICE account. The payment out will be broken down on the Cash Book into two credit entries, showing the net amount and the VAT separately. The corresponding debit entries will show the net amount only on the client ledger account, and the VAT will be shown on the VAT (HMRC) account.

Thus:

On the Cash Book:
CREDIT Net amount paid   Office account.
CREDIT VAT separately   Office account.
On the Client ledger account:
DEBIT Net amount   Office account.
On the Customs and Excise VAT account:
DEBIT the VAT   Office account.

Note from the above that at the time of payment only the NET amount will be shown as debited to the client ledger account, Office account.

EXAMPLE

1 The firm pays an expert a fee of £800 plus VAT £140 on behalf of their client Leith. The invoice from the expert was made out to the firm. The firm are holding £1,000 on general account of costs on client account.

Note that the firm MUST use office account here, as the Principal method is being used and the VAT paid must be recorded on the VAT (HMRC) account.

Cash Account

Date	Details	Office account			Client account		
		DR	CR	Bal	DR	CR	Bal
	Leith balance						1,000 DR
	Leith expert		800	800 CR			
	HMRC VAT		140	940 CR			

Client ledger account for Leith

Date	Details	Office account			Client account		
		DR	CR	Bal	DR	CR	Bal
	Balance on a/c					1,000	1,000 CR
	Cash expert	800		800 DR			
	(Note VAT 140)						

HMRC VAT account

Date	Details	Office account		
		DR Tax paid	CR Tax charged	Bal
	Cash VAT paid	140		140 DR

Billing the client and charging VAT Stage 2

When the client is billed, the firm will then charge the client VAT on the profit costs AND on the disbursement. The client ledger account will therefore record the Profit Costs and then the VAT on both the Profit Costs and the disbursement previously paid.

On the Client ledger account

DEBIT the Profit Costs/bill OFFICE account.
DEBIT the TOTAL VAT on the Profit Costs and the disbursement OFFICE account.

On the Profit Costs account

CREDIT the Profit Costs OFFICE account.

On the HMRC VAT account

CREDIT the TOTAL VAT charged on both the Profit Costs/bill and the disbursement OFFICE account.

Thus on the HMRC account the VAT paid on the disbursement will have been shown in the debit column, and the VAT charged to the client in the credit column. The firm will account to Customs and Excise for the balance. Ultimately it is the client who will bear the total VAT.

Continuing the example

Stage 2 The firm sends a bill to Leith for £400 plus VAT.

Client ledger account for Leith

Date	Details	Office account			Client account		
		DR	CR	Bal	DR	CR	Bal
	Balance on a/c					1,000	1,000 CR
(1)	Cash expert	800		800 DR			
(1)	(Note VAT 140)						
(2)	Profit Costs	400		1,200 DR			
	HMRC						
	VAT (140 + 70)	210		1,410 DR			

HMRC VAT account

Date	Details	Office account		
		DR	CR	Bal
(1)	Cash VAT paid	140		140 DR
(2)	Leith tax charged		210	70 CR

Profit Costs account

Date	Details	Office account		
		DR	CR	Bal
(2)	Leith bill		400	400 CR

Note from the HMRC account that the solicitors have already paid the £140 VAT which is offset against the amount of VAT charged, leaving a balance due to HMRC of £70.

Below is set out an example of the tax invoice to the client in respect of the above transaction.

TAX INVOICE

	Supply	VAT	
Name of client Leith			
Address of client			
VAT number			
(the solicitor's VAT registration number)			
To supply of legal services (Profit costs)	400		
VAT at 17.5%		70	
Taxable disbursement paid by us			
Expert fee	800		
VAT at 17.5% on fee		140	
TOTAL DUE	1,200	210	1,410

13.5 Agency method—summary

(a) The invoice is made out to the client.

(b) OFFICE or CLIENT account may be used.

(c) On payments show the total figure paid, including the VAT. Do not show the VAT separately, as the HMRC VAT account is not used.

13.6 Principal method—summary

(a) The invoice is made out to the firm of solicitors.

(b) OFFICE account must be used.

(c) On the client ledger account show the NET amount paid only. (The VAT paid will be shown on the HMRC VAT account.)

(d) When the bill is sent to the client, debit the profit costs and debit the VAT on the profit costs and on the disbursement previously paid, on the client ledger OFFICE account.

13.7 VAT relief for bad debts

As the HMRC account is credited when the bill is sent to the client, then this sum will have to be accounted for to HMRC. If the client is unable to pay, then the firm may write off the total bad debt including the VAT. This is hard on a business and so VAT relief is available where the debt has not been paid for at least 6 months.

The entries to write off a bad debt where VAT is recoverable are:

CREDIT the client ledger account with the Profit Costs and the VAT written off (shown as separate entries) OFFICE account.

DEBIT the Bad Debts accounts with the profit costs written off OFFICE account.
DEBIT the HMRC VAT account with the VAT OFFICE account.

EXAMPLE VAT RELIEF

The firm delivered a bill to their client Hardy for £200 plus VAT £35. Hardy was then adjudicated bankrupt and the debt was written off.

Hardy

Date	Details	Office account			Client account		
		DR	CR	Bal	DR	CR	Bal
(1)	Profit costs	200		200 DR			
(1)	HMRC VAT	35		235 DR			
(2)	Bad debt written off		200	35 DR			
	HMRC VAT		35	–			

HMRC VAT account

Date	Details	Office account		
		DR	CR	Bal
(1)	Hardy VAT on profit costs		35	35 CR
(2)	Hardy VAT written off	35		–

Profit Costs account

Date	Details	Office account		
		DR	CR	Bal
(1)	Hardy bill		200	200 CR

Bad Debts account

Date	Details	Office account		
		DR	CR	Bal
(2)	Hardy written off	200		200 DR

The above example shows that when the Bad Debt is written off with VAT relief, the firm will only lose the profit costs element, and not the VAT.

13.8 Check list

By the end of this chapter you should be able to:

1. know when a solicitor should register for VAT;
2. understand that a registered firm will account to HMRC for the VAT charged by the firm less the VAT paid by the firm;
3. make the entries required on the accounts in respect of the payment of VAT;
4. understand how a solicitor should deal with disbursements paid on behalf of clients and the difference between the principal method and the agency method in dealing with disbursements;
5. make the entries required on the accounts in respect of the agency method and the principal method in dealing with disbursements;
6. understand when VAT relief is available in respect of bad debts written off;
7. complete the self-test exercises at the end of the chapter.

13.9 Exercises on ledger accounts including VAT

1 Allow 5 to 10 minutes.
You are acting for Lucy Blue. A surveyor has been instructed by Lucy to prepare a report. The surveyor sends a bill addressed to Lucy Blue for £120 plus VAT £21. You are holding £200 on account of costs and disbursements in client account. On 7 November you pay the surveyor's bill. On 1 December you deliver a bill of costs to Lucy for £200 plus VAT.
   Show Lucy Blue's ledger account.

2 Allow 15 to 20 minutes.
You are acting in litigation for your client Jenny Green. You instruct a consulting engineer to prepare a report. The engineer sends you a bill for £200 plus VAT £35 addressed to your firm. You are holding £300 in client account for Jenny Green. On 23 September you pay the engineer's bill. In November the case is concluded and on 21 November you send a bill of costs to Jenny Green of £120 plus VAT.
   Show Jenny Green's ledger account, the cash account, the HMRC account and the Profit Costs account to record the above.

3 Allow around 15 minutes.
You are acting for Lyndon Tree. In the month of October the following events occur:

1 October	Pay enquiry agent's fee £75. The enquiry agent is not registered for VAT.
3 October	Pay surveyor's fee £160 plus £28 VAT. The bill is made out to Lyndon Tree.
4 October	Pay expert's fee £200 plus £35 VAT. The fee note is made out to you.
8 October	Receive a payment on account of costs and disbursements of £600 from Lyndon Tree.
9 October	Deliver a bill of costs to Lyndon Tree of £80 plus VAT. Transfer moneys due to you from client to office account and account to Lyndon Tree for the balance.

Show Lyndon Tree's ledger account to record the above transactions.

13.10 Suggested answers to exercises on ledger accounts including VAT

1 Lucy Blue account

Date	Details	Office account			Client account		
		DR	CR	Balance	DR	CR	Balance
	Balance					200	200 CR
7 Nov	Cash: surveyor				141		59 CR
1 Dec	Profit costs	200					
	VAT	35		235 DR			

The Agency method has been used here, as the invoice was made out to Lucy. The HMRC account will not be used.

2 Jenny Green account

Date	Details	Office account			Client account		
		DR	CR	Balance	DR	CR	Balance
	Balance					300	300 CR
23 Sept	Cash: engineer (VAT £35)	200		200 DR			
21 Nov	Profit costs	120		320 DR			
	VAT (£21 + £35)	56		376 DR			

The Principal method has been used here, as the invoice was made out to the firm. The £300 on the client account cannot be used as the payment must go through office account.

Cash account

Date	Details	Office account			Client account		
		DR	CR	Balance	DR	CR	Balance
23 Sept	Jenny Green: engineer's fee		200	200 CR			
	HMRC (J.G.)		35	235 CR			

HMRC VAT account

Date	Details	Office account		
		DR tax paid	CR tax charged	Balance
23 Sept	Cash—engineer (JG) VAT	35		35 DR
21 Nov	Jenny Green bill VAT		56	21 CR

Profit Costs account

Date	Details	Office account		
		DR	CR	Bal
21 Nov	Jenny Green		120	120 CR

3 **Lyndon Tree account**

Date	Details	Office account			Client account		
		DR	CR	Balance	DR	CR	Balance
1 Oct	Cash: enquiry agent	75		75 DR			
3 Oct	Cash: surveyor's fee	188		263 DR			
4 Oct	Cash: expert (Note: VAT £35)	200		463 DR			
8 Oct	Cash: you					600	600 CR
9 Oct	Profit costs	80					
	VAT (£14 + £35)	49		592 DR			
	Cash: transfer costs		592	—	592		8 CR
	Cash: you				8		—

The Principal method was used on 3 October and the Agency method on 4 October.

14

Financial statements and property transactions

14.1 Introduction

This chapter deals with the following:

1. Financial statements to clients.
2. A summary of the basic financial transactions in respect of a client's sale and purchase of property.
3. Receipt of deposit on exchange of contracts, as agent for the seller or as stakeholder and the entries required on the accounts.
4. Treatment of mortgage advances and mortgage repayment.
5. Completion of a sale and purchase and the financial statement sent to the client.
6. Entries required on the accounts on completion of a sale and purchase.

14.2 Financial statements to clients

Solicitors dealing with receipts of money and payments out on behalf of clients will have to account to the client for such receipts and payments. These will be shown on a financial statement, or statement of account, which will often be sent to the client at the same time as the bill of costs. This is common in, e.g., property transactions, or probate or trust matters. Other examples would be in respect of debt collection for a client, or any matter where funds have been received and held for a client.

Although there is no set form for such statements of account, they must be clear, contain a record of all receipts and payments, be relatively easy for the client to understand and show at the end the amount due to or from the client.

In property transactions it is a good idea to show a clear distinction between receipts and payments regarding the purchase of property, and receipts and payments regarding the sale of property. In probate and trust matters, a clear distinction between capital and interest should be made.

Later in this chapter some examples are given of financial statements in respect of property transactions.

14.3 Property transactions—a summary

Note that where a client is selling one property and buying another, rather than have two ledger cards for the client, one for the sale and one for the purchase, it is usually more convenient to deal with both purchase and sale on one client ledger card, as the proceeds of sale will be used towards the purchase of the new property. A summary of the most common financial transactions found in respect of a client's sale and purchase is set out below. This is a guide only, as obviously these will vary.

(a) Discuss finance with the client, giving details of solicitor's own charges, disbursements, e.g., search fees, stamp duty land tax (SDLT), land registry fees, estate agent's commission. If there is a mortgage on the property to be sold, obtain details of the amount required to pay off the mortgage. If there is a mortgage on the purchase, discover how much will be available, less any costs.

(b) Money may be received from the client on account of costs generally.

(c) Pay any search fees, fees for official copies, etc.

(d) If the client has instructed a surveyor to check the property in respect of the purchase, surveyor's fees may be paid.

(e) Money may be received from the client or a third party, e.g., the bank, to meet the deposit payable on the purchase.

(f) On exchange of contracts, a deposit will be received in respect of the sale. This may be held as stakeholder, when a separate stakeholder client ledger card will be opened—it cannot be used towards the deposit payable regarding the purchase—or it may be held as agent for the seller, when it may be credited direct to the client ledger card and can be used towards the deposit payable regarding the purchase. Note that a solicitor should now account for interest on stakeholder money held, where appropriate. See **Chapter 15** on deposit interest generally.

Payment of a deposit on the purchase will usually be made to the seller's solicitors, either as agent for the seller, or as stakeholder.

(g) Completion statements will be sent in respect of the sale and the purchase, showing how much money will be required on completion, taking account of the deposit already paid, and any other adjustments, e.g., additional amounts in respect of carpets, fittings, etc. Note that these are merely for information—no entries will be made on the accounts until the sale and purchase are completed.

(h) A financial statement will be sent to the client, showing all the receipts and payments out in respect of the sale and purchase, together with the solicitor's bills of costs and the amount that will either be due to the client, or needed from the client to complete. Note that at this stage, as the bills have been sent out, the solicitor's costs and VAT will be debited to the client ledger card. Note that all other disbursements, receipts, etc. are entered only when actually paid or received.

(i) Any mortgage money in respect of the purchase will be received before completion as will any money required from the client, if applicable.

(j) Complete the sale first, receive the net proceeds, i.e., the purchase price less any deposit paid, together with any other adjustments regarding fittings, etc.

If the deposit on the sale was held as stakeholder, then the money should be transferred from the stakeholder account to the client ledger card. This should also be separately recorded on a transfer sheet or journal.

Pay out the amount needed to redeem the mortgage.

Complete the purchase. Ensure that mortgage moneys are available before paying out the amount required to complete the purchase, again less the deposit which has been paid, and take account of any other adjustments needed.

(k) Pay the estate agent's commission on sale if instructed to do so. There should be sufficient money on client account to do this.

(l) Pay stamp duty land tax (SDLT) regarding purchase, again from client account if the money is available. The rates at present are 0–£125,000 nil; over £125,000 to £250,000 1%; over £250,000 to 500,000 3%; and over £500,000 4%.

(m) Pay Land Registry fees, from client account if possible.

(n) Transfer costs and disbursements due to the firm from client account to office account.

(o) Pay any balance to the client.

14.4 Receipt of deposit on exchange of contracts

A solicitor receiving a deposit on behalf of a client may hold the deposit as:

(a) agent; or

(b) stakeholder.

14.4.1 Receipt of deposit as agent

If a solicitor receives a deposit on exchange of contracts which is to be held as agent, it is held on behalf of the client seller. To record the receipt of a deposit as agent, the solicitor will make entries in the accounts to record a receipt of clients' money on behalf of the client seller.

EXAMPLE

The firm acts for White, the seller of Whiteacre, which is being sold for £70,000. On 23 September the firm receives a 10% deposit to hold as agents for the seller.

White: sale of Whiteacre

Date	Details	Office account			Client account		
		DR	CR	Balance	DR	CR	Balance
23 Sept	Cash: purchaser's solicitor, deposit					7,000	7,000 CR

Cash account

Date	Details	Office account			Client account		
		DR	CR	Balance	DR	CR	Balance
23 Sept	White Cash: purchaser's solicitor, deposit				7,000		7,000 DR

14.4.2 Receipt of deposit as stakeholder

When a solicitor receives a deposit as stakeholder, it is not held on deposit for the client seller, or for the buyer, but held between the parties, therefore the receipt of a stakeholder deposit should not be recorded in the client seller's ledger account.

A separate account, the stakeholder account, is opened to record dealings with deposits held by a solicitor as stakeholder. The deposit is held in the stakeholder account until completion, when it belongs to the seller.

The stakeholder account only records dealings with clients' money; the money belongs to the client(s) not the solicitor.

When the firm receives a deposit as stakeholder, the following entries are made:

(a) CREDIT the Stakeholder ledger account, client column.

(b) DEBIT the Cash account client column.

EXAMPLE

Assume that in the example in **14.4.1** the firm receives the 10% deposit as stakeholder.

Stakeholder account

Date	Details	Office account			Client account		
		DR	CR	Balance	DR	CR	Balance
23 Sept	Cash: deposit re White sale of Whiteacre					7,000	7,000 CR

The double entry will be in the Cash account as in the example in **14.4.1**.

On completion of the sale the deposit is transferred from the stakeholder account to the client seller's account. The bookkeeping entries are those to record a transfer from one client ledger account to another.

EXAMPLE

Continuing the example, assume that completion takes place on 24 October.

Stakeholder account

Date	Details	Office account			Client account		
		DR	CR	Balance	DR	CR	Balance
23 Sept	Cash: deposit re White sale of Whiteacre					7,000	7,000 CR
24 Oct	White: transfer sheet				7,000		—

White: re sale of Whiteacre

Date	Details	Office account			Client account		
		DR	CR	Balance	DR	CR	Balance
24 Oct	Stakeholder: transfer sheet					7,000	7,000 CR

14.5 Mortgage advances

14.5.1 Acting for mortgagee and purchaser

Rule 32(6) of the Solicitors' Accounts Rules 1998 provides that a solicitor acting for a borrower and lender on a mortgage advance in a property transaction shall not be required to open separate ledger accounts for the borrower and lender provided that:

(a) the funds belonging to each client are clearly identifiable; and

(b) the lender is an institutional lender which provides mortgages on standard terms in the normal course of its business, for example, a building society or bank.

Thus, if the solicitor is acting for a buyer and a building society provides the mortgage advance, the transactions can all be recorded in the client buyer's ledger account, without the need to open a separate ledger account for the building society.

However if the solicitor is acting for a buyer and a private lender, then separate ledger accounts must be opened for each.

In (a) above, 'clearly identifiable' requires the solicitor to ensure that the buyer's ledger account states unambiguously the nature and owner of the mortgage advance. Care therefore needs to be taken in completing the details entry. For example, if the Branchester Building Society makes an advance of £50,000 to Smith who is purchasing Greenacre, Smith's ledger account should state, when the advance is received:

'Cash: mortgage advance from Branchester Building Society: £50,000.'

Note that the mortgage money credited to the account still belongs to the lender, not the borrower, until completion takes place.

EXAMPLE (INSTITUTIONAL LENDER)

The firm acts for Red who is purchasing Cosy Villa for £150,000. Red has obtained a mortgage advance of £100,000 from the High Finance Building Society for which the firm also acts. Red is providing the balance from his own funds. The firm receives the mortgage advance on 16 October, with the usual instruction that the cheque is not to be negotiated until completion. Red has been informed that he will be required to pay £50,517 prior to completion. He brings a cheque to the office on 17 October. Completion takes place on 18 October and on the same date the firm sends two bills of costs to Red, one for £400 plus VAT for the conveyancing and one for £40 plus VAT for acting on behalf of the building society in respect of the mortgage, which is to be paid by Red. The transactions will be recorded as follows.

Red: re purchase of Cosy Villa

Date	Details	Office account			Client account		
		DR	CR	Balance	DR	CR	Balance
17 Oct	Cash—you					50,517	50,517 CR
18 Oct	Cash: mortgage advance from High Finance Building Society					100,000	150,517 CR
	Cash: seller's solicitor				150,000		517 CR
	Profit costs	400					
	VAT	70		470 DR			
	Profit costs (High Finance Building Society re mortgage)	40					
	VAT	7		517 DR			
	Cash: transfer costs		517	—	517		—

EXAMPLE (PRIVATE LENDER)

In the above example assume that Red is borrowing £100,000 from Uncle Black, for whom the firm also acts. On 16 October Uncle Black pays the firm £100,000 and both give written authority for that money to be transferred and used towards Red's purchase of Cosy Villa. The costs of the mortgage are to be paid by Red. The transactions will be recorded as follows:

Red: re purchase of Cosy Villa

Date	Details	Office account			Client account		
		DR	CR	Balance	DR	CR	Balance
18 Oct	Cash—you					50,517	50,517 CR
	Uncle Black: transfer mortgage advance					100,000	150,517 CR
	Cash: seller's solicitors				150,000		517 CR
	Profit costs	400					
	VAT	70		470 DR			
	Uncle Black: transfer costs	47		517 DR			
	Cash: transfer costs		517	—	517		—

Uncle Black: re mortgage advance

Date	Details	Office account			Client account		
		DR	CR	Balance	DR	CR	Balance
16 Oct	Cash—you					100,000	100,000
18 Oct	Profit costs	40					
	VAT	7		47 DR			
	Red: transfer sheet mortgage advance				100,000		—
	Red: transfer costs		47	—			

Note that Uncle Black is billed first and then the amount payable by Red is transferred.

When this method is used the lender's costs are transferred from the buyer's account to the lender's account by making the following entries:

(a) DEBIT purchaser's ledger card office account with costs and VAT.

(b) CREDIT lender's ledger card office account with costs and VAT.

As an alternative to transferring the gross advance from Uncle Black to Red, the solicitor could have transferred the net advance, after deducting costs, in which case Uncle Black's account would have appeared as follows:

Uncle Black: re mortgage advance

Date	Details	Office account			Client account		
		DR	CR	Balance	DR	CR	Balance
16 Oct	Cash—you					100,000	100,000 CR
18 Oct	Profit costs	40					
	VAT	7		47 DR			
	Red: transfer net advance					99,953	47 CR
	Cash: transfer costs		47	—	47		—

A further alternative is that the solicitors could have paid the net advance to the seller's solicitors out of Uncle Black's account. No entry would be made in Red's account in respect of the payment of the net advance.

14.5.2 Solicitor acting for mortgagee only

The accounting entries when the solicitor acts for the mortgagee only are:

(a) The solicitor opens an account for the mortgagee.

(b) When the mortgage advance is received, the solicitor makes entries in the mortgagee's account to record a receipt of client money.

(c) On completion, the solicitor makes entries in the mortgagee's account to record the delivery of a bill of costs to the mortgagee.

(d) On completion, the solicitor pays the net advance to the purchaser's solicitor and records this in the mortgagee's account as a payment of clients' money.

(e) Following completion, the solicitor transfers the costs from client to office account.

EXAMPLE

The firm acts for the High Finance Building Society which is making a mortgage advance of £100,000 to Red in connection with his purchase of Cosy Villa. Red's solicitors are Bagnets. The firm's costs for acting for the building society are £120 plus £21 VAT. The mortgage advance is received on 16 October and completion takes place on 18 October. Costs are transferred on 18 October.

High Finance Building Society

Date	Details	Office account			Client account		
		DR	CR	Balance	DR	CR	Balance
16 Oct	Cash—you					100,000	100,000 CR
18 Oct	Profit costs	120					
	VAT	21		141 DR			
	Cash: Bagnets				99,859		141 CR
	Cash: transfer: costs			141	—	141	—

14.5.3 Solicitor acting for buyer/borrower only

The accounting entries when the solicitor acts for the buyer/borrower only are:

(a) An account is opened for the buyer. No account is opened for the mortgagee because the mortgagee is not a client.

(b) On completion the firm records the receipt of the net advance as a receipt of client's money, in the buyer's ledger account.

(c) On completion the firm records the payment of the net advance to the seller's solicitor, as a payment of clients' money, in the buyer's ledger account.

(d) Entries are made in the cash account and the buyer's ledger account to record receipt and payment of clients' money, even if the cheque from the mortgagee is endorsed in favour of the seller's solicitor.

EXAMPLE

The firm acts for Red with regard to his purchase of Cosy Villa. Red is obtaining a mortgage advance of £100,000 from the High Finance Building Society. The solicitors acting for the building society have stated that their costs, which are to be paid by Red, will be £120 plus £21 VAT. It has been agreed that these costs will be deducted from the mortgage advance. On completion on 18 October, the building society's cheque for £99,859 is received by the firm and a cheque for that amount is paid to Gallops, the seller's solicitor.

Red

Date	Details	Office account			Client account		
		DR	CR	Balance	DR	CR	Balance
18 Oct	Cash: High Finance					99,859	99,859
	Cash: Gallops				99,859		—

14.6 Mortgage repayment

14.6.1 Usual method

The firm will treat the repayment as a normal payment out of client money, like any other disbursement.

14.6.2 Acting for the seller and a lender

Rule 32(6) of the Solicitors' Accounts Rules 1998 may not apply on redemption of a mortgage. Thus, if the solicitor acts for the seller and a lender, separate accounts will need to be opened for the seller and the lender. NB: this will be uncommon in practice.

(a) *Entries on completion.* When completion takes place the sale proceeds belong to the seller and are shown as a receipt of client's money in the client seller's account.

EXAMPLE

The firm acts for George with regard to the sale of Somehut. Completion takes place on 28 January when £140,000 is received.

George: re sale of Somehut

Date	Details	Office account			Client account		
		DR	CR	Balance	DR	CR	Balance
28 Jan	Cash: sale proceeds					140,000	140,000 CR

(b) *Costs.* The solicitor's costs for acting on the redemption will be recorded in the lender's account, although in practice they will be paid by the seller client.

EXAMPLE

The firm's costs for acting on behalf of Andover Building Society, which has a mortgage on Somehut, of £55,000, and for whom the firm also acts, are £40 plus VAT £7.

Andover Building Society: re mortgage redemption (George)

Date	Details	Office account			Client account		
		DR	CR	Balance	DR	CR	Balance
28 Jan	Profit costs VAT	40 7		 47 DR			

As the redemption costs will be paid by the borrower, a transfer of the costs and VAT will be made from the borrower's account to the lender's account. The transfer will be effected by making the following entries in the accounts.

(i) DEBIT the seller's ledger account office column.

(ii) CREDIT the lender's ledger account office column.

(c) *Redemption*. When the mortgage is redeemed a transfer of the redemption money is made from the seller's account to the lender's account. The payment of the redemption money to the lender is then shown as a payment of client money from the ledger account.

EXAMPLE

The firm's costs for acting for George on the sale of Somehut are £200 plus VAT £35. The redemption figure for the mortgage is £55,000. The mortgage is redeemed and costs transferred on 28 January. On the same date a cheque is sent to George for the balance due to him. The entries in the ledger accounts for George and Andover Building Society will be as follows:

George: re sale of Somehut

Date	Details	Office account			Client account		
		DR	CR	Balance	DR	CR	Balance
28 Jan	Cash: sale proceeds					140,000	140,000 CR
	Andover: transfer mortgage redemption				55,000		85,000 CR
	Profit costs	200					
	VAT	35		235 DR			
	Andover: transfer costs	47		282 DR			
	Cash: transfer costs		282	—		282	84,718 CR
	Cash—you				84,718		—

Andover: re mortgage redemption (George)

Date	Details	Office account			Client account		
		DR	CR	Balance	DR	CR	Balance
28 Jan	Profit costs	40					
	VAT	7		47 DR			
	George: transfer redemption money					55,000	55,000 CR
	George: transfer costs		47	—			
	Cash—you (mortgage redemption)				55,000		—

14.7 Completion

14.7.1 Financial statement

Before completion of a sale or purchase on behalf of a property client, a financial statement will be sent to the client. This will show the amount which the client will have to provide for completion or the balance due to the client following completion. There is no set form of financial statement, but whichever form is used it is essential that the statement should show all moneys received from and on behalf of the client and all payments made on his or her behalf.

The following is a suggested method of presentation of a financial statement when a solicitor is acting for a client selling and buying property simultaneously. Note that firms may use different methods of presentation, all of which are equally valid.

FINANCIAL STATEMENT

TO: A CARTRIGHT
SALE OF 'BLACKACRE' AND PURCHASE OF 'WHITEACRE'

SALE OF 'BLACKACRE'
Sale price		180,000	
LESS Mortgage repayment		40,200	
		139,800	

LESS payments
Estate agents' fees inc. VAT	4,230		
Official copies	10		
Profit Costs on sale inc. VAT	235		
		4,475	
NET SALE PROCEEDS		135,325	

PURCHASE OF 'WHITEACRE'
PURCHASE PRICE		220,000	
LESS mortgage advance		80,000	
		140,000	
LESS paid by you in advance		4,000	
		136,000	

ADD
Payments out
SDLT	2,200		
Land Registry fees	300		
Search fees	160		
Profit costs on purchase inc. VAT	470		
Profit costs on mortgage inc. VAT	94		
		3,224	
Balance due on purchase		139,224	

Amount required to complete purchase	139,224
LESS net amount received on sale	135,325
	3,899

OR (if net sale proceeds are more than amount required on purchase)
Net amount received on sale
LESS amount required to complete purchase.

14.7.2 Exercises on financial statements

1 You act for Virgil who is selling 'Olympus' for £50,000. On 1 April you receive a 10% deposit as stakeholder, 'Olympus' is subject to a mortgage of £15,000. You receive an account from the estate agent for £600 plus VAT £105. Your costs for acting on the sale are £200 plus VAT £35. Prepare a financial statement for Virgil.

2 You act for Samuel who is buying 'The Temple' for £180,000. He is borrowing £140,000 from the building society for whom you also act. Your local search costs £75. You receive a bridging loan of £18,000 from your client's bank for the deposit. You exchange contracts and pay the deposit. You pay bankruptcy search fee £1. Your costs for acting for the building society are £80 plus VAT and these are to be paid by Samuel. Your costs are £400 plus VAT £70, the land registry fee is £90, and stamp duty land tax £1,800. Samuel's bank informs you that the interest on the bridging loan is £75. Prepare a financial statement for Samuel.

3 Black and Co. solicitors acted for Hall in respect of the purchase of a house, 10 Arden Way for £100,000 and the sale of her existing house, 25 James Street for £80,000. The mortgage repayment on 25 James Street was £40,000, and a new mortgage was taken out on 10 Arden Way for £60,000. Black and Co. paid the following disbursements, local search fee £100, estate agents' charges on the sale £1,200 plus VAT, search fee £10, land registry fee of £200. Their profit costs on the sale were £200 plus VAT, on the purchase £400 plus VAT and on the mortgage £80 plus VAT.

Draw up a financial statement for Hall, showing the amount required from her on completion.

14.7.3 Answers to exercises on financial statements

1. FINANCIAL STATEMENT DATE

TO: VIRGIL
SALE OF 'OLYMPUS'

Sale price		50,000
LESS mortgage repayments		15,000
		35,000
LESS payments		
Estate agents' fees inc. VAT	705	
Profit Costs on sale inc. VAT	235	
		940
NET SALE PROCEEDS		34,060

2. FINANCIAL STATEMENT DATE

TO: SAMUEL
PURCHASE OF THE TEMPLE

PURCHASE PRICE		180,000
LESS mortgage advance		140,000
		40,000
ADD		
Payments out		
SDLT	1,800	
Land Registry fees	90	
Search fees (75 +1)	76	
Bank loan interest	75	
Profit costs on purchase inc. VAT	470	
Profit costs on mortgage inc. VAT	94	
		2,605
Balance due on purchase		42,605

3 FINANCIAL STATEMENT DATE

TO: HALL

SALE OF 25 JAMES STREET AND PURCHASE OF 10 ARDEN WAY

SALE OF 25 JAMES STREET

Sale price		80,000
LESS mortgage repayment		40,000
		40,000
LESS payments		
Estate agents' fees inc. VAT	1,410	
Profit Costs on sale inc. VAT	235	
		1,645
NET SALE PROCEEDS		38,355

PURCHASE OF 10 ARDEN WAY

PURCHASE PRICE		100,000	
LESS mortgage advance		60,000	
		40,000	
ADD			
Payments out			
Land Registry fees	200		
Search fee	10		
Local search fee	100		
Profit costs on purchase inc. VAT	470		
Profit costs on mortgage inc. VAT	94		
		874	
Balance due on purchase		40,874	
Amount required to complete purchase			40,874
LESS net amount received on sale			38,355
Balance due from you			2,519

14.7.4 Sale completions

The solicitor's accounts must reflect all the transactions involved in completing the sale of a property on the client's behalf. The following entries will usually have to be made on the completion of a sale:

(a) Entries to record the delivery of a bill of costs to the client for acting on the client's behalf with regard to the sale.

EXAMPLE

The firm acts for Ali with regard to the sale of 'Church Cottage' at a price of £60,000. On 3 May a bill of costs is delivered to Ali in the sum of £200 plus £35 VAT. Ali's account will appear as follows:

Ali

Date	Details	Office account			Client account		
		DR	CR	Balance	DR	CR	Balance
3 May	Profit costs	200					
	VAT	35		235 DR			

(b) Entries to record the receipt of the sale proceeds from the purchaser's solicitor (i.e., entries to record a receipt of clients' money).

Continuing the example:

Completion of Ali's sale takes place on 3 May. The firm receives a bank draft for £54,000. A deposit of £6,000 was paid to the firm as stakeholders on 3 April. Ali's account will appear as follows:

Ali

Date	Details	Office account			Client account		
		DR	CR	Balance	DR	CR	Balance
3 May	Profit costs	200					
	VAT	35		235 DR			
	Cash: purchaser's solicitor on completion					54,000	54,000 CR

(c) Entries to record the transfer of the deposit from stakeholder account to the client's ledger account if the deposit was paid to the seller's solicitor as stakeholder on exchange of contracts.

Continuing the example:

Stakeholder account

Date	Details	Office account			Client account		
		DR	CR	Balance	DR	CR	Balance
3 Apr	Cash: deposit re Ali					6,000	6,000 CR
3 May	Ali: transfer sheet				6,000		

Ali

Date	Details	Office account			Client account		
		DR	CR	Balance	DR	CR	Balance
May 3	Profit costs	200					
	VAT	35		235 DR			
	Cash: purchaser's solicitor on completion					54,000	54,000 CR
	Stakeholder: transfer sheet					6,000	60,000 CR

(d) Entries to record the redemption of a mortgage.

Continuing the example:

Assume that there is a mortgage to the Timberwell Building Society on 'Church Cottage'. The mortgage of £18,000 is redeemed on 4 May. Ali's account would appear as follows:

Ali

Date	Details	Office account			Client account		
		DR	CR	Balance	DR	CR	Balance
May 3	Profit costs	200					
	VAT	35		235 DR			
	Cash: purchaser's solicitor					54,000	54,000 CR
	Stakeholder: transfer sheet					6,000	60,000 CR
May 4	Cash: Timberwell Building Society				18,000		42,000 CR

(e) Entries to record the payment of any outstanding disbursements, e.g., estate agent's fees.

Continuing the example:

Assume that on 6 May the firm pays an estate agent's charges of £705. Ali's account would appear as follows:

Ali

Date	Details	Office account			Client account		
		DR	CR	Balance	DR	CR	Balance
May 3	Profit costs	200					
	VAT	35		235 DR			
	Cash: purchaser's solicitor					54,000	54,000 CR
	Stakeholder: transfer sheet					6,000	60,000 CR
May 4	Cash: Timberwell Building Society: redemption				18,000		42,000 CR
May 6	Cash: estate agent				705		41,295 CR

(f) Entries to record the transfer of costs from client to office account and to record the payment to the client of any balance owed.

Continuing the example:

Assume that on 6 May costs are transferred and the balance remaining in client account is paid to Ali.

Ali's account will appear as follows:

Ali

Date	Details	Office account			Client account		
		DR	CR	Balance	DR	CR	Balance
3 May	Profit costs	200					
	VAT	35		235 DR			
	Cash: purchaser's solicitor					54,000	54,000 CR
	Stakeholder: transfer sheet					6,000	60,000 CR
4 May	Cash: Timberwell Building Society: redemption				18,000		42,000 CR
6 May	Cash: estate agent				705		41,295 CR
	Cash: transfer: costs		235	—	235		41,060 CR
	Cash—you				41,060		—

14.7.5 Purchase completions

The solicitor's accounts must reflect all the transactions involved in completing the purchase of a property on the client's behalf. The following entries will usually have to be made on the completion of a purchase.

(a) Entries to record the delivery of a bill of costs to the client for acting with regard to the purchase.

EXAMPLE

The firm acts for Alfred with regard to the purchase of 'Costa Blanca' at a price of £95,000. On 3 May a bill of costs is delivered to Alfred in the sum of £320 plus VAT £56. The firm also acted for the mortgagee, Tall Trees Building Society, and its costs are £80 plus VAT £14. Alfred's account will appear as follows:

Alfred

Date	Details	Office account			Client account		
		DR	CR	Balance	DR	CR	Balance
200—							
3 May	Profit costs	320					
	VAT	56		376 DR			
	Profit costs: Building Society	80					
	VAT	14		470 DR			

(b) Entries to record the receipt of the balance of the purchase money from the client, if required, as shown on the financial statement.

Continuing the example:

A financial statement has been delivered to Alfred, showing a balance due from him on completion of £6,070. On 3 May Alfred pays the sum of £6,070 to the firm. Alfred's account will appear as follows:

Alfred

Date	Details	Office account			Client account		
		DR	CR	Balance	DR	CR	Balance
200—							
3 May	Profit costs	320					
	VAT	56		376 DR			
	Profit costs: Building Society	80					
	VAT	14		470 DR			
	Cash—you					6,070	6,070 CR

(c) Entries to record the receipt of the mortgage advance from the building society. Note: if the mortgage was from a private lender for whom the firm was acting, a separate ledger account would be opened for the lender and the mortgage advance would be shown as a transfer from the lender's account.

Continuing the example:

Alfred has obtained a mortgage advance of £80,000 from the Tall Trees Building Society for whom the firm also acts.

Alfred

Date	Details	Office account			Client account		
		DR	CR	Balance	DR	CR	Balance
3 May	Profit costs	320					
	VAT	56		376 DR			
	Profit costs: Building Society	80				6,070	6,070 CR
	VAT	14		470 DR			
	Cash: Tall Trees Building Society, mortgage advance					80,000	86,070 CR

(d) Entries to record the payment of the balance of the purchase moneys to the seller's solicitors.

Continuing the example:

Completion takes place on 3 May. On 3 April a 10% deposit of £9,500 had been paid to the seller's solicitors, Redhen and Co. The balance payable to Redhen and Co. on completion is £85,500. Alfred's account would appear as follows:

Alfred

Date	Details	Office account			Client account		
		DR	CR	Balance	DR	CR	Balance
3 May	Profit costs	320					
	VAT	56		376 DR			
	Profit costs: Building Society	80					
	VAT	14		470 DR			
	Cash—you					6,070	6,070
	Cash: Tall Trees Building Society, mortgage advance					80,000	86,070 CR
	Cash: Redhen & Co.				85,500		570 CR

(e) Entries to record the payment of any disbursements after completion, e.g., SDLT or Land Registry fees.

Continuing the example:

On 5 May the firm pays Land Registry fees of £100. Alfred's account will appear as follows:

Alfred

Date	Details	Office account			Client account		
		DR	CR	Balance	DR	CR	Balance
3 May	Profit costs	320					
	VAT	56		376 DR			
	Profit costs: Building Society	80					
	VAT	14		470 DR			
	Cash—you					6,070	6,070 CR
	Cash: Tall Trees Building Society, mortgage advance					80,000	86,070 CR
	Cash: Redhen & Co.				85,500		570 CR
5 May	Cash: Land Registry fees				100		470 CR

(f) Entries to record the transfer of costs from client to office account.

Continuing the example:

Costs are transferred to office account on 7 May. Alfred's account will appear as follows:

Alfred

Date	Details	Office account			Client account		
		DR	CR	Balance	DR	CR	Balance
3 May	Profit costs	320		376 DR			
	VAT	56					
	Profit costs: Building Society	80					
	VAT	14		470 DR			
	Cash—you					6,070	6,070 CR
	Cash: Tall Trees Building Society, mortgage advance					80,000	86,070 CR
	Cash: Redhen & Co.				85,500		570 CR
5 May	Cash: Land Registry fees				100		470 CR
7 May	Cash: transfer: costs		470	—	470		—

14.7.6 Simultaneous sale and purchase

When acting for a client with regard to a simultaneous sale and purchase, entries will be made in the accounts as in **14.7.4** and **14.7.5**.

14.7.6.1 Example

Swift & Co., solicitors, acted for Gulliver in the purchase of 'Lilliput' for £350,000 and sale of 'Lagado' for £300,000 and for the Academy Building Society in respect of an advance. The following events took place.

200—

2 September	Paid search fees of £65 in respect of the purchase of 'Lilliput' by Gulliver.
9 September	Paid survey fee of £940 including VAT in respect of the purchase of 'Lilliput'.
10 September	The Academy Building Society instructed the firm to act in respect of an advance of £125,000.
15 September	Received from Yahoo Limited a cheque for £35,000, being a bridging loan in respect of 'Lilliput'.
17 September	Exchanged contracts for the sale of Gulliver's house, 'Lagado', the deposit of 10% (£30,000) having been paid to the estate agent by the buyer. On the same day contracts were exchanged for the purchase of 'Lilliput' and the deposit of £35,000 was paid to the seller's solicitor to hold as stakeholder.
24 September	Received completion statement from the seller's solicitor in respect of 'Lilliput', showing £315,000 due on completion.
27 September	Sent completion statement to the solicitors acting for the buyer of 'Lagado', showing the balance due of £270,000.

2 October		Received cheque for £125,000 from the building society. The profit costs to be charged regarding the advance are £120 plus VAT.
5 October		Sent financial statement to Gulliver showing the balance of money required from him on completion of the sale and purchase, together with bills of costs in respect of the sale, purchase and mortgage advance. The statement includes, amongst other items, the following information:
	Solicitor's costs on sale	£400 plus VAT
	Solicitor's costs on purchase	£600 plus VAT
	Estate agent's commission inc VAT	£7,050
	Stamp duty land tax	£10,500
	Land Registry fees	£250
	Amount to redeem mortgage	£60,500
7 October		Cheque received from Gulliver, being the balance of purchase money and payment of costs.
12 October		Completed the sale and purchase. The amount due to redeem the mortgage is paid the same day. A cheque for £22,950 is received from the estate agents, being the deposit less their charges.
14 October		The bridging loan of £35,000 is paid to Yahoo Limited. Gulliver has paid the interest due on the loan direct to Yahoo Limited.
15 October		Paid stamp duty land tax.
25 October		Paid Land Registry fees. Transferred costs and disbursements from client account to office account.

Draw up the ledger account of Gulliver, showing all entries necessary to deal with the above events, and prepare a financial statement, suitable for presentation to Gulliver on 5 October 200—, showing the balance due from him on completion.

FINANCIAL STATEMENT 5 OCTOBER 200—

TO: GULLIVER

SALE OF 'LAGADO' AND PURCHASE OF 'LILLIPUT'

SALE OF 'LAGADO'

Sale price		300,000
LESS mortgage repayment		60,500
		239,500
LESS payments		
Estate agents' fees inc. VAT	7,050	
Profit costs on sale inc. VAT	470	
		7,520
NET SALE PROCEEDS		231,980

PURCHASE OF 'LILLIPUT'

PURCHASE PRICE		350,000
LESS mortgage advance		125,000
		225,000

ADD

Payments out

Survey fee	940	
Search fees	65	
Stamp duty land tax	10,500	
Land registry fees	250	
Profit costs on purchase inc. VAT	705	
Profit costs on mortgage inc. VAT	141	
		12,601
Balance due on purchase		237,601

Amount required to complete purchase	237,601
LESS net amount received on sale	231,980
Balance due from you	5,621

Gulliver

Sale of 'Lagado'; purchase of 'Lilliput'

Date	Details	Office account			Client account		
		DR	CR	Balance	DR	CR	Balance
200—							
2 Sept	Cash search fee	65		65 DR			
9 Sept	Cash survey fee	940		1,005 DR			
15 Sept	Cash: Yahoo Ltd re deposit					35,000	35,000 CR
17 Sept	Cash: deposit on purchase				35,000		—
2 Oct	Cash: mortgage advance Academy Building Society					125,000	125,000 CR
5 Oct	Costs on sale	400					
	VAT	70		1,475 DR			
	Costs on purchase	600					
	VAT	105		2,180 DR			
	Costs re advance	120					
	VAT	21		2,321 DR			
7 Oct	Cash—you to complete					5,621	130,621 CR
12 Oct	Cash balance proceeds sale					270,000	400,621 CR
	Cash: estate agent's deposit on sale less their commission					22,950	423,571 CR
	Cash: re purchase				315,000		108,571 CR
	Transfer re redemption				60,500		48,071 CR
14 Oct	Cash: bridging loan				35,000		13,071 CR
15 Oct	Cash: stamp duty land tax				10,500		2,571 CR
25 Oct	Cash: Land Registry fee				250		2,321 CR
	Cash: transfer costs and disbursements		2,321	—	2,321		—

14.8 Check list

By the end of this chapter you should be able to:

1. appreciate that a financial statement to the client should be clear, containing a full record of all receipts and payments;
2. understand the basic financial steps in a property transaction;
3. understand the difference between the receipt of a deposit as agent for the seller and as stakeholder and make the relevant entries on the accounts;
4. note the special requirements where a firm records the receipt of a mortgage advance on the borrower's/purchaser's account and make the relevant entries on the accounts;
5. make the entries required for a mortgage advance if acting for both a private lender and a borrower;
6. make the entries required for a mortgage advance if acting for the lender only, or if acting for the borrower only;
7. make the entries required for repayment of a mortgage;
8. draw up a financial statement to be sent to a client before completion of a sale and purchase;
9. make all entries required in respect of the sale and purchase of properties on behalf of a client;
10. complete the self-test exercises at the end of the chapter.

14.9 Exercises on property transactions

1 Allow 5 to 10 minutes.

Kumar and Co. act for Deakin in respect of the sale of his property, 1, Langdale Close for £180,000, and the purchase of 23, Harwood Grove, for £250,000. On 2 April the firm receives a cheque for £25,000 from Deakin for the deposit on the purchase.

On 10 April the firm exchanges contracts on the sale and purchase, receiving the 10% on the sale as stakeholder and paying the 10% deposit on the purchase. Show the entries on the client ledger account for Deakin.

Show the entries on the client ledger account for Deakin.

2 Allow around 10 minutes.

Your firm acts for Sinclair in respect of the sale of 2, Athens Avenue for £300,000 and the purchase of 1, Beech Park for £400,000. The firm has exchanged contracts on the sale and purchase. Sinclair paid the 10% deposit on the purchase and the firm received the 10% deposit on the sale as stakeholder. Show the entries required on Sinclair's client ledger account in respect of the following transactions:

1 March   The firm receives a mortgage for £150,000 from Wakefield Building Society

3 March   The firm completes the sale of 2, Athens Avenue, transferring the amount due from stakeholder account and receiving the balance of the sale proceeds. It also completes the purchase of 1, Beech Park, paying the balance of the purchase price. It redeems the mortgage on 2, Athens Avenue by paying £35,625.

3 Allow about 15 minutes.

Farrell and Co. acted for Keeble in the sale of his house 'Rosewood' for £50,000 and for the Burnley Building Society who were owed approximately £15,000 by way of mortgage on the house. The following events took place:

200—

8 May	Received cheque for £45,000 from the buyer's solicitors, being the balance of purchase moneys. The amount required to redeem the mortgage including interest is £15,325. The amount due to the building society is paid by cheque.
9 May	Mann and Co., estate agents, acting for Keeble, send a cheque for £3,590, being the deposit less their commission of £1,200 plus VAT £210.
10 May	Sent cheque for £594 including VAT to Oliver in respect of pre-sale repairs to the property.
13 May	Bill of costs sent to Keeble for £240 plus VAT.
15 May	Costs and disbursements are transferred to office account and the balance due to Keeble is paid to him.

Write up the client's ledger account for Keeble, showing all necessary entries to record the above transactions. VAT is to be calculated at 17.5%.

(Law Society Examination, revised.)

4 Allow about 30 minutes.

Your firm acts for Andrew Arbuthnot who is purchasing 'Holywell House' for £60,000 with a private mortgage of £30,000 from Lancelot Lake, for whom the firm also acts. The following events take place:

2003

2 December	Pay search fee £18.
16 December	Receive cheque for £6,000 from Andrew for the deposit.
17 December	Contracts exchanged. Paid £6,000 to the seller's solicitors.
20 December	Receive completion statement from seller's solicitors showing £54,000 payable on completion.
31 December	Send statement to Andrew showing amount required for completion including:
	Costs on sale: £120 plus VAT
	Costs on mortgage: £40 plus VAT
	Search fee: £18 already paid
	Bill of costs also sent.

2004

12 January	Receive mortgage advance and Andrew's cheque for the balance of the completion money.
15 January	Complete the purchase.
16 January	Transfer costs and disbursements to office account.

Prepare the ledger accounts for Andrew and Lancelot Lake and the cash account, together with the financial statement sent to Andrew on 31 December.

5 Allow about 1 hour.

Guppy and Jobling, solicitors, acted for Smallweed in respect of the purchase of a house 'The Badgers' and the sale of his existing house 'Chesney'. 'The Badgers' was being purchased for £180,000 and 'Chesney' was to be sold for £140,000.

200—

8 May	Paid local search fees of £50.
14 May	Instructions received from the Dedlock Building Society to act in connection with the advance to Smallweed of £28,000 regarding 'The Badgers'.
20 May	Received £18,000 from Smallweed, being the deposit on 'The Badgers'.
25 May	Exchanged contracts for the sale of 'Chesney' and received 10% deposit as stakeholder. Also exchanged contracts for purchase of 'The Badgers' and paid 10% deposit to the seller as stakeholder.
10 June	Seller's solicitors sent completion statement showing the balance of purchase money due, being the purchase price less the deposit paid.
15 June	Sent financial statement to Smallweed, showing the amount due from him on completion, together with bills of costs in respect of the sale and the purchase. Costs on sale were £280 plus VAT, costs on the purchase were £360 plus VAT, costs in respect of the mortgage advance were £80 plus VAT.
23 June	Smallweed sent a cheque for the amount shown as due on the financial statement.
24 June	Paid petty cash search fees of £10.
25 June	Received advance cheque from the Dedlock Building Society.
27 June	Completed the sale and purchase of the properties.
30 June	Paid the estate agent's charges, being £2,800 plus VAT. Paid stamp duty land tax of £1,800.
10 July	Paid Land Registry fees of £400. Transferred costs and disbursements from client account to office account.

Draw up the financial statement for Smallweed and the client ledger card.

6 Allow about 1 hour.

Team Players & Co act for Mr and Mrs Plum in respect of the sale of their property 8, Pleasant Avenue for £450,000 and the purchase of 'Top Hole' for £600,000. There is a mortgage of approximately £100,000 on 8, Pleasant Avenue, due to the Trusty Building Society.

The High Flyers Bank Limited has agreed to advance £200,000 in respect of the new purchase. The bank will also assist with bridging finance in respect of the deposit due on the purchase. The balance required for the purchase will come from a bonus that Mr Plum is expecting.

200—

1 June	Local land charge search fee £100 paid.
9 June	Bridging loan in respect of the balance required for the deposit on the purchase is received in the sum of £15,000.
14 June	Contracts are exchanged in respect of the sale of 8 Pleasant Avenue the deposit of £45,000 being received as agents for the sellers. Contracts are also exchanged in respect of the purchase of Top Hole and a cheque for £60,000 is forwarded to the solicitors for the sellers who are holding as stakeholders.
20 June	A completion statement is sent to the buyers solicitors in respect of the sale of 8, Pleasant Avenue showing the balance due of £405,000 and a sum of £10,000 in respect of carpets, curtains and furnishings.

Financial statements and property transactions 229

	The solicitors acting for the seller of Top Hole confirm that the balance due on the purchase will be £540,000.
21 June	An invoice is received from the estate agents acting for Mr and Mrs Plum showing the commission due to them of £9,000 plus VAT.
24 June	The firm sends bills of costs in respect of the sale and purchase to Mr and Mrs Plum. Profit costs on the purchase are £1,200 plus VAT, profit costs on the sale are £800 plus VAT. Profit costs in respect of the mortgage advance amount to £200 plus VAT.
25 June	Mr Plum sends a a cheque to cover the balance required on purchase and all costs and disbursements. The High Flyers Bank Ltd send a draft for £200,000 in respect of the mortgage advance.
4 July	Completed sale of 8, Pleasant Avenue and purchase of Top Hole. The bridging loan is repaid to the bank, together with interest of £140. The mortgage on 8, Pleasant Avenue is redeemed in the sum of £99,500. Costs and disbursements due are transferred from client account to office account.
	Stamp duty land tax of £24,000 is paid.
10 July	Paid the estate agent's commission plus VAT. Paid the Land Registry fees of £300.

Draw up a financial statement showing the amount required from Mr and Mrs Plum to complete the transactions, and show the account of Mr and Mrs Plum.

7 Allow up to 1 hour 20 minutes.
You act for Dinah Dobbs in the sale of 'Green Trees' and the purchase of 'Red Roofs'. The sale price of 'Green Trees' is £40,000 and the purchase price of 'Red Roofs' is £80,000. She is purchasing 'Red Roofs' with a mortgage of £55,000 from the Lendalot Building Society. 'Green Trees' is mortgaged to a private lender, her nephew Charles. You have also received instructions from the Lendalot Building Society and Charles. The following events occur:

200—

2 August	Pay search fee £18 out of petty cash.
5 August	Receive instructions from the Lendalot Building Society in connection with the mortgage.
16 August	A bridging loan is obtained from the Mid-West Bank for £8,000 and that sum is transferred by the bank into Dinah's client account.
19 August	Exchange contracts. Receive deposit of £4,000 on 'Green Trees' as stake-holder. Pay £8,000 deposit on 'Red Roofs'.
23 August	Receive invoice from Sellalot estate agents for their commission, £400 plus VAT. The invoice is addressed to Dinah. Receive completion statement from seller's solicitors showing amount due to complete purchase of 'Red Roofs'.
30 August	Send completion statement of purchaser's solicitors showing balance of £36,000 due on completion of sale of 'Green Trees'.
2 September	Charles informs you that the amount required to redeem the mortgage on 'Green Trees' will be £10,425. Your costs will be £40 plus VAT, payable by Dinah. You ascertain from the Mid-West Bank that the interest on the bridging loan is £83.

4 September	Send a financial statement together with bills of costs to Dinah showing: costs on sale £120 plus VAT, on the purchase £400 plus VAT and on the mortgage advance £60 plus VAT; Land Registry fee £175.
12 September	Receive mortgage advance, held to order until 16 September.
16 September	Complete sale and purchase. Send cheques to Charles to redeem mortgage and to the Mid-West Bank to pay the bridging loan and interest.
17 September	Pay land registry fees and estate agent's commission. Send balance due to Dinah and transfer costs and disbursements.

Prepare the financial statement sent to Dinah on 4 September and make the necessary entries in Dinah's ledger account, Charles's ledger account and the cash account to record the above transactions. VAT is assumed to be 17.5%.

14.10 Suggested answers to exercises on property transactions

1 Deakin – sale of 1, Langdale Close; purchase of 23, Harwood Grove

Date	Details	Office account			Client account		
		DR	CR	Bal	DR	CR	Bal
2 Apr	Cash—you deposit					25,000	25,000 CR
10 Apr	Cash—deposit on purchase				25,000		—

Note that the £18,000 deposit paid as stakeholder will be credited to the stakeholder account, not Deakin's account, and then it will be transferred back to Deakin's account on completion of the sale.

2 Sinclair – sale of 2, Athens Avenue; purchase of 1, Beech Park

Date	Details	Office account			Client account		
		DR	CR	Bal	DR	CR	Bal
1 Mar	Cash—mortgage Advance Wakefield Building Society					150,000	150,000 CR
3 Mar	Transfer sheet—stakeholder deposit					30,000	180,000 CR
	Cash—balance sale proceeds					270,000	450,000 CR
	Cash—balance purchase monies				360,000		90,000 CR
	Cash—repay mortgage				35,625		54,375 CR

3 Farrell and Co.
Keeble: re sale of 'Rosewood'

Date	Details	Office account			Client account		
		DR	CR	Balance	DR	CR	Balance
200—							
8 May	Cash: sale proceeds					45,000	45,000 CR
	Cash: Burnley Building Society: mortgage redemption				15,325		29,675 CR
9 May	Cash: Mann & Co. (less commission £1,410)					3,590	33,265 CR
10 May	Cash: I. Oliver				594		32,671 CR
13 May	Profit costs	240					
	VAT	42		282 DR			
15 May	Cash: transfer: costs		282	—	282		32,389 CR
	Cash—you				32,389		—

FINANCIAL STATEMENT

TO: ANDREW ARBUTHNOT

PURCHASE OF HOLYWELL HOUSE

PURCHASE PRICE		60,000
LESS mortgage advance		30,000
		30,000
LESS deposit paid by you		6,000
		24,000
ADD		
Payments out		
Profit costs on purchase inc VAT	141	
Profit costs on mortgage inc VAT	47	
Search fees	18	
		206
Balance due on purchase		24,206

4 Client: Andrew Arbuthnot
Matter: purchase of 'Holywell House'

Date	Details	Office account			Client account		
		DR	CR	Balance	DR	CR	Balance
2003							
2 Dec	Cash: search fee	18		18 DR			
16 Dec	Cash—you					6,000	6,000 CR
17 Dec	Cash: deposit				6,000		—
	Profit costs (purchase)	120					
	VAT	21		159 DR			
2004							
12 Jan	Cash—you					24,206	24,206 CR
15 Jan	Lancelot Lake transfer advance					30,000	54,206 CR
	Cash: completion				54,000		206 CR
	Lancelot Lake transfer costs	47		206 DR			
	Cash: transfer costs		206	—		206	—

Lancelot Lake

Date	Details	Office account			Client account		
		DR	CR	Balance	DR	CR	Balance
2003							
31 Dec	Profit costs	40					
	VAT	7		47 DR			
2004							
12 Jan	Cash—you					30,000	30,000 CR
15 Jan	Arbuthnot transfer sheet				30,000		
	Arbuthnot: transfer costs		47	—			—

Cash account

Date	Details	Office account			Client account		
		DR	CR	Balance	DR	CR	Balance
200—							
2 Dec	Arbuthnot: search fee		18	18 CR			
16 Dec	Arbuthnot				6,000		6,000 DR
17 Dec	Arbuthnot: deposit					6,000	—
200—							
12 Jan	Lancelot Lake mortgage advance				30,000		30,000 DR
	Arbuthnot				24,206		54,206 DR
15 Jan	Arbuthnot: completion					54,000	206 DR
16 Jan	Arbuthnot: transfer: costs	206		188 DR		206	—

5 Guppy and Jobling

FINANCIAL STATEMENT DATE

TO: SMALLWEED

SALE OF CHESNEY AND PURCHASE OF THE BADGERS

SALE OF CHESNEY

Sale price		140,000
LESS payments		
Estate agents' fees inc. VAT	3,290	
Profit costs on sale inc. VAT	329	
		3,619
NET SALE PROCEEDS		136,381

PURCHASE OF THE BADGERS

PURCHASE PRICE		180,000	
LESS mortgage advance		28,000	
		152,000	
LESS paid by you in advance		18,000	
		134,000	
ADD			
Payments out			
SDLT	1,800		
Land Registry fees	400		
Search fees	60		
Profit costs on purchase inc VAT	423		
Profit costs on mortgage inc VAT	94		
		2,777	
Balance due on purchase		136,777	
Amount required to complete purchase			136,777
LESS net amount received on sale			136,381
			396

Smallweed: re sale of 'Chesney' and purchase of 'The Badgers'

Date	Details	Office account			Client account		
		DR	CR	Balance	DR	CR	Balance
200—							
8 May	Cash: local search fee	50		50 DR			
20 May	Cash—you re deposit					18,000	18,000 CR
25 May	Cash: deposit on sale				18,000		—
15 June	Profit costs on sale	280		330 DR			
	VAT	49		379 DR			
	Profit costs on purchase	360		739 DR			
	VAT	63		802 DR			
	Profit costs re advance	80		882 DR			
	VAT	14		896 DR			
23 June	Cash—you to complete					396	396 CR
24 June	Petty cash search fees	10		906 DR			
25 June	Cash: mortgage advance Dedlock Building Society					28,000	28,396 CR
27 June	Cash: sale proceeds					126,000	154,396 CR
	Transfer stakeholder Transfer sheet					14,000	168,396 CR
	Cash: seller's solicitors				162,000		6,396 CR
30 June	Cash: estate agents inc. VAT				3,290		3,106 CR
	Cash: stamp duty land tax				1,800		1,306 CR
10 July	Cash: Land Registry fees				400		906 CR
	Cash: transfer from client to office		906	—	906		—

6 FINANCIAL STATEMENT DATE

TO: MR AND MRS PLUM

SALE OF 8 PLEASANT AVENUE AND PURCHASE OF 'TOP HOLE'

SALE OF 8 PLEASANT AVENUE

Sale price	450,000
ADD re carpets curtains, etc.	10,000
	460,000
LESS mortgage repayment	99,500
	360,500

LESS payments
Estate agents' fees inc. VAT   10,575
Profit costs on sale inc. VAT   940
                                                         11,515
NET SALE PROCEEDS   348,985

PURCHASE OF 'TOP HOLE'

PURCHASE PRICE   600,000
LESS mortgage advance   200,000
                                                        400,000

ADD
Payments out
SDLT   24,000
Land Registry fees   300
Search fees   100
Profit costs on purchase inc. VAT   1,410
Profit costs on mortgage inc. VAT   235
                                                         26,185
Balance due on purchase   426,185

Amount required to complete purchase   426,185
LESS net amount received on sale   348,985
                                                                    77,200

Client: Mr and Mrs Plum
Matter: sale of 8, Pleasant Avenue and purchase of 'Top Hole'

Date	Details	Office account			Client account		
		DR	CR	Balance	DR	CR	Balance
200—							
1 June	Cash: search fee	100		100 DR			
9 June	Cash: High Flyers Bank: deposit					15,000	15,000 CR
14 June	Cash: deposit on sale					45,000	60,000 CR
	Cash: deposit on purchase				60,000		—
24 June	Profit costs on purchase	1,200		1,300 DR			
	VAT	210		1,510 DR			
	Profit costs on sale	800		2,310 DR			
	VAT	140		2,450 DR			
	Profit costs on mortgage	200		2,650 DR			
	VAT	35		2,685 DR			

Date	Details	Office account			Client account		
		DR	CR	Balance	DR	CR	Balance
25 June	Cash—you balance due					77,200	77,200 CR
	Cash: mortgage advance					200,000	277,200 CR
4 July	Cash: balance on sale					415,000	692,200 CR
	Cash: balance on purchase				540,000		152,200 CR
	Cash: repay bridging loan plus interest				15,140		137,060 CR
	Cash: mortgage redemption				99,500		37,560 CR
	Cash: stamp duty land tax				24,000		13,560 CR
	Cash: transfer costs from client to office account	2,685	—		2,685		10,875 CR
10 July	Cash: Estate agents				10,575		300 CR
	Cash: Land Registry fee				300		—

7 FINANCIAL STATEMENT DATE

TO: DINAH DOBBS
SALE OF 'GREEN TREES' AND PURCHASE OF 'RED ROOFS'
SALE OF 'GREEN TREES'

Sale price		40,000
LESS mortgage repayment		10,425
		29,575
LESS payments		
Estate agents' fees inc. VAT	470	
Profit Costs on sale inc. VAT	141	
Costs on redemption inc. VAT	47	
		658
NET SALE PROCEEDS		28,917

PURCHASE OF 'RED ROOFS'

PURCHASE PRICE		80,000
LESS mortgage advance		55,000
		25,000
ADD		
Payments out		
Bridging loan interest	83	
Land Registry fee	175	
Search fees	18	
Profit costs on purchase inc. VAT	470	
Profit costs on mortgage inc. VAT	70.50	

	816.50
Balance due on purchase	25,816.50
Net amount received on sale	28,917
LESS amount required to complete purchase	25,816.50
	3,100.50

Client: Dinah Dobbs
Matter: sale of 'Green Trees'; purchase of 'Red Roofs'

Date	Details	Office account DR	Office account CR	Office account Balance	Client account DR	Client account CR	Client account Balance
200—							
2 Aug	Petty cash: search fees	18		18 DR			
16 Aug	Cash: bridging loan					8,000	8,000 CR
19 Aug	Cash: deposit paid				8,000		—
4 Sept	Costs: sale	120		138 DR			
	VAT	21		159 DR			
	Purchase	400		559 DR			
	VAT	70		629 DR			
	Costs: mortgage advance	60		689 DR			
	VAT	10.50		699.50 DR			
16 Sept	Cash: sale proceeds					36,000	36,000 CR
	Stakeholder Transfer sheet					4,000	40,000 CR
	Cash: Lendalot Building Society mortgage advance					55,000	95,000 CR
	Cash: purchase				72,000		23,000 CR
	Charles: transfer mortgage redemption				10,425		12,575 CR
	Cash: Mid-West Bank: repay loan				8,083		4,492 CR

Date	Details	Office account DR	Office account CR	Office account Balance	Client account DR	Client account CR	Client account Balance
17 Sept	Cash: Land Registry				175		4,317 CR
	Cash: estate agent				470		3,847 CR
	Charles: transfer: redemption costs	47		746.50 DR			
	Cash: transfer costs		746.50	—	746.50		3,100.50 CR
	Cash—you				3,100.50		—

Client: Charles
Matter: mortgage redemption

Date	Details	Office account			Client account		
		DR	CR	Balance	DR	CR	Balance
200—							
4 Sept	Costs	40		47 DR			
	VAT	7					
16 Sept	Dinah: transfer: redemption money					10,425	10,425 CR
	Cash—you (redemption)				10,425		—
17 Sept			47	—			

Cash account

Date	Details	Office account			Client account		
		DR	CR	Balance	DR	CR	Balance
200—							
16 Aug	Dinah: bridging loan				8,000		8,000 DR
19 Aug	Stakeholder re Dinah deposit				4,000		12,000 DR
	Dinah: deposit paid					8,000	4,000 DR
12 Sept	Dinah: mortgage advance (Lendalot Building Society)				55,000		59,000 DR
16 Sept	Dinah: sale proceeds				36,000		95,000 DR
	Dinah: purchase					72,000	23,000 DR
	Charles: mortgage redemption					10,425	12,575 DR
	Dinah: loan repayment					8,083	4,492 DR
	Dinah: Land Registry fees					175	4,317 DR
	Dinah: estate agent's fees					470	3,847 DR
	Dinah: transfer: costs	746.50		746.50 DR		746.50	3,100.50 DR
	Dinah: payment of balance					3,100.50	—

Deposit interest and interest payable to clients

15.1 Introduction

This chapter deals with the following:

1. The two methods of paying interest to clients on money held on their behalf.
2. Entries required when placing money on a special designated deposit account for a client.
3. When solicitors should pay a client interest from office account if the money has not been placed on a special deposit account.
4. Example of entries made to record interest payable to the client.
5. Earning interest on clients' money on a general deposit account.
6. Solicitor/trustees duties.

15.2 Paying interest to the client, rules 24 and 25

As solicitors often hold large sums of money on behalf of their clients for some time, in many cases they are obliged to pay interest to their clients on the sums held. There are two ways of doing this:

(1) placing the sum held for a particular client on a special designated deposit account for that client (in the name of the firm) to earn interest, which will be paid to the client;

OR

(2) paying the client interest equivalent to that which would have been earned had they done so. (This will come out of office account. See rule 24.)

Clearly the first method will only be used if the solicitors know that the money will be held for some time. Its advantage for solicitors is that the bank will calculate the interest payable. This method may also be useful where trust money is involved (see **15.4**).

The second method may be used by solicitors where they have placed a substantial part of client monies on a general deposit account; this will earn interest for the firm, and the interest will be paid into office account. The firm can then pay individual clients interest out of this. Usually a higher rate of interest will be earned on this general client account than the amount payable on the individual accounts for clients, and so the solicitors and their clients can benefit from the difference.

15.2.1 Placing money on special designated deposit account

The solicitor will ask the bank to transfer the client's money from the firm's client account at the bank to a separate deposit account in the client's name (see rule 14(5). The solicitor must account to the client for all the interest earned on this account (see rule 24(1). The money, together with interest, will be transferred back to the ordinary client account before paying the client.

EXAMPLE

The firm acts for Madden in a personal injury claim and received £50,000 in settlement of the claim on 3 September. Madden is not sure how to invest the money and on 5 September asks you to hold it for some time. The firm transfers the £50,000 to a designated deposit account.

1. The entries on the accounts will show a receipt into client account.
   Then the entries on the accounts will show a payment out of the client account, and a receipt into the deposit account.
2. Payment out of the firm's Client account:

   CREDIT the Cash account Client account.
   DEBIT the Client ledger account Client account.
3. Receipt into the firm's designated deposit account for the client:

   DEBIT the Deposit Cash account (this will be a combined account for all the designated deposit accounts; see Rule 32(3)(a)).
   CREDIT a separate Client ledger account for the deposit Client account. See rule 32(3)(b).

Cash account

Date	Details	Office account			Client account		
		DR	CR	BAL	DR	CR	BAL
3 Sept	Madden: settlement of claim(1)				50,000		50,000 DR
5 Sept	Madden: transfer to Deposit account (2)					50,000	—

Madden account

Date	Details	Office account			Client account		
		DR	CR	BAL	DR	CR	BAL
3 Sept	Cash: settlement of claim (1)					50,000	50,000 CR
5 Sept	Cash: transfer to Deposit (2)				50,000		—

Deposit Cash account

Date	Details	Office account			Client account		
		DR	CR	BAL	DR	CR	BAL
5 Sept	Madden: held on deposit (3)				50,000		50,000 DR

Madden

Held on deposit

Date	Details	Office account			Client account		
		DR	CR	BAL	DR	CR	BAL
5 Sept	Deposit cash account (3)					50,000	50,000 CR

All that has happened is that the money has been moved from the main client bank account to the deposit account, and a separate client ledger account for Madden has been opened to record this.

4. When the interest is earned the entries are:

    DEBIT The Deposit Cash account Client account.

    CREDIT Madden Held on deposit Client ledger Client account.

Continuing the example—Interest earned on 1 December is £120.

Deposit Cash account

Date	Details	Office account			Client account		
		DR	CR	BAL	DR	CR	BAL
5 Sept	Madden: held on deposit (3)				50,000		50,000 DR
1 Dec	Madden: deposit interest (4)				120		50,120 DR

Madden

Held on Deposit account

Date	Details	Office account			Client account		
		DR	CR	BAL	DR	CR	BAL
5 Sept	Deposit Cash (3)					50,000	50,000 CR
1 Dec	Deposit Cash: interest (4)					120	50,120 CR

Continuing the example:

When the firm wants to pay Madden the total amount, as the deposit account will not have a cheque book, the total money held on deposit will be transferred back to the ordinary client bank account before paying Madden.

The entries for transferring the money back from deposit account are:

5. Payment out of deposit account:

    CREDIT the Deposit Cash account.

    DEBIT Madden Held on Deposit account client account.

6. Receipt into ordinary client bank account:

    DEBIT Cash Account client account.

    CREDIT Madden Client ledger account client account.

Deposit Cash account

Date	Details	Office account			Client account		
		DR	CR	BAL	DR	CR	BAL
5 Sept	Madden: held on deposit (3)				50,000		50,000 DR
1 Dec	Madden: deposit interest (4)				120		50,120 DR
	Madden held on deposit (5)					50,120	—

Madden

Held on Deposit account

Date	Details	Office account			Client account		
		DR	CR	BAL	DR	CR	BAL
5 Sept	Deposit Cash (3)					50,000	50,000 CR
1 Dec	Deposit Cash: interest (4)					120	50,120 CR
1 Dec	Deposit Cash account (5) transfer back				50,120		—

Cash account

Date	Details	Office account			Client account		
		DR	CR	BAL	DR	CR	BAL
3 Sept	Madden: settlement of claim (1)				50,000		50,000 DR
5 Sept	Madden: transfer to Deposit account (2)					50,000	—
1 Dec	Madden: transfer from Deposit account (6)				50,120		50,120 DR

Madden account

Date	Details	Office account			Client account		
		DR	CR	BAL	DR	CR	BAL
3 Sept	Cash: settlement of claim (1) Cash account transfer to Deposit (2)				50,000	50,000	50,000 CR —
1 Dec	Cash account: back from Deposit (6)					50,120	50,120 CR

7. Then a normal payment out of client money to Madden can be made:

CREDIT the Cash account.
DEBIT Madden account.

Cash account

Date	Details	Office account			Client account		
		DR	CR	BAL	DR	CR	BAL
3 Sept	Madden: settlement of claim (1)				50,000		50,000 DR
	Madden: transfer to Deposit account (2)					50,000	—
1 Dec	Madden: transfer back from Deposit account (6)				50,120		50,120 DR
	Madden: balance due (7)					50,120	—

Madden account

Date	Details	Office account			Client account		
		DR	CR	BAL	DR	CR	BAL
3 Sept	Cash—settlement of claim (1)					50,000	50,000 CR
	Cash Account transfer to Deposit (2)				50,000		—
1 Dec	Cash Account: back from Deposit (6)					50,120	50,120 CR
	Cash account—you (7)				50,120		—

Rule 32(3)(b) SAR gives an alternative to opening a separate client ledger account for the Deposit money held. The firm may have an additional column on the client ledger card recording the amount held on deposit. Using the above example the account for Madden would be as follows:

Madden account

Date	Details	Office account			Client account			Deposit client account		
		DR	CR	BAL	DR	CR	BAL	DR	CR	BAL
3 Sept	Cash: settlement of claim					50,000	50,000 CR			
5 Sept	Cash—Account transfer to Deposit				50,000		—			
5 Sept	Deposit Cash								50,000	50,000 CR
1 Dec	Deposit Cash interest								120	50,120 CR
1 Dec	Deposit Cash transfer back							50,120		—
1 Dec	Cash account: back from deposit					50,120	50,120 CR			—
	Cash account: you				50,120		—			

15.2.2 Paying the client equivalent interest from office account, rule 24

If the firm does not place money held for the client on deposit, then the solicitor should pay an equivalent sum under rule 24, but not if:

(a) the amount of interest calculated is £20 or less; or

(b) the sum of money held does not exceed the amount shown below for a time not exceeding the period shown:

£1,000 for 8 weeks;
£2,000 for 4 weeks;
£10,000 for 2 weeks;
£20,000 for 1 week.

If a sum over £20,000 is held for less than a week, a firm need only account for interest if it is fair and reasonable to do so.

Note that there are other exceptions to the payment of interest in rule 24.

If clients have not been paid interest they may apply to the Office for the Supervision of Solicitors for a certificate as to whether interest should have been paid, and the amount payable.

If a firm pays a sum out of office account as interest to the client, a business expense has been paid. To record payments of interest, an expense account, the Interest Payable account, is opened. This is an office account only. The firm may pay the interest by a cheque drawn on office account, and send a separate cheque, drawn on client account for the money held. Alternatively the firm may transfer the interest payable from office account to client account, and pay one cheque to the client for the balance together with the interest.

EXAMPLES

A. The firm has held £10,000 for their client Floyd for one month and on 10 December pays a cheque from office account for interest of £25, together with a cheque from client account for the £10,000. Note that the interest payable will also have to be recorded on the client ledger account, office account column under rule 32(4)SAR.

1. Thus the entries to show the interest payable are:

    DEBIT the Interest Payable account Office account.
    CREDIT Floyd's Client ledger account Office account.
    Then when the two cheques are sent the entries would be:

2. Payment of interest payable:

    CREDIT the Cash account Office account.
    DEBIT Floyd's Client ledger account Office account.

3. Payment of amount held on Client account:

    CREDIT the Cash account Client account.
    DEBIT Floyd's Client ledger account Client account.

Interest Payable account—Expense account

Date	Details	Office account		
		DR	CR	BAL
10 Dec	Floyd (1)	25		25 DR

Floyd account

Date	Details	Office account			Client account		
		DR	CR	BAL	DR	CR	BAL
10 Dec	Balance held Interest payable (1) Cash you: interest (2) Cash you: balance due (3)	25	25	25 CR —	10,000		10,000 CR —

Cash account

Date	Details	Office account			Client account		
		DR	CR	BAL	DR	CR	BAL
	Balance Floyd interest (2) Floyd balance due (3)		25	10,000 DR 25 CR		10,000	—

B. If the solicitor decides to send one cheque drawn on client account, then the entries will be as follows:

1. Record the interest payable as before:

    DEBIT the Interest Payable account Office account.
    CREDIT Floyd's Client ledger account Office account.

2. Transfer the interest payable to Client account:

    CREDIT the Cash account Office account.
    DEBIT Floyd's Client ledger account Office account.
    DEBIT the Cash account Client account.
    CREDIT Floyd's Client ledger account Client account.

3. Pay the client the total due from Client account:
    CREDIT the Cash account Client account.
    DEBIT Floyd's Client ledger account Client account.

    The accounts would therefore be as follows:

Interest Payable account—Expense account

Date	Details	Office account		
		DR	CR	BAL
10 Dec	Floyd (1)	25		25 DR

Floyd account

Date	Details	Office account			Client account		
		DR	CR	BAL	DR	CR	BAL
10 Dec	Balance held Interest Payable (1) Cash transfer— interest (2) Cash you: balance due (3)	25	25	25 CR —	10,025	25	10,000 CR 10,025 CR —

Cash account

Date	Details	Office account			Client account		
		DR	CR	BAL	DR	CR	BAL
	Balance						10,000 DR
	Floyd: transfer interest (2)		25	25 CR	25		10,025 DR
	Floyd: balance due (3)					10,025	—

15.3 Earning interest on clients' money on a general deposit account

As stated in **15.2** solicitors may transfer part of their client money to a general deposit account. Any interest earned on this is office money (see rule 13 note (xi)(b)) and will be credited direct to office account. This can then be used to pay interest to individual clients, where appropriate.

When a solicitor transfers clients' money from current account to deposit account the following entries in the accounts are made:

(a) CREDIT the cash account client column.

(b) DEBIT the deposit cash account client column.

EXAMPLE

The firm has a balance of £100,000 on its client current account. The partners decide to place £30,000 of this on deposit on 9 September.

Cash account

Date	Details	Office account			Client account		
		DR	CR	Balance	DR	CR	Balance
	Balance						100,000 DR
9 Sept	Deposit cash: general deposit					30,000	70,000 DR

Deposit cash account

Date	Details	Office account			Client account		
		DR	CR	Balance	DR	CR	Balance
9 Sept	Cash: general deposit, clients' money				30,000		30,000 DR

Interest earned on the general deposit account is practice income and the firm will open an income account, the Interest Received account, to record this income.

When the bank notifies the firm that interest has been earned on the client deposit account, the following bookkeeping entries will be made:

(a) Credit the Interest Received account.

(b) Debit the Cash account office column.

EXAMPLE

On 8 May the bank credits £1,000 interest to office account on money held on general deposit.

Interest Received account/office account

Date	Details	DR	CR	Balance
8 May	Cash (general deposit)		1,000	1,000 CR

Cash account

Date	Details	Office account			Client account		
		DR	CR	Balance	DR	CR	Balance
8 May	Cash (general deposit): interest receivable	1,000		1,000 DR			

15.4 Solicitor/Trustees

If a solicitor is a trustee then under general law trustees should not profit from a trust. Either the trust money will be placed on a designated deposit account, with all the interest being paid to the trust, or the solicitor will have to account for all interest that would have been earned had the money been placed on deposit. If the trust money is paid into a general client account the solicitor must be careful not to obtain any indirect benefit from the money being placed into the client account. As the solicitor may benefit from an increased rate of interest by virtue of trust money it may be safer to place all trust money into a separate client bank account.

15.5 Check list

By the end of this chapter you should be able to:

1. understand when interest should be paid to a client;
2. understand the two methods of paying interest to clients;
3. make the entries in respect of:
    (a) the transfer to a deposit account,
    (b) the receipt of interest earned on the deposit account,
    (c) the transfer back to general client bank account,
    (d) payment to the client;
4. make the entries to show interest payable to the client;
    (a) when a separate cheque drawn on office account is sent to the client,
    (b) when the interest payable is transferred to client account before being paid to the client;

15.6 Exercises on deposit interest and interest payable

1. Allow up to 25 minutes.
   On 1 March Cooper asked his solicitors to hold the net proceeds of sale of his cottage, previously received by them, being £100,000, until he had taken full investment advice. The money was placed on a designated deposit account immediately, and on 1 October the sum of £102,000, including interest earned was transferred back to the client current account, before a cheque was sent to Cooper for the total. Draw up all the relevant accounts for the above.

2. Allow up to 15 minutes.
   A firm of solicitors acted for Booth in respect of debt collection. The firm received £14,000 from a debtor on behalf of Booth on 5 January, and Booth asked the firm to hold this until 20 March. The firm then allowed interest of £100 and paid a cheque drawn on client account for the total of £14,100 to Booth on that date.

15.7 Suggested answers to exercises on deposit interest and interest payable

1. Cooper—sale of cottage

Date	Details	Office account			Client account		
		DR	CR	BAL	DR	CR	BAL
	Balance (sale proceeds)						100,000 CR
1 Mar	Cash: transfer to deposit (1)				100,000		—
1 Oct	Cash: from deposit (5)					102,000	102,000 CR
	Cash: you (6)				102,000		—

Cooper
Held on Deposit account

Date	Details	Office account			Client account		
		DR	CR	BAL	DR	CR	BAL
1 Mar	Deposit Cash (2)					100,000	100,000 CR
1 Oct	Deposit Cash—interest (3)					2,000	102,000 CR
1 Oct	Deposit Cash account (4)				102,000		—

Cash account

Date	Details	Office account			Client account		
		DR	CR	BAL	DR	CR	BAL
	Cooper: balance						100,000 DR
1 Mar	Cooper: transfer to deposit account (1)					100,000	—
1 Oct	Cooper: transfer from deposit account (5)				102,000		102,000 DR
	Cooper: balance due (6)					102,000	—

Deposit Cash account

Date	Details	Office account			Client account		
		DR	CR	BAL	DR	CR	BAL
1 Mar	Cooper: held on deposit (2)				100,000		100,000 DR
1 Oct	Cooper: deposit interest (3)				2,000		102,000 DR
	Cooper: deposit transfer back (4)					102,000	—

2. Booth account—debt collection

Date	Details	Office account			Client account		
		DR	CR	BAL	DR	CR	BAL
5 Jan	Cash: debtor (1)					14,000	14,000 CR
20 Mar	Interest payable (2)		100	100 CR			
	Cash transfer interest (3)	100		—		100	14,100 CR
	Cash you balance due (4)				14,100		—

Interest payable account

Date	Details	Office account			Client account		
		DR	CR	BAL	DR	CR	BAL
20 Mar	Booth—interest (2)	100		100DR			

Cash account

Date	Details	Office account			Client account		
		DR	CR	BAL	DR	CR	BAL
5 Jan	Booth: debtor (1)				14,000		14,000 DR
20 Mar	Booth: transfer interest (3)		100	100CR	100		14,100 DR
	Booth: balance due (4)					14,100	—

16

Probate transactions

16.1 Introduction

These occur when a firm acts in connection with the administration of an estate. A summary of some common financial transactions is set out below:

(a) A grant of probate or letters of administration will be required, probate fees will be paid and, where applicable, inheritance tax. It may be necessary to obtain a loan from the bank to the executors in respect of the inheritance tax payable. This may be paid direct from the loan account to the Inland Revenue, or the money may be paid into the firm's client account before payment is made to the Inland Revenue.

(b) Payments will be made regarding advertisements.

(c) Once probate has been obtained the firm will use it to collect all the assets of the deceased, for example bank account moneys, building society moneys, life policy proceeds. Some of this may be used to pay back the bank loan for inheritance tax, together with any interest due on the loan.

(d) Property belonging to the deceased may be sold, e.g., house and household contents.

(e) Debts due from the estate of the deceased will be paid, as will funeral expenses.

(f) Pecuniary legacies will be paid.

(g) The firm will charge costs (plus VAT) regarding administration and any sale of property, and transfer such costs from client account to office account with the agreement of the executors.

(h) The balance of the estate will be distributed to the beneficiary/beneficiaries, together with any interest due from the firm, either from moneys held on designated deposit or interest in lieu.

16.2 Exercises on probate transactions

1 Olde, Bayley & Co., solicitors, are instructed by the executors of Passway, deceased, to administer the estate on their behalf. The gross value of the estate amounts to £62,000 and consists of a house valued at £45,000 (subject to a mortgage of £12,000) and personalty valued at £17,000. There are various debts due by the estate amounting to £1,892. The following events take place:

7 October	Probate fees of £50 are paid by the firm's cheque.
15 October	A cheque for £16 is drawn in respect of the statutory advertisements, the cost of the local advertisement (£8) being met by a payment out of petty cash.

Date	Description
18 October	The balance remaining in the Standoff Building Society (£223) is paid into client account.
21 October	Proceeds of life policy received, being £5,000.
28 October	The household contents are sold and a cheque for £5,890 is received from the auctioneer. Commission of £620 had already been deducted.
4 November	Contracts for the sale of the house (£44,500) are exchanged, and a deposit of £4,450 is received by Olde, Bayley & Co., for them to hold as stakeholders.
18 November	Debts amounting to £1,927 are paid.
25 November	Paid funeral expenses £432.
4 December	The sale of the house is completed and a bank draft (£40,050) for the balance of the purchase money is received. The mortgage is redeemed by the payment of £12,367 which is inclusive of accrued interest.
11 December	A pecuniary legacy of £5,000 is paid to a legatee.
12 December	Bill of costs re sale of the house is prepared and agreed with the executors, profit costs being £440 plus VAT, and cash disbursements £20 (no VAT) are paid. Paid estate agents their commission £720 plus VAT.
16 December	Bill of costs for the administration of the estate, profit costs £520 (plus VAT) and disbursements, sent to executors, and after receiving their agreement, all moneys due to the firm from the estate are transferred to office account.
17 December	The balance of moneys now held by Olde, Bayley & Co., on behalf of the executors, is paid over to Rich, the residuary legatee, in accordance with their instructions. This includes the interest allowed on the money held by the firm on behalf of the executors of £208.

Show the client ledger card of the executors of Passway deceased. The rate of VAT is to be taken as 17.5%.

2 The firm is informed that Saturn died on 26 February, and the executors appointed in the will instruct the firm to act in the administration of the estate generally. The estate consists of a house 'Eudestar' valued at £70,000 and personalty valued at £47,500. There are various debts due by the estate (£1,500) together with a loan from an insurance company (secured on a life insurance policy) amounting to £5,000. The residue of the estate has been left to Neptune, a nephew who is in the process of buying a cottage, 'The Wild Leap', a matter which is being dealt with by the firm.

During the administration, the following events take place:

Date	Description
8 March	House insurance premium (£95) on 'Eudestar', now due, and the firm debits the Executors' account, the amount being transferred to the account of the insurance company, for whom the firm acts.
14 March	Probate fees of £70 are paid by cheque.
19 March	The grant is received and registered with the bank.
26 March	The amount invested by the deceased with the Constellation Building Society is, after registration of the grant, withdrawn, the balance amounting to £590 being paid into client account.

27 March	The firm draws a cheque in respect of statutory advertisements (£22), and pays £12 out of petty cash in respect of the local advertisement.
29 March	Received cheque from the Pluto Insurance Co. Ltd, for the sum of £6,342, being the net sum receivable from the company after the deduction of £5,158 in respect of the loan together with accrued interest.
1 April	Debts amounting to £1,500, together with funeral expenses of £1,000, are paid out of client account. The executors have agreed to an interim distribution of £4,000 to Neptune, which is transferred to Neptune's client account. The firm then sends a cheque (£4,000) to the solicitors acting for the vendor of the cottage 'The Wild Leap', for them to hold as stakeholders, contracts being exchanged the same day.
5 April	Exchanged contracts for the sale of 'Eudestar', the deposit of £7,000 having been received by the firm for them to hold as stakeholders.
12 April	Sundry fees (£3) paid from office account re the transmission of shares to Virgo, a beneficiary in the estate of Saturn, deceased.
26 April	Received completion statement in respect of 'The Wild Leap', showing £36,000 due, being the balance of purchase money. Sent financial statement to Neptune same day, showing profit costs of £280 excluding VAT (as per bill of costs attached thereto), Land Registry fees £70. Paid £10 from petty cash, in respect of bankruptcy search.
30 April	Completed purchase of 'The Wild Leap', the balance of purchase moneys being received by the firm from the Bank of Aries as a loan, an undertaking having been given that the sum would be repaid to them from the proceeds of sale of 'Eudestar'. The executors had previously agreed to this arrangement.
2 May	Completed sale of 'Eudestar', receiving a bank draft (£63,000) in respect of the balance of purchase moneys. Paid Land Registry fees re 'The Wild Leap'.
9 May	The firm agrees the bills of cost for the sale of the house and the administration of the estate with the executors. Profit costs with regard to the sale amount to £440 (excluding VAT), and with regard to the administration £680 (excluding VAT), together with disbursements in both cases. With the executors' agreement, a sum amounting to £36,146 is transferred from the account of the executors to the account of Neptune, and a cheque for this amount is sent to the Bank of Aries in accordance with the firm's undertaking.
16 May	All moneys due to the firm from the estate are transferred to office account.
17 May	The balance of moneys held by the firm on behalf of the executors is transferred to the account of Neptune at the request of the executors, such sum being inclusive of interest allowed by the firm of £567. All moneys due to the firm from Neptune are transferred to office account, the balance due to Neptune being held pending further instructions.

You are required to show the ledger accounts of:

(i) Neptune;

(ii) the executors of Saturn, deceased.

The rate of VAT is to be taken as 17.5%.

In making the necessary entries, it is important that the account in which the corresponding entry would be made is clearly identified by the appropriate entry in the details column. (Solicitors' Final Examinations, amended.)

16.3 Suggested answers to exercises on probate transactions

1 Executors of Passway deceased

Date	Details	Office account			Client account		
		DR	CR	Balance	DR	CR	Balance
7 Oct	Cash: probate fees	50		50 DR			—
15 Oct	Cash: advertisements	16		66 DR			
	Petty cash: advertisements	8		74 DR			
18 Oct	Cash: Standoff Building Society					223	223 CR
21 Oct	Cash: life policy					5,000	5,223 CR
28 Oct	Cash: auctioneer (less commission £620)					5,890	11,113 CR
18 Nov	Cash: debts				1,927		9,186 CR
25 Nov	Cash: funeral expenses				432		8,754 CR
4 Dec	Cash: sale proceeds					40,050	48,804 CR
	Stakeholder: transfer					4,450	53,254 CR
	Cash: mortgage redemption				12,367		40,887 CR
11 Dec	Cash: legacy				5,000		35,887 CR
12 Dec	Costs: sale	440					
	VAT	77		591 DR			
	Petty cash: disbursements	20		611 DR			
	Cash: estate agent				846		35,041 CR
16 Dec	Costs: re estate	520					
	VAT	91		1,222 DR			
	Cash: transfer: costs		1,222	—	1,222		33,819 CR
17 Dec	Interest payable		208	208 CR			
	Cash transfer interest payable	208		—		208	34,027 CR
	Cash: Rich				34,027		—

2 Executors of Saturn deceased re administration of estate

Date	Details	Office account			Client account		
		DR	CR	Balance	DR	CR	Balance
8 Mar	Cash: transfer: insurance premium: client account: 'Eudestar'	95		95 DR			
14 Mar	Cash: probate fees	70		165 DR			
26 Mar	Cash: Constellation Building Society					590	590 CR
	Cash: statutory advertisement				22		568 CR
	Petty cash: local advertisement	12		177 DR			
29 Mar	Cash: Pluto Insurance Co. Ltd					6,342	6,910 CR
1 Apr	Cash: debts				1,500		5,410 CR
	Cash: funeral expenses				1,000		4,410 CR
	Neptune: transfer				4,000		410 CR
12 Apr	Cash: fees: transmission of shares to Virgo	3		180 DR			
2 May	Cash: purchaser's of 'Eudestar'					63,000	63,410 CR
	Stakeholder: transfer sheet					7,000	70,410 CR
9 May	Costs: sale	440					
	VAT	77		697 DR			
	Costs: administration	680					
	VAT	119		1,496 DR			
	Neptune: transfer			—	36,146		34,264 CR
16 May	Cash: transfer: costs		1,496	—	1,496		32,768 CR
	Interest payable		567	567 CR			
17 May	Cash: transfer: from office account in lieu of interest	567		—		567	33,335 CR
	Neptune: transfer residue				33,335		—

Neptune: re purchase of 'Wild Leap'

Date	Details	Office account			Client account		
		DR	CR	Balance	DR	CR	Balance
1 Apr	Executors of Saturn deceased: transfer					4,000	4,000 CR
	Cash: deposit re 'The Wild Leap'				4,000		—
26 Apr	Costs	280		329 DR			
	VAT	49					
	Petty cash: bankruptcy search	10		339 DR			
30 Apr	Cash: Bank of Aries					36,000	36,000 CR
	Cash: purchase of 'The Wild Leap'				36,000		—
2 May	Cash: Land Registry	70		409 DR			
9 May	Executors of Saturn deceased: transfer					36,146	36,146 CR
	Cash: Bank of Aries				36,146		—
17 May	Executors of Saturn deceased: transfer: residue					33,335	33,335 CR
	Cash: transfer: costs		409	—	409		32,926 CR

17

Further transactions

17.1 Introduction

This chapter deals with the following transactions:

1. Reducing the client's bill and VAT (abatements).
2. Dishonoured cheques on:
    (a) office account;
    (b) client account.
       Including drawing against uncleared cheques and entries required to correct any breach of the Solicitors' Accounts Rules.
3. Small transactions.
4. Bad debts—a reminder.

The following transactions are further examples of the operation of the Solicitors' Accounts Rules 1998, the Solicitors' Practice Rules 1990 and the Solicitors' Financial Services (Scope) Rules 2001.

17.2 Abatements

After a bill of costs has been delivered to the client, a solicitor may decide to reduce the profit costs.

When an abatement of costs is made, a credit note is sent to the client, showing the reduction in costs and VAT.

The solicitor will make the following entries in the accounts to record an abatement:

(a) CREDIT the client's ledger account office column with the reduction in profit costs and VAT (on separate lines).

(b) DEBIT the profit costs account with the costs abatement.

(c) DEBIT the Customs and Excise account with the reduction in VAT.

EXAMPLE

On 30 June 200— the firm delivers a bill of costs to Charles, the executor of Fred, deceased, for £600 plus VAT. After discussing the matter with Charles, the firm agrees to reduce its bill to £400 and records the abatement in its account on 31 July 200—.

Executor of Fred deceased

Date	Details	Office account			Client account		
		DR	CR	Balance	DR	CR	Balance
200—							
30 June	Profit Costs	600					
	VAT	105		705 DR			
31 July	Costs: abatement		200				
	VAT: abatement		35	470 DR			

Costs account (Office account)

Date	Details	DR	CR	Balance
200—				
30 June	Profit Costs: executor of Fred deceased		600	600 CR
31 July	Profit Costs: abatement: executor of Fred deceased	200		400 CR

Customs and excise account (Office account)

Date	Details	DR	CR	Balance
200—				
30 June	Executor of Fred deceased		105	105 CR
31 July	Executor of Fred deceased: VAT: abatement	35		70 CR

17.3 Dishonoured cheques

17.3.1 Dishonoured cheque paid into office account

If a cheque paid into office account is later dishonoured, the solicitor will make the following entries in the accounts:

(a) DEBIT the client ledger account office column with the value of the dishonoured cheque.

(b) CREDIT the Cash account office column.

EXAMPLE

There is a debit balance of £235 on Peter's office account on 1 November 200— in respect of costs previously charged to Peter. On 21 November Peter pays the costs by cheque. On 26 November the firm's bank notifies it that Peter's cheque has been returned by the paying banker. To record the above transactions, the following entries will be made in Peter's account.

Peter

Date	Details	Office account			Client account		
		DR	CR	Balance	DR	CR	Balance
200—							
1 Nov	Balance b/d			235 DR			
21 Nov	Cash—you		235	—			
26 Nov	Cash: dishonoured cheque	235		235 DR			

The cash account will appear as follows:

Cash account

Date	Details	Office account			Client account		
		DR	CR	Balance	DR	CR	Balance
200—							
21 Nov	Peter	235		235 DR			
26 Nov	Peter (dishonoured cheque)		235	—			

17.3.2 Dishonoured cheque paid into client account

If a cheque paid into client account is later dishonoured, the solicitor will make the following entries in the accounts:

(a) DEBIT the client's ledger account client column with the value of the cheque.

(b) CREDIT the Cash account client column.

EXAMPLE

On 4 February 200— Jane paid the sum of £200 on account of costs and disbursements by cheque. On 7 February the firm's bankers notified it that Jane's cheque had been returned. The following entries will be made in the accounts to record these events.

Jane

Date	Details	Office account			Client account		
		DR	CR	Balance	DR	CR	Balance
200—							
4 Feb	Cash—you					200	200 CR
7 Feb	Cash: dishonoured cheque				200		—

Cash account

Date	Details	Office account			Client account		
		DR	CR	Balance	DR	CR	Balance
200—							
4 Feb	Jane				200		200 DR
7 Feb	Jane (dishonoured cheque)					200	—

17.3.3 Drawing against uncleared cheques in client account

The Solicitors' Accounts Rules 1998 do not prevent a solicitor from drawing against an uncleared cheque paid into client account but, if the cheque is later dishonoured, the solicitor is in breach of the Solicitors' Accounts Rules, Rules 1(d) and 22(5), and must make an immediate transfer from office to client account of the amount by which the client account is overdrawn. See Rule 7(1).

When a solicitor has drawn on client account against a cheque which is later dishonoured, the following entries will be made in the accounts:

(a) Entries to record the dishonour of a client account cheque (i.e., those entries in **17.3.2**).

(b) Entries to record the transfer from office account to client account of the amount by which client account is overdrawn.

Note: it is not necessary to transfer the full value of the cheque which has been dishonoured unless the client account is overdrawn by this amount.

Continuing the example from **17.3.2**:

Assume that on 5 February the firm drew a cheque on client account for £55 in respect of court fees. The cheque was then dishonoured on 7 February.

Jane

Date	Details	Office account			Client account		
		DR	CR	Balance	DR	CR	Balance
200—							
4 Feb	Cash—you					200	200 CR
5 Feb	Cash: court fee				55		145 CR
7 Feb	Cash: dishonoured cheque					200	55 DR
	Cash: transfer to remedy breach	55		55 DR		55	—

Cash account

Date	Details	Office account			Client account		
		DR	CR	Balance	DR	CR	Balance
200—							
4 Feb	Jane				200		200 DR
5 Feb	Jane (court fee)					55	145 DR
7 Feb	Jane (dishonoured cheque)					200	55 CR
	Jane (transfer to client account)		55	55 CR	55		—

17.4 Small transactions

When a solicitor does work which involves only one accounting transaction—the charging of costs, for example, for drafting a will, the solicitor may open a ledger account for the client and record the delivery of a bill of costs and receipt of payment of costs in the usual way.

Alternatively the solicitor may make entries only to record the receipt of costs, as follows:

(a) DEBIT the Cash account office column with costs and VAT (on separate lines).

(b) CREDIT the costs account with costs.

(c) CREDIT the HM Revenue and Customs account with VAT.

17.5 Bad debts—a reminder

If no VAT relief is available the firm will have to write off the total amount due, including VAT. If VAT relief is available (see **13.1.2**) the VAT element can be debited to the HMRC VAT account, thus offsetting the VAT due to HMRC.

17.6 Check list

By the end of this chapter you should be able to:

1. make the entries required in respect of a reduction (abatement) of a client's bill of costs on the relevant accounts;
2. make the entries required in respect of a dishonoured cheque;
3. make the entries required where a payment has been made from client account against a cheque which is then dishonoured;
4. note small transactions and VAT relief on bad debts.

17.7 Exercises on further transactions

1. On 12 February 2002 a firm of solicitors receives £100 from its client Green on account of his pending divorce action costs. On 13 February the sum of £75 is paid out of moneys received from Green, to an enquiry agent. On 17 February the bank notifies the firm that the cheque from Green for £100 has been returned by the paying bankers. Green intimates that he will be in funds within the next two weeks. Prepare the account of Green.

2. You act for A who is purchasing a house:

1 May	Receive a cheque for £6,000 for the deposit.
2 May	Send a cheque for £6,000 to seller's solicitors.
6 May	Bank notifies you that cheque has been returned.

   Prepare the account for A and the cash account to record the above. The cash account need not be balanced.

3. (a) On 20 January you deliver a bill of costs to Ann for £200 plus VAT £35. On 27 January you agree to reduce the cost to £160 plus VAT.

   (b) On 20 January Adam sends a cheque for £500: £141 is in payment of a bill you have delivered to him and the balance is for payment to the Wilshire county court for an action which he lost. On 21 January you pay the money due to the county court. On 22 January Adam's cheque is dishonoured. On 28 January Adam brings in cash to replace the dishonoured cheque.

   Show the client ledger accounts and the Cash account to record the above.

4. During the month of November, Teepot, Cupp & Saucer, solicitors, deal with the following events, and you are required to show all the relevant entries on the clients' ledger accounts, which are to be balanced. The rate of VAT is to be taken as 17.5%.

1 November	£6,000 is being held as stakeholder for Lemon. Cheque received (£4,000) from Peter, who is not a client of the firm, being the deposit on the sale of a house by Milko, for whom the firm acts. The firm is to hold the money as stakeholders. Exchanged contracts for the sale of Milko's house, and paid petty cash disbursements of £6 (no VAT) on his behalf, on the same day.
4 November	Banker's draft received (£54,000) on completion of the sale of Lemon's house, stake money of £6,000 being transferred from stakeholder account. The mortgagee of Lemon's house, Alexander, had already instructed the firm to act on his behalf in the redemption of his charge on Lemon's house, and the redemption money (£9,675) is transferred to his account. It has been agreed that the mortgagee's costs (£40 plus VAT) will be borne by Lemon. (Assume that Alexander is not an institutional lender.)
5 November	Paid by cheque the sum of £10,000 in respect of a debt which had been incurred by Lemon to Cupp, a partner in the firm, Lemon having previously agreed to this action. The amount due to the mortgagee of Lemon's house is paid by cheque, and the estate agent's fee (£1,200 plus VAT), is paid by the firm since the invoice was addressed to them.

	A bill of costs is rendered to Lemon, showing profit costs of £800 plus VAT. The firm writes off the sum of £70.50 (inclusive of VAT £10.50) as a bad debt, the amount having been owed to the firm by Smith since March 2000. Smith has now been adjudicated bankrupt.
11 November	The designated deposit account opened by the firm re Orange, in respect of an amount of £10,000 held by them for the period of six months, is closed, and a cheque for the sum, together with interest of £150 credited by the bank, is sent to Orange.
14 November	Cheque sent to Lemon in respect of balance of moneys held on his behalf, including agreed interest of £124. The amount due to the firm is transferred to office account and Lemon's account is then closed.
25 November	Bill of costs rendered to Milko, showing profit costs (£320 plus VAT) together with disbursements already incurred.
29 November	The sale of Milko's house is completed, a banker's draft for £36,000 being received from the purchaser's solicitors. The amount due to the firm is transferred to office account, and a cheque for the balance due to Milko is sent to him.

(Solicitors' Final Examination amended.)

17.8 Suggested answers to exercises on further transactions

1 Green

Green

Date	Details	Office account			Client account		
		DR	CR	Balance	DR	CR	Balance
12 Feb	Cash—you					100	100 CR
13 Feb	Cash: enquiry agent				75		25 CR
17 Feb	Cash: returned cheque				100		75 DR
	Cash: transfer	75		75 DR		75	—

2 A. account

Date	Details	Office account			Client account		
		DR	CR	Balance	DR	CR	Balance
1 May	Cash—you					6,000	6,000 CR
2 May	Cash: deposit paid				6,000		—
6 May	Cash: dishonoured cheque				6,000		6,000 DR
	Cash: transfer to correct breach	6,000		6,000 DR		6,000	—

Cash account

Date	Details	Office account			Client account		
		DR	CR	Balance	DR	CR	Balance
1 May	A: monies received				6,000		6,000 DR
2 May	A: deposit paid					6,000	—
6 May	A: dishonoured cheque					6,000	6,000 CR
	A: transfer to correct breach		6,000	6,000 CR	6,000		

3 (a) **Ann**

Date	Details	Office account			Client account		
		DR	CR	Balance	DR	CR	Balance
20 Jan	Profit costs	200					
	VAT	35		235 DR			
27 Jan	Costs abatement		40				
	VAT abatement		7	188 DR			

(b) **Adam account**

Date	Details	Office account			Client account		
		DR	CR	Balance	DR	CR	Balance
20 Jan	Balance			141 DR			
	Cash—you		141	—		359	359 CR
21 Jan	Cash: Wilshire County Court				359		—
22 Jan	Cash: dishonoured cheque	141		141 DR		359	359 DR
	Cash: transfer to correct breach	359		500 DR		359	—
28 Jan	Cash—you		500	—			

Cash account

Date	Details	Office account			Client account		
		DR	CR	Balance	DR	CR	Balance
	Adam split cheque	141		141 DR	359		359 DR
21 Jan	Adam: Wilshire County Court					359	—
22 Jan	Adam: dishonoured cheque		141	BREACH —		359	359 CR
	Adam: transfer to correct breach		359	359 CR	359		—
28 Jan	Adam:	500		141 DR			

4 Teepot, Cupp & Saucer

Milko

Date	Details	Office account			Client account		
		DR	CR	Balance	DR	CR	Balance
1 Nov	Petty cash: disbursement	6		6 DR			
25 Nov	Profit Costs	320		326 DR			
	HMRC VAT	56		382 DR			
29 Nov	Cash: sale proceeds					36,000	36,000 CR
	Stakeholder: transfer: deposit					4,000	40,000 CR
	Cash: transfer: costs from client to office account		382	—	382		39,618 CR
	Cash—you				39,618		—

Lemon

Date	Details	Office account			Client account		
		DR	CR	Balance	DR	CR	Balance
4 Nov	Cash: sale proceeds					54,000	54,000 CR
	Stakeholder: transfer: deposit					6,000	60,000 CR
	Alexander: transfer: redemption				9,675		50,325 CR
	Alexander: transfer: redemption costs	47		47 DR			
5 Nov	Cash: Cupp				10,000		40,325 CR
	Cash: estate agent	1,200		1,247 DR			
	Profit Costs	800					
	HMRC VAT (210+140)	350		2,397 DR			
	Interest allowed		124	2,273 DR			
14 Nov	Cash: transfer interest allowed	124		3,397 DR		124	40,449 CR
	Cash: transfer: costs		2,397	—	2,397		38,052 CR
	Cash—you				38,052		—

Alexander

Date	Details	Office account			Client account		
		DR	CR	Balance	DR	CR	Balance
4 Nov	Profit Costs	40					
	VAT	7		47 DR			
	Lemon: transfer: redemption					9,675	9,675 CR
	Lemon: transfer: redemption costs		47	—			
5 Nov	Cash—you				9,675		—

Smith

Date	Details	Office account			Client account		
		DR	CR	Balance	DR	CR	Balance
8 Nov	Balance Bad debt HMRC VAT		60 10.50	70.50 DR — 			

Orange

Date	Details	Office account			Client account		
		DR	CR	Balance	DR	CR	Balance
	Cash account: back from deposit Cash: you				 10,150	10,150	10,150 CR

Orange

Held on deposit

Date	Details	Office account			Client account		
		DR	CR	Balance	DR	CR	Balance
	Balance Deposit interest Deposit cash: transfer back				 10,150	 150	10,000 CR 10,150 CR

Stakeholder account

Date	Details	Office account			Client account		
		DR	CR	Balance	DR	CR	Balance
 1 Nov 4 Nov 29 Nov	Balance Cash: Milko Lemon: transfer Milko: transfer				 6,000 4,000	6,000 4,000	6,000 CR 10,000 CR 4,000 CR —

18

Short-answer questions and revision questions on solicitors' accounts

18.1 Introduction

This chapter contains the following questions on solicitors' accounts:
1. Set A. These questions require a statement of the principles or rules involved.
2. Set B. These questions require a statement of the principles or rules involved and the entries on the accounts.
3. Two long questions requiring you to make entries in a series of transactions.

18.2 Revision questions—Set A

Explain how a firm of solicitors should deal with the following. You should state the principles/rules involved. There is no need to state the debit and credit entries involved.

Allow 5 to 10 minutes for each question.

1. The firm is dealing with a probate matter and the deceased's bank agrees to advance £20,500 to the executors in respect of inheritance tax. A loan account is opened by the bank for the executors and a cheque for £20,500 is drawn by the executors, payable to HMRC, and handed to the firm of solicitors.

2. The firm has held the net proceeds of sale of a house on behalf of its client David for the past two months. David now asks for the net proceeds, totalling £10,000, to be sent to him.

3. Jane, a client, owes the firm £940, being £800 re costs and £140 re VAT. Seven months after the bill was delivered the firm writes off the debt.

4. The firm receives cash of £600 on behalf of its client Clarke in settlement of a claim. Clarke has asked that the firm pay this cash over to Boswell in payment of a debt due from Clarke to Boswell.

5. The firm acts for Ruby, a partner in the firm, and her friend John, who is a legal executive in the firm. They are selling a cottage and purchasing a larger house in town. The firm receives a cheque for £30,000 to hold as agent for the seller.

6. The firm receives a cheque for £400 on general account of costs from their client Ian. A disbursement of £415 (no VAT payable) is paid by the firm on behalf of Ian.

7. The firm receives a cheque for £770 from their client Lisa. This is in respect of the firm's bill for £400 plus VAT, which had been sent to Lisa, and counsel's fees of £300 (no VAT) which have not yet been paid.

18.3 Suggested answers to revision questions—Set A

1. No entries need be shown on the solicitors' accounts at all, as the loan account at the bank belongs to the executors and not the firm. The cheque is made out to HMRC, so it does not belong to the firm and it should merely be forwarded to HMRC.

2. As £10,000 has been held for two weeks or more, here two months, then the money should have been placed on a designated deposit account to earn interest for David. The proceeds plus the interest should be paid to him. See Rule 24(1). If the money has not been placed on a designated deposit account for David then the firm should pay an amount at least equivalent to the amount that would have been earned. Interest payable will come from the firm's office account.

3. As the debt is at least six months old the firm may claim bad debt relief. Thus the amount of £800 will be recorded as a bad debt, and the VAT of £140 can be debited to the HMRC account, thus reducing the VAT payable to HMRC.

4. Although normally a firm of solicitors must pay money received on behalf of a client into a client bank account, under r. 17(a) of the Solicitors' Accounts Rules 1998, where money is received in cash and is without delay paid in cash in the ordinary course of business to the client or on the client's behalf there is no need to pay into the client bank account. The firm can therefore pay the money to Boswell. However, entries must be made on the accounts showing the receipt and payment out of client money. Take care re money laundering.

5. Although money received on behalf of partners in the firm is not client money, Rule 13 Note (xii), where the money is received on behalf of a partner together with a non partner then the money will be client money and as this is held as agent for the seller, it can be recorded on a client ledger card for Ruby and John.

6. The £400 on general account of costs should have been paid into client account, Rule 13 Note (i)(d). The firm cannot pay the total disbursement of £415 from client account, Rule 22(5). Although it would be technically possible for the firm to pay two cheques, one for £400 from client account and one for £15 from office account, this would seem odd, and the better course would be to pay £415 from office account, and then transfer £400 from client account. It is also possible for the firm to advance money to fund the payment under r. 15. It may be necessary to ask the client for further funds if these are needed for other disbursements.

7. This is mixed office/client money, Rules 19 & 20. The sum of £470, being £400 plus VAT £70, is office account money. The remaining £300 should be held on client account until counsel's fees are paid. The cheque may be split or, more usually, the whole amount paid into client account, and then £470 transferred to office account within 14 days. Alternatively the entire sum may be paid into office account and counsel's fees paid or the money transferred to client account by the end of the second working day following receipt, Rule 19.

18.4 Self-assessment questions—Set B

Decide whether the following transactions should be dealt with through client account or office account, and show or explain the entries that would be made on the accounts.

Allow about 10 minutes for each question.

1. A solicitor receives £400 on general account of costs from Janet.

2 A solicitor receives £470 as an agreed fee in respect of work to be done for Harold. The firm has not yet sent a bill to Harold.

3 The solicitor holds £200 on general account of costs from Ethel. An enquiry agent is paid £150 (no VAT is payable).

4 The firm is acting for one of the partners, John, in respect of his sale of a flat in Mersey Quays. The sale price of £54,000 is received on completion from the purchaser's solicitors.

5 The firm is acting on behalf of one of its employees, Patsy, in respect of the sale of a house. Sale proceeds are received in the sum of £90,000.

6 The firm is acting for one of its partners, Jane, together with her husband in respect of the sale of a house. Sale proceeds are received in the sum of £150,000.

7 The firm has £80,000 on general client account. The office account is overdrawn at the bank. A disbursement of £50 has to be paid on behalf of their client Brian, who has not yet sent any money on account of costs.

8 The firm sent out a bill to Anthony for £800 plus VAT £140. Counsel's fees are due but not yet paid in the sum of £600. Anthony sends a cheque for £1,540.

9 The firm receives £5,000 in respect of Derek's sale of 'The Gables', to hold as stakeholder.

10 The firm receives £6,000 in respect of Mary's sale of 8, Beaumont Square, to hold as agent for the seller. The sum of £5,000 is paid out in respect of her purchase of 10, Bloxham Road.

11 A cheque made out to client James for £300 is received by the firm.

12 The firm receives £60 cash on behalf of their client Cecil. Later that day the cash is handed to Cecil who has called into the office.

13 A cheque is received made out to the firm for £9,000 in respect of a debt due from Agnes to their client Joe.

14 The firm sent out a bill of costs for £800 plus VAT to their client, Tim. The firm later agreed with Tim to reduce the bill to £600 plus VAT.

18.5 Suggested answers to self-assessment questions—Set B

1 Money on general account of costs is client money and must be paid into client account (see r. 13).

Janet

Date	Details	Office account			Client account		
		DR	CR	Balance	DR	CR	Balance
	Cash—you on account of costs					400	400 CR

Cash book

Date	Details	Office account			Client account		
		DR	CR	Balance	DR	CR	Balance
	Janet: on account costs				400		400 DR

2 An agreed fee is office money and must be paid into office account (see r. 19(5)). So:

   (a) CREDIT Harold client ledger card office account.

   (b) DEBIT the cash book office account.

3 The £200 on general account of costs would have been paid into client account. As this money is available, and VAT is not involved, the enquiry agent can be paid from client account.

Ethel

Date	Details	Office account			Client account		
		DR	CR	Balance	DR	CR	Balance
	Cash—you on account of costs					200	200 CR
	Cash: enquiry agent				150		50 CR

Cash book

Date	Details	Office account			Client account		
		DR	CR	Balance	DR	CR	Balance
	Ethel: on a/c costs				200		200 DR
	Ethel: enquiry agent					150	50 DR

4 Client's money does not include money to which the only person entitled is the solicitor himself or herself or, in the case of a firm of solicitors, one or more of the partners in the firm: see the notes to r. 13. The money cannot be paid into client account; it must be held on an office account in the name of John.

John

Date	Details	Office account			Client account		
		DR	CR	Balance	DR	CR	Balance
	Cash: sale proceeds		54,000	54,000 CR			

Cash book

Date	Details	Office account			Client account		
		DR	CR	Balance	DR	CR	Balance
	John: re sale	54,000		54,000 DR			

5 Patsy does not fall within the exception in **Answer 4** above: she is a client and the money will be paid into client account on her behalf. So:

   (a) CREDIT Patsy client ledger card client account.

   (b) DEBIT the Cash book client account.

6 Provided Jane's husband is not a partner in the firm, the money is again client money: see **Answer 4** above, i.e., Jane is not the only person entitled. So:

   (a) CREDIT Jane and husband client ledger card client account.

   (b) DEBIT the Cash book client account.

7 Although there are sufficient funds on client account to pay the disbursement, as the firm is not holding any money on behalf of Brian, the payment cannot be made out of client account, it must be made out of office account. See r. 22(8), which makes it clear that money drawn cannot exceed the total held on account of the client. So:

   (a) DEBIT Brian client ledger card Office account.

   (b) CREDIT the Cash book office account.

8 A solicitor may only pay money into office account in respect of, *inter alia*, 'costs', which excludes counsel's fees which have not yet been paid. On the assumption that no VAT is payable in respect of counsel's fees in this case then £940 is office money, and £600 is client money. The cheque may be split, i.e., £940 paid into office account and £600 into client account, or all the money may be paid into client account, and then £940 transferred to office account within 14 days or all the money may be paid into office account and then either counsel's fees paid or transferred to client account, within 2 working days, see r. 19.

Entries where the money is split:

Anthony

Date	Details	Office account			Client account		
		DR	CR	Balance	DR	CR	Balance
	Costs	800		800 DR			
	VAT	140		940 DR			
	Cash—you		940	—		600	600 CR

The cash book would be debited £940 on office account, and debited £600 on client account.

Entries where the money is paid into client account and then transferred:

Anthony

Date	Details	Office account			Client account		
		DR	CR	Balance	DR	CR	Balance
	Balance re costs and VAT			940 DR			
	Cash—you					1,540	1,540 CR
	Cash: transfer costs		940	—	940		600 CR

Cash book

Date	Details	Office account			Client account		
		DR	CR	Balance	DR	CR	Balance
	Anthony				1,540		1,540 DR
	Anthony: transfer costs	940		940 DR		940	600 DR

9 The money does not belong to Derek until completion of the sale. It must be paid into stakeholder account, a client ledger card, client account. So:

   (a) CREDIT the stakeholder account client ledger card client account.

   (b) DEBIT the Cash book client account.

10 As this money is held for Mary it may be paid into her client ledger card, client account and used in respect of the deposit payable on the purchase.

Mary: Sale 8, Beaumont Square; purchase 10, Bloxham Road

Date	Details	Office account			Client account		
		DR	CR	Balance	DR	CR	Balance
	Cash deposit: agent for vendor					6,000	6,000 CR
	Cash deposit on purchase				5,000		1,000 CR

The other entries would have been to debit the cash book client account with £6,000, and to credit the cash book client account in respect of the deposit paid on purchase, i.e., £5,000.

11 As the cheque is made out to the client, it cannot be paid into the solicitor's bank accounts, whether office account or client account. No entries need be made on the accounts, although a note may be made if required.

12 Although the rules do not require this money to be paid into client account at the bank, client's money has still been received and then paid out.
Receipt:

   (a) CREDIT the client ledger card of Cecil client account.

   (b) DEBIT the cash book client account.

   Payment out:

   (a) DEBIT the client ledger card of Cecil client account.

   (b) CREDIT the cash book client account.

13 As the cheque is made out to the firm it can be paid into the firm's bank account. The money is received on behalf of Joe and is client money. So:

   (a) CREDIT Joe's client ledger card client account.

   (b) DEBIT the Cash book client account.

14 **Tim**

Date	Details	Office account			Client account		
		DR	CR	Balance	DR	CR	Balance
	Profit Costs	800		800 DR			
	VAT	140		940 DR			
	Abatement		200	740 DR			
	VAT		35	705 DR			

Profit costs account Office account

Date	Details	DR	CR	Balance
	Tim: bill of costs		800	800 CR
	Tim: abatement	200		600 CR

HM Revenue and Customs VAT account Office account

Date	Details	DR	CR	Balance
	Tim: bill of costs		140	140 CR
	Tim: abatement	35		105 CR

18.6 Test on further transactions

Allow about 40 to 45 minutes to complete this test.
Harriet, Peter and Alex are solicitors, and they deal with the following events:

3 January	Paid by cheque the sum of £2,000 on behalf of Black, and received later the same day from Black, a cheque for £1,500 in partial satisfaction. The balance is to be paid from the proceeds of the sale of his house, which will be received within a few days' time.
7 January	Received cheque, in respect of the sale of Black's house, amounting to £22,634, being the balance of purchase money. The sum of £2,500 is transferred from stakeholder account the same day. The firm also acts for the mortgagees of Black, the Savall Building Society, and £7,436 is sent to that company to redeem the mortgage. The bill of costs is sent to the building society. The costs of redemption of Black's mortgage (£20 plus VAT) are to be borne by Black.
10 January	Bill of costs sent to Black (£240 plus VAT).
13 January	Pink repays a personal loan of £1,000 made by Peter, a partner in the firm.
16 January	Grey pays £200 on account of her pending divorce action costs, and petty cash disbursements of £16 are paid in respect of this on the same day.
22 January	Paid enquiry agent, on behalf of Grey, the sum of £40 (no VAT), the cheque being drawn on client account.
24 January	The bank notifies the firm that the cheque from Grey has been returned unpaid by the paying bankers.
29 January	The sum of £1,000, which has been held on behalf of Blue for some three months, is repaid to Blue, together with agreed interest of £40. The payment is made by means of a cheque drawn on client account. The money has not been deposited in a designated deposit account.

Write up the client's ledger accounts, showing all relevant entries. All accounts are to be balanced. The rate of VAT is to be taken as 17.5%.

(Law Society Final Examination, amended.)

18.7 Suggested answer to test on further transactions

Black

Date	Details	Office account			Client account		
		DR	CR	Balance	DR	CR	Balance
3 Jan	Cash	2,000		2,000 DR			
3 Jan	Cash—you		1,500	500 DR			
7 Jan	Cash: purchaser's solicitors					22,634	22,634 CR
	Stakeholder: transfer					2,500	25,134 CR
	Cash: Savall Building Society: redemption				7,436		17,698 CR
10 Jan	Profit Costs	240		740 DR			
	VAT	42		782 DR			
	Costs (mortgage redemption)	20		802 DR			
	VAT	3.50		805.50 DR			
13 Jan	Cash: transfer: costs		805.50	—	805.50		16,892.50 CR

Grey—divorce

Date	Details	Office account			Client account		
		DR	CR	Balance	DR	CR	Balance
16 Jan	Cash: you					200	200 CR
	Petty cash: disbursements	16		16 DR			
22 Jan	Cash: enquiry agent				40		160 CR
24 Jan	Cash: returned cheque				200		40 DR
	Cash: transfer to correct breach	40		56 DR		40	

Blue

Date	Details	Office account			Client account		
		DR	CR	Balance	DR	CR	Balance
29 Jan	Balance						1,000 CR
	Interest payable		40	40 CR			
	Cash: transfer interest	40				40	1,040 CR
	Cash: you amount due				1,040		—

Note: an account is not opened for Peter as he is a partner in the firm and it would be in breach of the Solicitors' Accounts Rules 1998 Rule 13 Note (xii) to pay the money received from Pink into client account.

18.8 Test on ledger accounts including VAT

Allow approximately 1 hour to complete this test.

Except where specifically referred to in the questions, taxation (including VAT) should be ignored.

Bread, Butter and Honey are solicitors, and they deal with the following events:

3 April	Paid £23.50 (including VAT £3.50) by cheque drawn on office account, in respect of the reproduction of documents. The invoice is made out to the client, Phantasia, for whom the firm are acting in a tax matter before the special commissioners.
4 April	Received banker's draft for £49,500 from the purchaser's solicitors, being the balance of purchase money re the sale by Smith of his house 'Figleaf'. On the same day the sum of £19,500 is sent by cheque to the mortgagees of the property, in full payment of the amount due to them.
7 April	Logger, Hedd and Co., the estate agents acting for Smith, send cheque to firm for £4,235, being the deposit on 'Figleaf' less their commission.
8 April	Received the sum of £300 from Phantasia on account of costs generally.
11 April	The firm acts for Jones in the collection of a debt due to her, amounting to £5,000. The debtor sends two cheques for the debt, each cheque being for the sum of £2,500 and dated 16 May and 16 June, respectively.
14 April	Sent cheque for £587.50 (including VAT £87.50) to A. Builder in respect of pre-sale repairs to 'Figleaf'. The invoice was addressed to the firm.
28 April	Paid fee of £235 (including VAT £35) to E. X. Pert, a witness who appeared on behalf of Phantasia. The payment was made out of client account.
29 April	Bill of costs sent to Smith (£300 plus VAT).
5 May	Paid from client account £94 (including VAT) in respect of transcripts obtained on behalf of Phantasia.
9 May	Profit costs and disbursements are transferred from client account to office account in respect of Smith.
20 May	Bill of costs in respect of tax matter is rendered to Phantasia, showing profit costs of £700 plus VAT.
16 June	Received cheque in settlement of Phantasia's account with the firm.
17 June	Bill of costs for £60 plus VAT delivered to Jones.
20 June	Both cheques from the debtor of Jones, having been presented and met, the total amount due, after deduction of costs but inclusive of interest allowed by the firm (£22), was paid over to Jones. The amount due to the firm is transferred from client to office account.
30 June	The firm allows interest of £250 for Smith, before paying the total due from client account.

You are required to show the ledger accounts of Phantasia, Smith and Jones, recording all the above transactions. The rate of VAT is to be taken as 17.5%.

(Law Society Final Examination, amended.)

18.9 Suggested answer to test on ledger accounts including VAT

Phantasia

Date	Details	Office account			Client account		
		DR	CR	Balance	DR	CR	Balance
3 Apr	Cash: production of documents	23.50		23.50 DR			
8 Apr	Cash—you					300	300 CR
28 Apr	Cash: E. X. Pert				235		65 CR
5 May	Cash: transcripts				94		29 DR
	Cash: transfer	29		52.50 DR			
	Cash: transfer					29	—
20 May	Costs	700					
	HMRC (VAT)	122.50		875 DR			
16 June	Cash—you		875	—			

Smith

Date	Details	Office account			Client account		
		DR	CR	Balance	DR	CR	Balance
4 Apr	Cash: purchaser's solicitors					49,500	49,500 CR
	Cash: redemption				19,500		30,000 CR
7 Apr	Cash: estate agent (less commission)					4,235	34,235 CR
14 Apr	Cash: A. Builder	500		500 DR			
29 Apr	Profit Costs	300					
	HMRC (VAT)	140		940 DR			
	87.50 + 52.50						
9 May	Cash: transfer: costs		940	—	940		33,295 CR
30 June	Interest payable		250	250 CR			
	Cash: transfer interest	250		—		250	33,545 CR
	Cash—you				33,545		—

Jones

Date	Details	Office account			Client account		
		DR	CR	Balance	DR	CR	Balance
16 May	Cash: debtor					2,500	2,500 CR
16 June	Cash: debtor					2,500	5,000 CR
17 June	Profit Costs	60					
	HMRC (VAT)	10.50		70.50 DR			
20 June	Interest payable		22	48.50 DR		22	5,022 CR
	Cash: transfer	22		70.50 DR			
	Cash: transfer		70.50	—	70.50		4,951.50 CR
	Cash—you				4,951.50		—

INDEX

A

abatements 257-8
accountants
   inspections by 175
Accountants' Report Rules (1991)
   inspection by accountant 175
   report to Law Society 175
accounting bases 96-7
accounting concepts
   accruals 96
   business entity 95
   consistency 96
   cost 95
   going-concern 96
   materiality 96
   money measurement 95
   prudence 96
accounting policies 96-7
accounts
   classification *see* **classification of accounts**
   consolidated *see* **consolidated accounts**
   double-entry bookkeeping *see* **double-entry bookkeeping**
   duty to keep 174-5
   final *see* **final accounts**
   interpretation *see* **interpretation of accounts; ratio analysis**
   presentation *see* **presentation of accounts**
   purpose 2
   reasons for study 1-2
   types to be kept 2
   see also individual accounts eg **client account; personal accounts**
accruals concept 96
acid test 144
adjustments
   check list 48
   closing stocks 43-4, 48
   exercises 48-52, 62-9
   expenses 39-41
   need for 39
   work in progress 44-7
agency
   receipt of deposit as agent 207
appropriation account 71-2
   change in partnership 76-7
assets 5
   balance sheet 29-30, 31, 32
   current assets ratio 143
   disposal of part of group 60-1
   final accounts
      disposal of part of group 60-1
      sale of assets 60-1
   sale 60-1

assumptions *see* **accounting concepts**
attorney, power of 167
auditors' report
   Companies Acts requirements 119-20
authorities
   retention of copies 174-5

B

bad debts *see* **debts**
balance sheet 27
   adjustments 41
   assets 29-30, 31, 32
   capital 30-1
   Companies Acts requirements 119-20
   company accounts 117-20
   consolidated accounts 128-32
   current assets 30, 31
   current liabilities 31
   definitions 29-31
   depreciation 59
   exercise 33-7
   fixed assets 30, 31
   liabilities 30
   long-term liabilities 31
   partnership 71, 72, 74-5
   vertical format 32-3, 117-19
balance, trial *see* **trial balance**
bases 96-7
bill of costs
   abatement 257-8
bonus issue 115-16
business entity concept 95

C

capital
   balance sheet 30-1
   gearing ratios 149-50
   redemption reserves 115
   return on capital employed 146, 150
   working capital ratio 145
capital account
   business proprietor 6-7
   partnerships 73
cash account 171-2
   double-entry bookkeeping 3-5
cheques
   dishonoured
      into client account 259-60
      into office account 258-9
   retention time 175
   split between office and client account 185-6
   third parties 171
   uncleared, drawing against 260-1

classification of accounts
   income and expenses accounts 5, 8–11
   personal accounts 5, 6
     of business proprietor 6–7
   real accounts 5, 7–8
   trading accounts 11–12
client account 12
   balance sheet 32–3
   cash at bank 33
   check list 175
   cheques
     dishonoured, paid into 259–60
     split 185–6
     uncleared, drawing against 260–1
   controlled trusts 166–7, 239
   definition of client money 162–3
   designated deposit 239–43
   disbursements from 168
   earned interest 246–7
   exercises 176–9
   mixed office/client money 185–6
   payments into 163–4, 168
     from Legal Services Commission 164
     from third party 164–5
   power of attorney 167
   receipt of 169–70
   separation from office money 162
   transfers
     between accounts 183–5
     from office account 182–3
     to office account 181–2
   withdrawals from 165, 170
   see also **interest payment**
client money 32, 33
clients
   financial statements to 205
closing stocks 43–4, 48
company accounts
   balance sheet
     example 119–20
     vertical form 117–19
   bonus issue of shares 115–16
   check list 120
   Companies Acts requirements 119–20
   consolidated *see* **consolidated accounts**
   debentures 106–7
   deferred taxation 110–11
   dividends 111–13
   exercises 120–6
   group companies *see* **consolidated accounts**
   liabilities 114
   limited companies 103–26
   preference shares 105–6
   premium shares 104–5
   profit and loss account 107–17
   profits, retained 113–14
   provisions 114
   public companies 119
   reserves 114
     capital reserves 115
     capitalisation 115–16
     revenue reserves 115
   retained profits 113–14
   share capital 103–6
   sinking funds 116–17
   taxation 108–9
     deferred 110–11
computerised systems
   hardcopy and reproduction capability 175

consistency concept 96
consolidated accounts 127–39
   acquisition of shares
     for less than book value 131–2
     for more than book value 130–1
   balance sheet 128–32, 134–5
   check list 136
   exercises 136–9
   holding majority interest in subsidiary 134–6
   profit and loss account 132–4, 135–6
controlled trusts 239
   definition 166
   delegation to outside manager 166
   indirect benefit 166
   interest on money 166
   rules 166
   solicitor co-trustee with outsider 167
conveyancing transactions 206–7
   check list 226
   completion
     financial statement 214–17
     purchase completion 220–3
     sale completion 217–20
     simultaneous sale and purchase 223–5
   exercises 226–38
   mortgage advances
     acting for buyer/borrower only 212
     acting for mortgagee only 211–12
     acting for mortgagee and purchaser 209–11
   mortgage redemption, acting for seller and lender 213–14
   receipt of deposit
     as agent 207
     as stakeholder 208–9
corporation tax 108–9
cost concept 95
costs
   abatement 257–8
Court of Protection receivers
   Solicitors' Accounts Rules (1998) 167
current accounts
   partnerships 74
current assets ratio 143

D

debentures
   issue at discount 106–7
debts
   bad *see* **debts, bad**
   collection 144
   doubtful 54–5, 61–2
debts, bad 61
   check list 62
   in final accounts
     effect 55–7
     recovery of written off debt 54
     writing off 53–4, 61
   VAT relief 200, 261
deferred taxation 110–11
deposit interest *see* **interest payment**
depreciation
   calculation 57–8
   check list 62
   final accounts 57–9
   recording in accounts 58–9
dividends
   appropriation 111–12, 113–14
   cover 151
   interim 112–13

payment 112
yield 150
double-entry bookkeeping
  cash account 3-5
  check list 14
  exercises 14-17
  layout 4-5
  principle 3-4
  worked example 12-14
drawings
  business proprietor 7
  partnerships 72
    cash 73
    end of year 73
  profit and loss account 29
duty to keep 174-5

E

earnings per share 150
efficiency ratio 148-9
errors
  of commission 21
  of compensating 20
  of entry 20
  of omission 21
  of principle 21
exercises
  adjustments 48-52, 62-9
  balance sheet 33-7
  client account 176-9
  company accounts 120-6
  consolidated accounts 136-9
  conveyancing transactions 226-38
  deposit interest 248-9
  double-entry bookkeeping 21-5
  final accounts 33-7, 62-9
    partnerships 78-90
  further transactions 261-6
  ledger entries 186-91
  manufacturing accounts 99-102
  office account 176-9
  partnership final accounts 78-90
  probate transactions 251-6
  profit and loss account 33-7
  ratio analysis 156-9
  revision questions 267-8
  self assessment questions 268-73
  trading accounts 99-102
  trial balances 21-5
  value added tax 201-3
expenses
  partnership 72

F

final accounts
  assets
    disposal of part of group 60-1
    sale 60-1
  balance sheet 27, 33-7
  check list 33
  closing accounts 28
  closing stocks 43-4
  debts
    doubtful, provisions 54-5, 61-2
    effect of bad debts 55-7
    recovery of written off debt 54
    writing off bad debts 53-4, 61

depreciation 57-9
  exercises 62-9
  partnerships *see* **partnerships**
  payment in advance 41-2
  presentation 29
  profit and loss 27, 29, 33-7
  sale of assets 60-1
  work in progress 44-7
final balances
  adjustments 41
financial accounting concepts *see* **accounting concepts**
financial statements
  conveyancing transactions 214-17
  to clients 205
  see also individual statements
format *see* **presentation of accounts**

G

gearing 149-50
going-concern concept 96

I

income and expenses accounts 5, 8-11
  interest receivable account 8
  profits cost account 8
  rent receivable account 8
interest payment
  check list 247
  clients' money 246-7
  deposit interest 240-3
  designated deposit 239-43
  equivalent money 239, 244-6
  exercises 248-9
  money in lieu 239, 244-6
  payment to client 239-46
  Rules 239-46
  solicitor trustee 247
  trust money 239, 247
interest receivable account 8
interpretation of accounts
  check list 155
  efficiency ratio 148-9
  factors outside the accounts 142
  gearing 149-50
  investment ratios 150-2
  liquidity ratios 143
  overtrading 145-6
  past years 142-3
  profitability ratios 146-7
  ratio analysis *see* **ratio analysis**
  trends 143
  use of accounts 141-2
investment ratios 150-2

L

Law Society
  accountant's report to 175
layout of accounts 29, 108, 117-20
ledger entries
  check list 186
  exercise 186-91
  including VAT 201-3, 275-6
letters of administration 251
limited companies *see* **company accounts**
liquidators
  Solicitors' Accounts Rules (1998) 167

liquidity ratios 143
long-term liabilities 31

M

manufacturing accounts 97-8
  check list 99
  example 98
  exercise 99-102
  stock 97-8
materiality concept 96
money measurement concept 95
mortgages
  advances
    acting for buyer/borrower only 212
    acting for mortgagee only 211-12
    acting for mortgagee and purchaser 209-11
  redemption, acting for seller and lender 213-14

O

office account 12
  check list 175
  definition of office money 167
  dishonoured cheque paid into 258-9
  exercises 176-9
  payments into 168, 181-2
  payments out of 168-9, 182-3
  receipt of office money 168
  split cheques 185-6
  transfer from client account 181-2
  transfer to client account 182-3
overtrading 145-6

P

partnerships
  appropriation account 71-2, 76-7
  balance sheet 71, 72, 74-5
  capital accounts 73
  changes in constitution 76-7
  check list 77
  current accounts 74
  drawings 72
    cash 73
    end of year 73
  expenses 72
  final accounts
    balance sheet 71, 72, 74-5
    example 75-6
    exercises 78-90
    expenses 72
    profit and loss account 71-2
    test 90-3
  general 71
  profit and loss account 71-2
  sole practitioner taking in partner 77
payment in advance
  final accounts 41-2
personal accounts 5, 6
personal accounts of business proprietor 6-7
  capital account 6-7
  drawings account 7
petty cash 171-2
policies 96-7
power of attorney 167
preference shares
  cumulative 105
  non-cumulative 105
  participating 105
  redeemable 105
  share capital account 106
presentation of accounts
  balance sheet 31-2, 117-20
  final accounts 29
  profit and loss account 29, 108
  vertical format 29, 108, 117-19
preservation period 174-5
price earnings ratio 151-2
probate transactions
  advertisement payments 251
  collection of assets 251
  costs 251
  distribution of estate 251
  exercises 251-6
  grant of letters of administration 251
  grant of probate 251
  property 251
profit
  gross profit percentage 146-7
  net profit percentage 147
  retained 113-14
profit and loss account 27
  consolidated 132-4
  depreciation 59
  drawings 29
  exercise 33-7
  limited companies 107-17
  notes on 29
  partnership 71-2
  vertical format 29, 108
  work in progress 45-7
profitability ratios 146-7
profits cost account 8
provisions
  company accounts 114
  doubtful debts 54-5, 61-2
prudence concept 96

R

ratio analysis 142
  acid test 144
  borrowings to shareholders' funds 150
  capital gearing ratios 149-50
  check list 155
  collection period 144
  current assets ratio 143
  debtors to creditors ratio 146
  dividend cover 151
  dividend yield 150
  earnings per share 150
  efficiency ratio 148-9
  example 152-5
  exercise 156-9
  gross profit percentage 146-7
  investment ratios 150-2
  liquidity ratios 143
  net profit percentage 147
  payment period 144-5
  price earnings ratio 151-2
  profitability ratios 146-7
  rate of stock turnover 148-9
  return on capital employed 146, 150
  return on ordinary shareholders interest 150
  trade creditors to purchases ratio 144-5
  trade debtors to sales ratio 144
  working capital ratio 145

real accounts 5, 7–8
receivers (Court of Protection)
    Solicitors' Accounts Rules (1998) 167
rent receivable account 8
reserves
    capital reserves 115
    capitalisation of 115–16
    revaluation reserve 115
    revenue reserves 115
retained profits 113–14
retention time
    accounts 174–5
    authorities 175
    paid cheques 175
return on capital employed 146, 150
return on ordinary shareholders interest 150
revaluation reserve 115

S

sale of assets
    final accounts 60–1
share capital 103–6
share premium account 115
shares
    acquisition
        for less than book value 131–2
        for more than book value 130–1
    bonus issue 115–16
    earnings per share 150
    preference 105–6
    premium 104–5
    Stock Exchange 119
sinking funds 116–17
small transactions 261
solicitors' accounts
    abatements 257–8
    agreed fees 174
    cash account 171–2
    cheques
        dishonoured
            into client account 259–60
            into office account 258–9
        split between office and client account 185–6
        third parties 171
    client account *see* **client account**
    controlled trusts 166–7, 239
    costs 173–4
    delivery of bills of costs 173–4
    duty to keep accounts 174–5
    further transactions
        exercises 261–6
        tests 273–4
    ledger entries exercise 186–91
    office account *see* **office account**
    petty cash 171–2
    trustees 166, 167
    value added tax
        account used 194
        accounting to Customs and Excise 194–9
        agency method 196–7, 199
        charging output tax 195–6
        disbursements 196–9
        exercises 201–3
        paying input tax 194–5
        principal method 197–9
        registering for 193

        tax invoices 194
        tax points 194
Solicitors' Accounts Rules (1998) 161–7, 174
    liquidator, trustees in bankruptcy and receivers 167
stakeholder
    receipt of deposit as 208–9
stock
    closing 43–4
    manufacturing accounts 97–8
stock Exchange
    sale of shares on 119
stock turnover rate 148–9
suspense accounts 19–20

T

taxation
    companies 108–11
    corporation tax 108–9
    deferred 110–11
    value added tax *see* **value added tax**
trading accounts 11–12, 97–8
    check list 99
    example 8
    exercises 99–102
transactions *see individual transactions eg* **conveyancing transactions**
trial balance
    check list 21
    errors not revealed by 20–1
    exercises 21–5
    preparation 19
    purpose 19
    suspense accounts 19–20
trustees
    solicitors as 166, 167
trustees in bankruptcy
    Solicitors' Accounts Rules (1998) 167
trusts *see* **controlled trusts**
types to be kept 2

V

value added tax
    account used 194
    accounting to Customs and Excise 194–9
    agency method 196–7, 199
    bad debt relief 200, 261
    checklist 201
    disbursements 196–9
    exercises 201–3
    input tax 194–5
    ledger accounts 201–3, 275–6
    output tax 195–6
    principal method 197–9
    registering for 193
    solicitors' accounts 193–203
    tax invoices 194
    tax points 194

W

work in progress
    closing 46–7
    profit and loss account 45–7
    worked example 46–7
working capital ratio 145